THE CAVALRY

THE CAVALRY

EDITED BY JAMES LAWFORD

THE BOBBS-MERRILL COMPANY
INDIANAPOLIS NEW YORK

Contents

FOREWORD by JAMES LAWFORD 5

PART 1 THE HORSE IN WAR 7
A pictorial review of the cavalry charger and the mounted soldier,
explaining their roles, equipment and training.

PART 2 THE STORY OF THE CAVALRY 31
Fifteen chapters that trace and assess the performance of cavalry
from the time of the Assyrians up to the end of World War I.

ORIGINS 32

THE HUNS 45

CHARLEMAGNE AND THE DAWN OF CHIVALRY 49

THE MONGOLS 57

DECLINE OF THE KNIGHT 63

THE THIRTY YEARS' WAR 73

THE ENGLISH CIVIL WAR 85

THE AGE OF THE SUN KING 93

THE AGE OF FREDERICK THE GREAT 107

THE MOGULS AND THE MAHRATTAS 123

THE NAPOLEONIC WARS 129

THE CRIMEAN WAR 143

INTERLUDE: COLONIAL CAVALRY 151

US CAVALRY AND THE CIVIL WAR 155

THE TWILIGHT OF THE CAVALRY 167

INDEX AND ACKNOWLEDGMENTS 174

COPYRIGHT © ROXBY PRESS LIMITED 1976
ISBN 0-672-52192-X
LIBRARY OF CONGRESS CATALOG CARD NUMBER 76-5986
ALL RIGHTS RESERVED, INCLUDING THE RIGHT OF
REPRODUCTION IN WHOLE OR IN PART IN ANY FORM
PUBLISHED BY THE BOBBS-MERRILL COMPANY INC
INDIANAPOLIS NEW YORK
FIRST US PRINTING
MADE BY ROXBY PRESS PRODUCTIONS,
98 CLAPHAM COMMON NORTHSIDE,
LONDON, SW4 9SG

EDITORIAL DIRECTOR MICHAEL LEITCH
ART DIRECTOR DAVID POCKNELL
PICTURE RESEARCH ANNE HORTON

PHOTOTYPESET BY TRADESPOOLS LTD, FROME, SOMERSET

PRINTED AND BOUND
IN BELGIUM BY H. PROOST & CIE, TURNHOUT

FOREWORD by JAMES LAWFORD

It is as well to begin by defining the word cavalry, now that lancers can be found driving tanks, horse artillery drop from aircraft and man enormous guns, and sky-cavalry charge onto their objectives in helicopters. Webster's Dictionary, published in 1924, defined cavalry as 'That part of a military force that serves on horseback and, while it may be dismounted to fight, in an emergency, is normally used to realise the advantages of the horse's mobility in manoeuvring and impetus in charging.' In this book the term has been applied, in general, to warriors or soldiers who normally fought on horseback; dragoons, who early showed a preference for remaining on their chargers in battle, have been admitted, as have mounted infantry, but only when discharging a true cavalry role. Soldiers on camels, elephants, chariots or other forms of vehicle, have for the most part been excluded.

It is not possible within the present limitations of space to cover every aspect of such a vast subject. We have tried to choose the important periods in the evolution of the cavalry, to analyse the strategy and tactics of the day, relating them to what was practised before, and finally in each period to describe a battle, generally fought by one of the masters of warfare, in which these tactics may be seen in action.

The book is a symposium, and as its general editor I have been glad to call on the writing talents of Brigadier Peter Young, R. A. Crosbie-Weston, Curt Johnson, Dr T. A. Heathcote, Lt-Col Alan Shepperd and David Chandler, all of whom have exceptional knowledge of the periods they have covered in their respective chapters. Thanks are due to many others who assisted in the book's production, in particular to Colonel E. C. Spenser who served in Palestine in 1918 with the Poona Horse and took part in a number of charges with the lance; he gave much invaluable advice. Mrs J. L. Spears, ALA, Librarian of the Prince Consort Library, Aldershot, rendered noble service, putting at our disposal the magnificent collection of uniform books in her library. Mr Derek White and Mr Richard Holmes, lecturers at the Royal Military Academy, Sandhurst, contributed some useful information about the French and German armies. Mr R. Goodall has been responsible for photographing many of the illustrations, particularly those from the Prince Consort Library. J.P.L.

PART 1
THE
HORSE
IN WAR
BY PETER YOUNG

THE ILLUSTRATED HORSE

Artists have presented us with a bewildering array of solutions to the common problem of depicting horsemen and their mounts. In the Middle Ages there was a tendency to draw the horse absurdly small in relation to the rider. This perhaps indicated man's over-lofty view of himself rather than a widespread inability to draw horses. After all, many centuries earlier the Assyrians in their stylized temple reliefs (see inset, from Nineveh) had shown they could successfully describe the appearance of their horses, even if they could not faithfully depict them in motion. As it turned out, not until Edward Muybridge's instantaneous photographs of 1878 were many of the secrets of equine motion revealed. The purpose of these opening pages is thus to alert the reader's eye to certain conventions adopted at various times in the portrayal of the cavalryman and his horse.

BELOW: A 15th-CENTURY BOHEMIAN KNIGHT, FROM A COLOURED PEN DRAWING BY JACOBUS DE CESULIS IN *MORIBUS ET OFFICIIS VIVENTIUM* (PRAGUE). THE KNIGHT IS WEARING FULL PLATE ARMOUR, WITH NO VESTIGE OF CHAIN-MAIL; HE IS NOT CARRYING A SHIELD BUT IS ARMED WITH A CURIOUSLY SHORT LANCE AND IS SEATED IN A HIGH JOUSTING OR TOURNEY SADDLE. HIS RIDICULOUSLY UNDERSIZED HORSE WEARS A TRAPPER OF MAIL MADE IN TWO HALVES MEETING AT THE SADDLE

LEFT: A ROMAN PARADE IN THE DAYS OF THE EMPEROR ANTONIUS PIUS (REIGNED AD 138–161). THE SCENE IS FROM THE BASE OF THE ANTONINE COLUMN, AND SHOWS A TROOP OF 17 HORSEMEN PRANCING AROUND A GROUP OF TWO STANDARD-BEARERS AND EIGHT FOOT SOLDIERS. FIVE OF THE HORSEMEN CARRY STANDARDS, AND ONE OF THESE IS ARMED WITH A SHORT SWORD; NONE OF THE OTHER RIDERS APPEARS TO BE ARMED. ALL THE RIDERS HAVE SADDLECLOTHS, BUT NO STIRRUPS. THE HORSES ARE RATHER SMALL, NOT UNLIKE WELSH COBS.

ABOVE: THE STONE OF HORNHAUSEN, A 7TH-CENTURY CARVING OF A SAXON HORSEMAN: THE BEARDED WARRIOR IS ARMED WITH LANCE AND SWORD, AND CARRIES A SHIELD. HE HAS NO STIRRUPS. ALTHOUGH THE HORSE HAS A STYLIZED OUTLINE, SEVERAL INTERESTING FEATURES ARE DISCERNIBLE, AMONG THEM HIS ARAB HEAD, WELL-PLACED SHOULDER AND VERY LONG BACK. THE STONE IS AN UNUSUAL WORK, BUT THE ARTIST WAS WORKING IN AN AWKWARD MEDIUM, AND FOR ALL THE APPARENT DISTORTION ONE IS LEFT WITH THE IMPRESSION THAT HE HAD A CONSIDERABLE UNDERSTANDING OF HORSES AND THEIR ANATOMY.

THE CAVALRY

LEFT: SPRIGHTLY, AND SOMEWHAT FANCIFUL, ILLUSTRATIONS BY CHARLES PARROCEL TO THE *ECOLE DE LA CAVALERIE* (1751) WHOSE AUTHOR, THE MARQUIS DE LA GUÉRINIÈRE, WAS A PIONEER OF MODERN *HAUTE ECOLE* EQUITATION.

LEFT: A PRUSSIAN UNDER-OFFICER OF THE 1st REGIMENT OF DRAGOONS RIDING A VERY ALERT, FIT-LOOKING GREY CHARGER. FROM *ROYAL PRUSSIAN CAVALRY*, BY LIEDER AND KRÜGER (BERLIN, 1825).

ABOVE: GUSTAVUS ADOLPHUS (1594–1632), KING OF SWEDEN. HE WEARS CUIRASSIER'S ARMOUR AND IS MOUNTED ON A HEAVY-LOOKING CHARGER WHOSE HEAD IS TOO SMALL FOR HIS THICK NECK. THE REARING HORSE WAS A TRADITIONAL POSTURE IN EQUESTRIAN PORTRAITS OF EMINENT MEN, AND IMPLIED THE PRESENCE OF A MAN OF ACTION. A HORSE AT REST, ON THE OTHER HAND, SUGGESTED A MAN OF AUTHORITY.

CENTRE BELOW: PHOTOGRAPH OF A BLACKFOOT BRAVE ON HIS PONY, *c.* 1910. THE PONY APPEARS TO HAVE MUCH IN COMMON WITH THE MONGOL MOUNT ON PAGE 59.

A REALISTICALLY DESCRIBED INCIDENT FROM THE CHARGE OF THE LIGHT BRIGADE, 1854. LT SIR GEORGE WOMBWELL, 17TH LANCERS, IS CAPTURED BY A TROOP OF COSSACKS. LITHOGRAPH BY W. BOOSEY AFTER A. DE PRADES.

CAVALRY HORSES IN PORTUGUESE ANGOLA IN 1972, WHERE THEY WERE USED BY THE COLONIAL POWER FOR COUNTER-INSURGENCY WORK. THAT ON THE LEFT IS A PALOMINO, PROBABLY OF IBERIAN ORIGIN.

9

THE LIGHT AND THE HEAVY

Given that there are not less than 86 different breeds of horse, many of them eminently suitable for cavalry work, it is not easy briefly to describe the qualities that a cavalryman looks for in a horse. Much, of course, depends on the role for which the horse is intended, and one may conveniently distinguish between heavy and light horses (and ponies, these being less than 14.2 hands, or 58 in/147 cm). In general, heavy cavalry were allocated to shock duties, literally to battering a path through the enemy's ranks, while light cavalry, although expected to take their place in the line of battle, were developed principally for outpost duties (patrols, ambushes, etc.) appropriate to their greater speed and mobility.

An interesting account of 'Blitz', considered an almost-ideal light cavalry horse, appears in a British War Office handbook of 1908 entitled *Animal Management*. Following the maxim that 'A good horse is one with many good, few indifferent and no bad points,' the writer emphasizes the horse's 'Arab type of head, long rein, well placed shoulder, short back, strong loin and well ribbed up middle piece, deepening through the heart. The quarter and thigh is muscular, the arm long, the cannon short, and the back tendons show no tendency to be

Long Magazine Lee Enfield rifle, carried in the short butt bucket in use from 1894.

The saddle is a Universal Pattern steel-arch type, introduced in 1890. A blanket is folded between the saddle and the numnah, the latter being a thick pad of felt or sheepskin.

'Hussar' stirrup with a brass slide close to the stirrup iron.

LIGHT HORSE

THE ILLUSTRATION SHOWS SERGEANT SEYMOUR, 2ND GORDON HIGHLANDERS, SERVING WITH A MOUNTED INFANTRY UNIT IN 1896. HE IS MOUNTED ON A COB, A SHORT-LEGGED, STRONGLY BUILT TYPE OF NOT MORE THAN 15 HANDS (60 IN/152 CM). MORE THAN 200 YEARS EARLIER, IN THE ENGLISH CIVIL WAR, COBS WERE SUPPLIED TO REGIMENTS OF DRAGOONS.

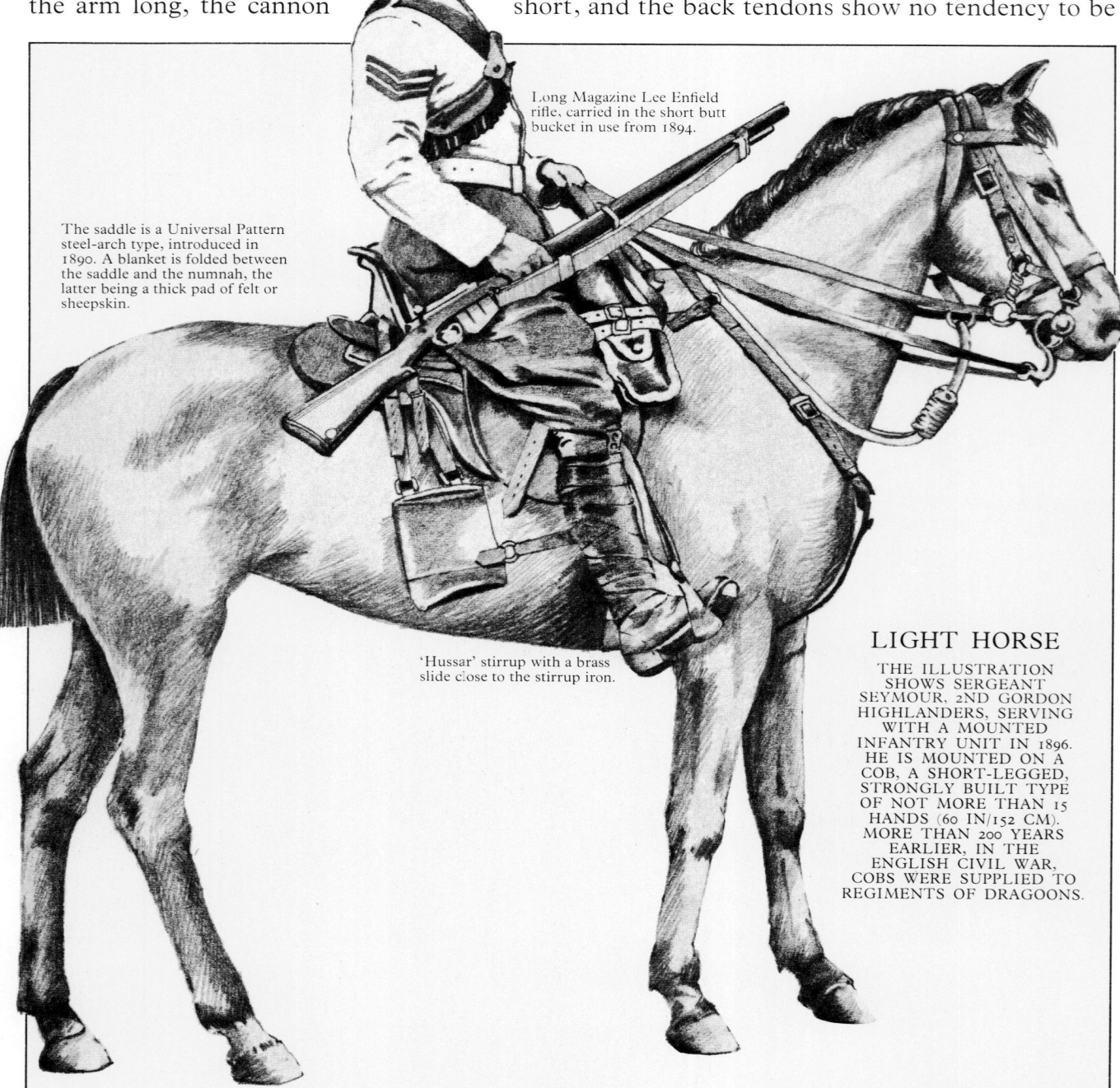

THE CAVALRY

tied in below the knee. This horse, "Blitz", an Arab, was a wonderful performer in his class, did an immense amount of work, left off sound, and [when described] was nearly twenty years of age'. (For an explanation of anatomical terms, see the 'Heavy Horse' illustration below.) It is worth for a moment considering Blitz's age: while a racehorse, for example, is classified as 'aged' at 12, a cavalry horse may still be a valuable asset between 12 and 18 – provided he is properly looked after by a well-trained trooper. A horse is not really useful for cavalry work until he is at least four years of age; at about eight or nine he begins to come to the height of his powers.

While 'Blitz' was a light horse, the Percheron stallion inset on this page is a fine example of the heavy horse. He is 17 hands, and in breeding condition weighed about a ton. Bred in the USA, he and others like him supplied the foundation stock of the Allies' most successful draught horse in World War I, large numbers serving with the artillery in 1916–18. A century before, he would have been typical of the chargers used by the French heavy cavalry: big, slow and powerful, such were the mounts of Napoleon's cuirassiers at Eylau and Waterloo. Under reasonable circumstances these horses could march 20–25 miles a day at about 4 mph.

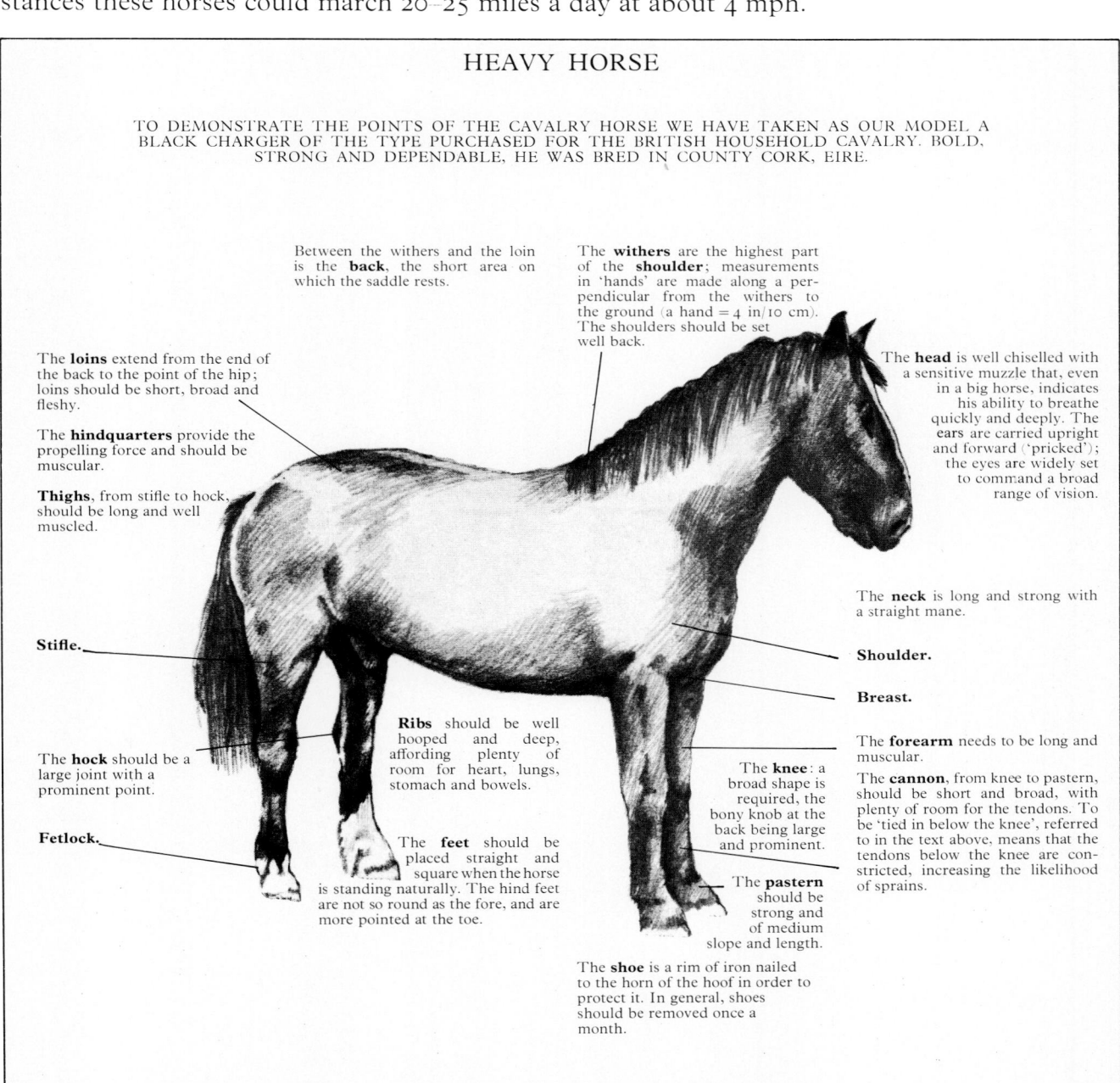

HEAVY HORSE

TO DEMONSTRATE THE POINTS OF THE CAVALRY HORSE WE HAVE TAKEN AS OUR MODEL A BLACK CHARGER OF THE TYPE PURCHASED FOR THE BRITISH HOUSEHOLD CAVALRY. BOLD, STRONG AND DEPENDABLE, HE WAS BRED IN COUNTY CORK, EIRE.

Between the withers and the loin is the **back**, the short area on which the saddle rests.

The **withers** are the highest part of the **shoulder**; measurements in 'hands' are made along a perpendicular from the withers to the ground (a hand = 4 in/10 cm). The shoulders should be set well back.

The **loins** extend from the end of the back to the point of the hip; loins should be short, broad and fleshy.

The **hindquarters** provide the propelling force and should be muscular.

Thighs, from stifle to hock, should be long and well muscled.

The **head** is well chiselled with a sensitive muzzle that, even in a big horse, indicates his ability to breathe quickly and deeply. The ears are carried upright and forward ('pricked'); the eyes are widely set to command a broad range of vision.

The **neck** is long and strong with a straight mane.

Shoulder.

Breast.

Stifle.

The **hock** should be a large joint with a prominent point.

Fetlock.

Ribs should be well hooped and deep, affording plenty of room for heart, lungs, stomach and bowels.

The **feet** should be placed straight and square when the horse is standing naturally. The hind feet are not so round as the fore, and are more pointed at the toe.

The **knee**: a broad shape is required, the bony knob at the back being large and prominent.

The **pastern** should be strong and of medium slope and length.

The **forearm** needs to be long and muscular.

The **cannon**, from knee to pastern, should be short and broad, with plenty of room for the tendons. To be 'tied in below the knee', referred to in the text above, means that the tendons below the knee are constricted, increasing the likelihood of sprains.

The **shoe** is a rim of iron nailed to the horn of the hoof in order to protect it. In general, shoes should be removed once a month.

EQUIPMENT FOR THE CHARGER

When asked why he never wore spurs, the eccentric King Frederick the Great replied, 'Try sticking a fork into your bare stomach and you will soon see why.' The accoutrements of the cavalry horse should be designed for simplicity and the comfort of both horse and rider. The main items are the saddle and bridle, though bits, stirrups and spurs are also briefly considered in these pages.

The earliest bridle was a simple halter of hide or thong round the animal's lower jaw, but by the 7th century BC the bridle had acquired its modern shape, with much the same combination of straps. Of these, the headstall has a headpiece passing behind the ears and joining a headband which runs across the forehead. Cheek-straps run down the sides of the head and are fastened to the two ends of the bit. There are innumerable types of bit, the two main ones being the curb and the snaffle, both of which are mentioned in Xenophon's essays on horsemanship (4th century BC). In the Middle Ages some of the bits that were invented look like instruments of torture, but nowadays the emphasis is on simplicity.

Assyrian monuments show decorated saddlecloths, some of them quilted: as time went by, these were secured by breast-band and crupper. The invention of the girth made riding much safer. A bronze figure of Alexander the Great riding Bucephalus shows a broad girth (see also page 37). The saddle proper was introduced by the 3rd or 4th century AD. There were no stirrups until the days of Emperor Maurice (6th century), the rider having to mount at a block or by vaulting. The medieval saddle was like the Oriental saddle of modern times, with high peaks before and behind. The modern riding saddle has a framework called the 'tree' with a projection, the pommel, at the front over the horse's withers. Side bars curve round into the cantle, as the arch at the back of the tree is known.

The spur is attached to the rider's heel, and is used to goad the horse into motion. The earliest spur was the prick type, known to the Greeks. In medieval times long spurs with rowels were introduced. A knight was entitled to wear gilded spurs, and if he fell into disgrace they were ceremonially hacked off with a cook's chopper. In general, the better the rider, and the better he knows his mount, the less he will need to encourage it with the spur.

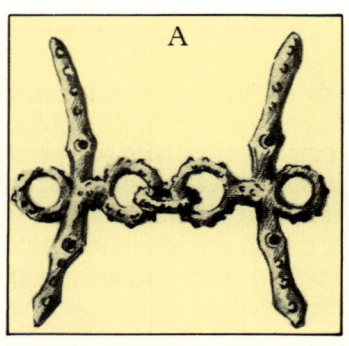

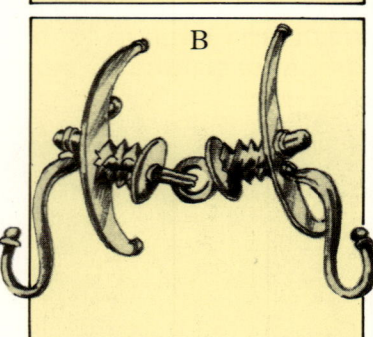

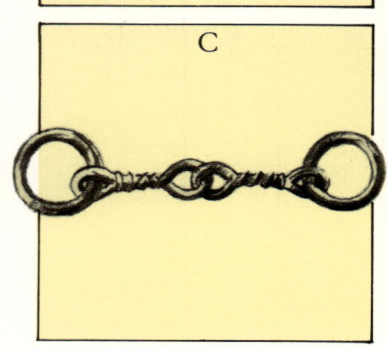

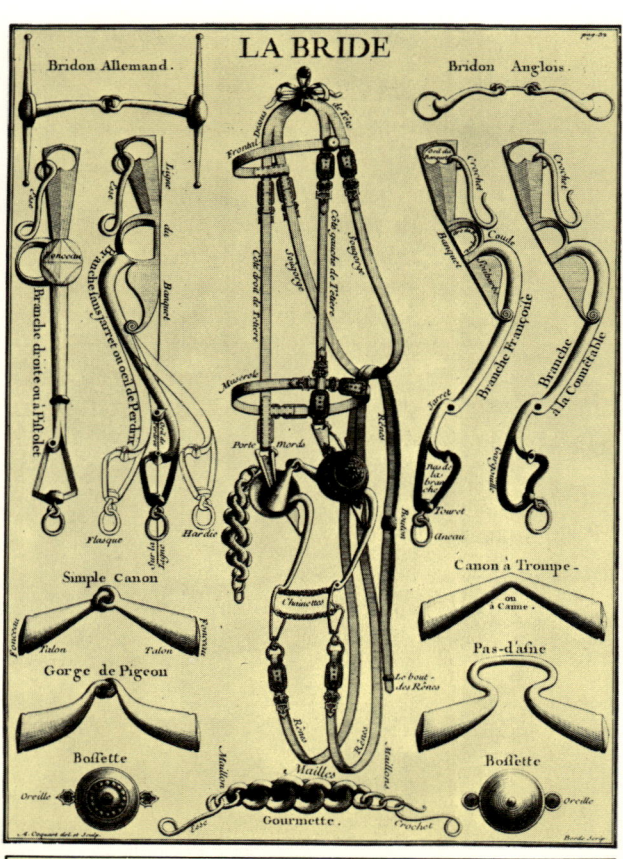

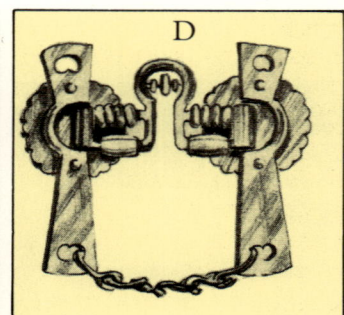

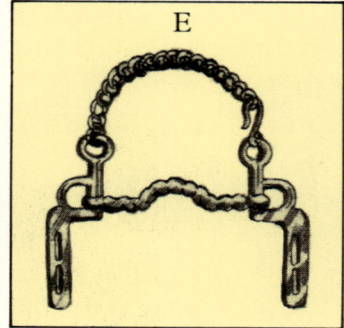

'THE BRIDLE', AS ILLUSTRATED BY CHARLES PARROCEL FOR THE MARQUIS DE LA GUÉRINIÈRE'S *ECOLE DE LA CAVALERIE* (1751). IN THE BRITISH ARMY A SIMILAR BIT AND BRIDLE WAS IN USE AS LATE AS 1838.

A AN ASSYRIAN BIT OF REMARKABLY MODERN APPEARANCE.

B BRONZE GREEK BIT OF THE 5TH CENTURY BC.

C BIT USED BY THE ROMAN CAVALRY

D MEDIEVAL FRENCH BIT, LATE 14TH CENTURY.

E MODERN BRITISH MILITARY BIT.

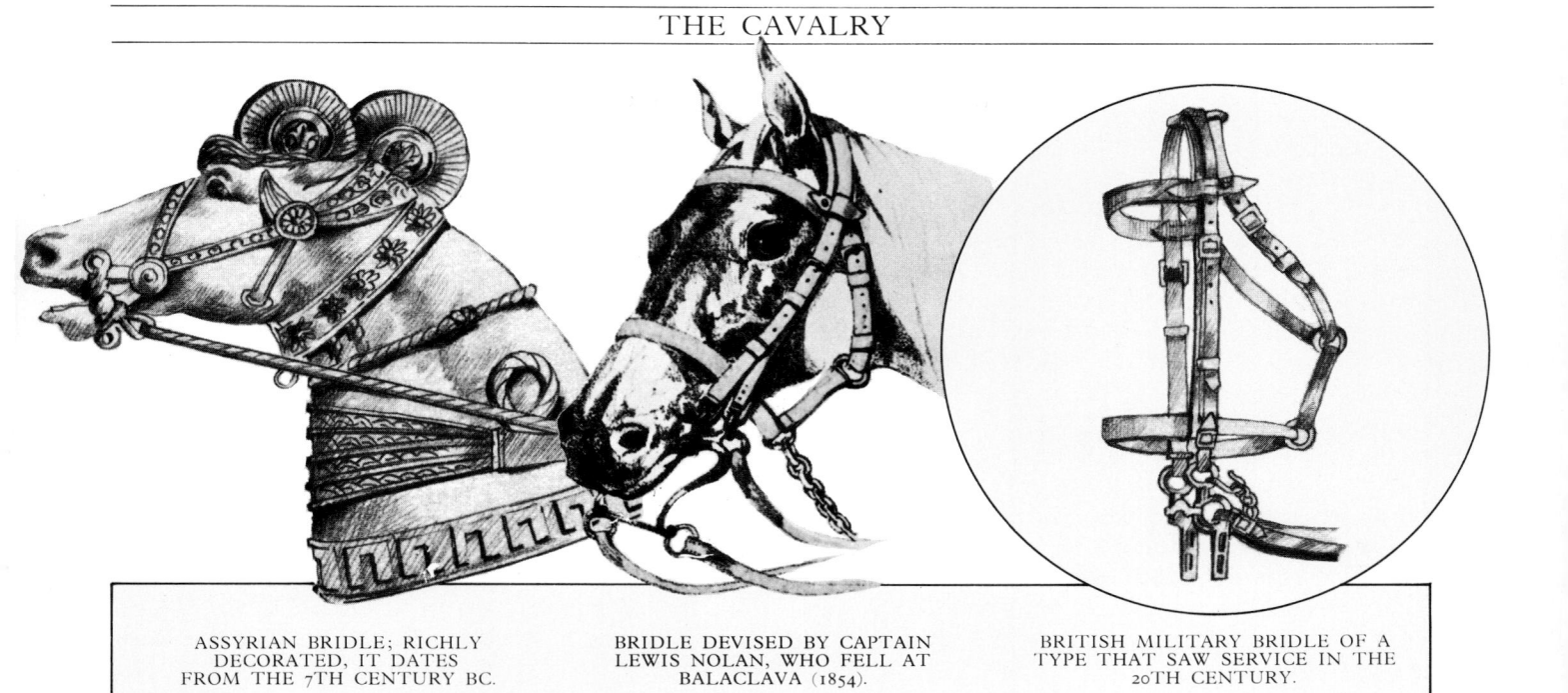

THE CAVALRY

ASSYRIAN BRIDLE; RICHLY DECORATED, IT DATES FROM THE 7TH CENTURY BC.

BRIDLE DEVISED BY CAPTAIN LEWIS NOLAN, WHO FELL AT BALACLAVA (1854).

BRITISH MILITARY BRIDLE OF A TYPE THAT SAW SERVICE IN THE 20TH CENTURY.

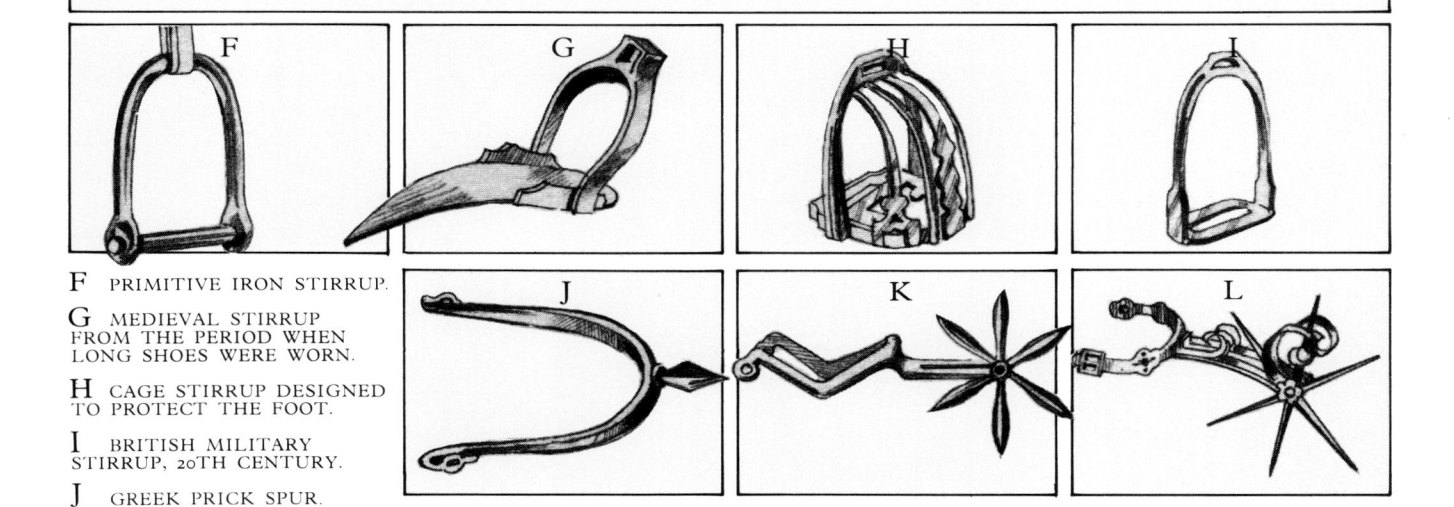

F PRIMITIVE IRON STIRRUP.
G MEDIEVAL STIRRUP FROM THE PERIOD WHEN LONG SHOES WERE WORN.
H CAGE STIRRUP DESIGNED TO PROTECT THE FOOT.
I BRITISH MILITARY STIRRUP, 20TH CENTURY.
J GREEK PRICK SPUR.
K ROWEL SPUR, 14TH CENTURY.
L A 15TH CENTURY ENGLISH SPUR FROM THE HEAVY ARMOUR PERIOD; THE POINTS ARE 3 IN/7.6 CM LONG.

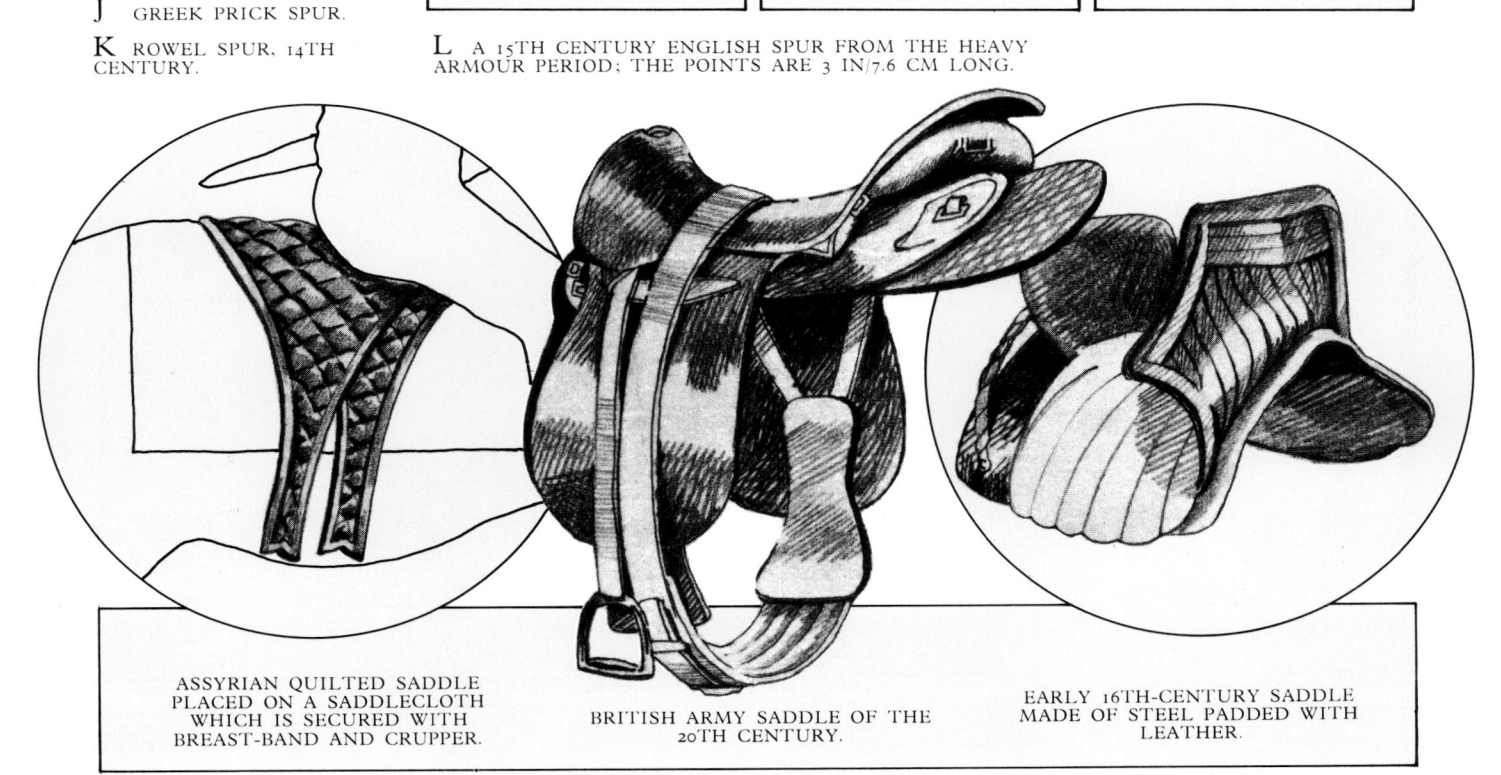

ASSYRIAN QUILTED SADDLE PLACED ON A SADDLECLOTH WHICH IS SECURED WITH BREAST-BAND AND CRUPPER.

BRITISH ARMY SADDLE OF THE 20TH CENTURY.

EARLY 16TH-CENTURY SADDLE MADE OF STEEL PADDED WITH LEATHER.

13

THE MILITARY HORSEMAN

In 1642 Richard Atkyns of Tuffley, Gloucestershire, employed his servant, Erwing, a Scot who had served in France in the *Gendarmes*, to 'train up my horse, and make them bold'. The training Atkyns had in mind was to accustom his horses to drums, colours, pistols and the various noises that may terrify a beast on the battlefield. This had been normal practice with cavalry from the earliest times, no commander ever having liked to take his men into action on untrained horses. However, it must often have been necessary to do so; the English Civil War, in which Atkyns fought as a Royalist captain, provides ample evidence. At Edgehill (23 October 1642) for example, the formations led by Prince Rupert and Sir William Balfour had been raised not more than three months previously – which may well account for some of the disorder and confusion that occurred on the day, as when, in the opening phase, the Royalist horse careered past the exposed Parliamentarian flanks and ran on into the streets of Kineton, where they fell to untimely looting.

Conversely, one might have assumed that the Scots Greys who in 1815 thundered forward at Waterloo, and in point of fact went much too far, would have been well trained. But, although they were an old regiment, they had not been on active service since 1794. In the scantily policed England of George III, their role for the previous 21 years had been that of aid to the civil power; with their troops dispersed far and wide, unit training had suffered.

A cavalry unit might enter upon a campaign well mounted on well-trained horses, but the first marches would then take as heavy a toll as the first skirmishes. This became all too clear in the Boer War (1899–1902) in which, it has been estimated, 750,000 horses were engaged of which 500,000 perished. The trouble was, as the future Field-Marshal Allenby, a truly great cavalryman, wrote of the Boer War generals, 'They don't care a straw about the horses... I've lost 32 horses in 9 days, only two in action. The rest have died from exhaustion or shortage of food.'

In South Africa the British went far afield for their remounts. To secure a good remount, even a veteran needed luck as well as ingenuity. From a train-load of Hungarian horses, Sergeant Jackson, serving with the 7th Mounted Infantry, picked the one that seemed the best. Sad to relate, his company commander agreed with his choice and took it for himself. Instead, Jackson got a 'heavy-footed, lumbering old beast with a head like a coal-scuttle and a canter that would fracture your skull!' Fortunately for him, a 'great raking black mare' ran away with some young soldier twice in a morning, and thereafter Jackson rode her until the peace.

THE TROOPER SHOULD CHECK HIS SADDLE AND BRIDLE, AND THE STATE OF HIS HORSE'S SHOES, BEFORE MOUNTING; IN PARTICULAR HE MUST ENSURE THAT THERE IS NO CHANCE OF THE SADDLE SLIPPING. THIS AND THE OTHER ILLUSTRATIONS ON THESE PAGES ARE FROM *LA TRAITÉ SUR LA CAVALERIE*, BY COUNT DRUMMOND DE MELFORT, FIELD MARSHAL OF THE KING'S ARMIES AND INSPECTOR GENERAL OF LIGHT TROOPS, PUBLISHED AT DRESDEN IN 1784 AND BASED MAINLY ON THE COUNT'S EXPERIENCES IN THE WAR OF THE AUSTRIAN SUCCESSION (1740–48) AND THE SEVEN YEARS' WAR (1756–63).

THE CAVALRY

THE AIM OF THESE EXERCISES IS TO TRAIN THE HORSEMAN AND MAKE HIM MASTER OF HIS HORSE. THE COUNT REMARKS THAT THERE ARE SOME WHO BELIEVE IN THE VIRTUES OF RIDING WITH A SHORT STIRRUP LEATHER, A VIEW TO WHICH HE DOES NOT SUBSCRIBE. TRAINING WITH THE SABRE IS IMPORTANT, THE COUNT BELIEVES, FOR IN HIS EXPERIENCE 90 OUT OF 100 CUTS ARE DELIVERED WITH THE FLAT; HENCE THE DUMMY HEADS MOUNTED ON POLES AT THE TRAINING GROUND. FIREARMS PRACTICE WITH PISTOL AND CARBINE IS ALSO SHOWN.

IN THIS SEQUENCE THE HORSE IS ACCUSTOMED TO THE SIGHTS AND NOISES OF THE BATTLEFIELD. DRUMBEATS, PISTOL SHOTS AND WAVING COLOURS PUT HIS TEMPERAMENT TO THE TEST, AND HE IS ALSO TRAINED TO CROSS DITCHES WITHOUT HESITATION.

THE ARMOURED KNIGHT

In the heavy armour period, begun in the 8th century by the military reforms of Charlemagne (742–814), the cavalryman was the undisputed champion of the battlefield. Against the mailed knight, supported by his esquires and mounted men-at-arms, the ill-equipped peasants comprising the enemy infantry could do little. This feudal *status quo* persisted largely unchallenged until the arrival of the crossbow and the longbow in the 12th century.

Early armour, made of chain-mail or small plates of metal or leather, was worn by Roman cavalry and their chargers; but in other parts of Europe, although knights might be heavily protected, it is rare to find evidence of armoured horses much before the 12th century. In its early form the horse's mail trapper was often covered by a textile housing that was both ornamental and warded off rust. By the early 14th century plate armour was coming in, lined with leather or cloth. For purposes of jousting, specialized armour was developed. In battle, as well as for the tourney, the knight's main offensive weapon was the lance: constructed of wood, usually poplar, it was painted in the knight's colours.

In the early 16th century, when its battlefield relevance had faded somewhat against the offensive power of cannon and arquebus, the armour of the knight and the bardings of his charger came to a peak of refinement. Suits were intricately decorated with etched patterns and by embossing with the hammer, but the reasons for this had more to do with prestige than protection. By the second half of the 16th century horse armour became increasingly discarded, and in a comparatively short time vanished from use.

A 14TH-CENTURY FRENCH CHAMFRON. IT IS MADE FROM SEVERAL THICKNESSES OF PARCHMENT GLUED TOGETHER, AND HAS METAL PIECES TO PROTECT THE EARS, NOSE AND EYES, AND A BAR TO GUARD THE MIDDLE OF THE FACE.

ARMOUR OF PHILIP II OF SPAIN (1527–98). HIS HORSE WEARS THE ALL-ROUND PROTECTION OF FRONTAL BREASTPLATE, FLANCHARD AT THE FLANK AND CRUPPER AT THE REAR. OVER THE UPPER PART OF THE HEAD IS A DEMI-CHAMFRON, AN ABBREVIATED VERSION OF THE PIECE WORN BY OTTO HEINRICH'S HORSE ON THE FACING PAGE.

THE CAVALRY

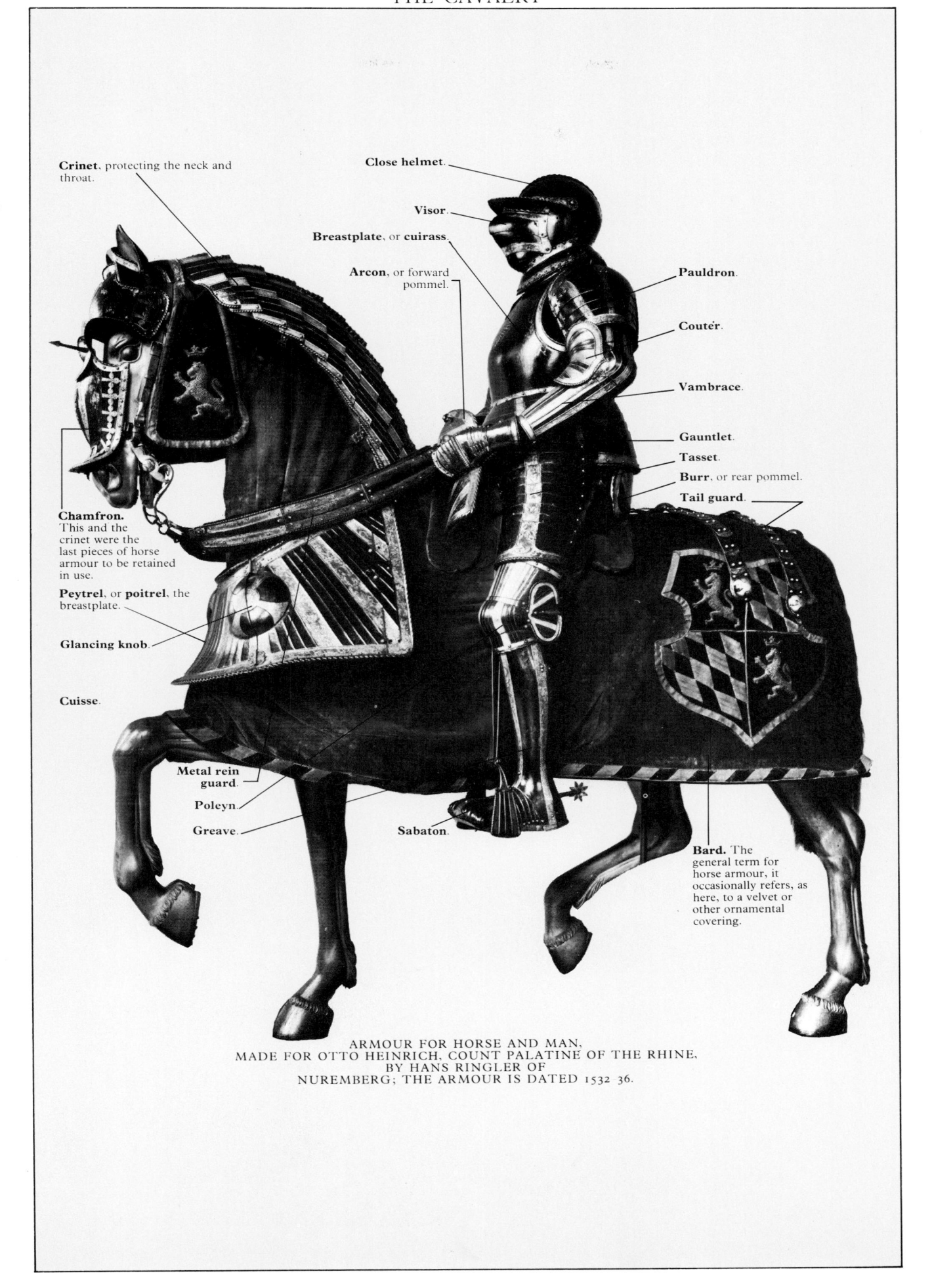

Crinet, protecting the neck and throat.

Close helmet.

Visor.

Breastplate, or **cuirass**.

Arcon, or forward pommel.

Pauldron.

Couter.

Vambrace.

Chamfron. This and the crinet were the last pieces of horse armour to be retained in use.

Gauntlet.

Tasset.

Burr, or rear pommel.

Tail guard.

Peytrel, or **poitrel**, the breastplate.

Glancing knob.

Cuisse.

Metal rein guard.

Poleyn.

Greave.

Sabaton.

Bard. The general term for horse armour, it occasionally refers, as here, to a velvet or other ornamental covering.

ARMOUR FOR HORSE AND MAN,
MADE FOR OTTO HEINRICH, COUNT PALATINE OF THE RHINE,
BY HANS RINGLER OF
NUREMBERG; THE ARMOUR IS DATED 1532–36.

THE CUIRASSIER

The heavy cavalry of the late Middle Ages, men-at-arms and *Gendarmerie*, gradually developed into cuirassiers. As early as 1484 the Emperor Maximilian of Austria, the 'last of the knights', had a corps of *Kyrissers*, 100 strong; and at the time of the Thirty Years' War (1618–48) cuirassiers wearing three-quarter armour were still fairly common. As the 17th century wore on, cuirassiers tended to abandon their armour, except for the back- and breastplates, although the Austrians retained the lobster-tailed helmet as late as the War of the Spanish Succession (1701–14).

The British heavy cavalry were among the first to rid themselves of armour, thus relieving their horses of unnecessary weight. The Prussians kept their breastplates until after the Seven Years' War (1756–63). In the French Army Napoleon I reduced his heavy cavalry, but made those he kept really heavy, forming the biggest men and horses into regiments of cuirassiers, of which by 1812 there were 14. These units were seldom used for outpost duty. Their role was to make massive strokes in a pitched battle, as at Eylau, Borodino and Waterloo. In the 19th century the French clung to the cuirass after other nations had mostly abandoned it; after the war of 1866, for example, the Austrians converted their cuirassiers into dragoons.

PRUSSIAN CUIRASSIER AT THE TIME OF THE SEVEN YEARS' WAR (1756-63). ONE IS REMINDED OF FREDERICK THE GREAT'S CAUSTIC COMMENT THAT WHEN HE CAME TO THE THRONE HIS CAVALRY CONSISTED OF 'GIANTS MOUNTED UPON ELEPHANTS'. ACTUALLY THE CHARGER DEPICTED HERE IS VERY HANDSOME, BUT THE TROOPER LOOKS A BIT ON THE STOUT SIDE. FROM *HEERSCHAU DER SOLDATEN FRIEDRICHS DES GROSSEN*, BY ADOLF MENZEL, PUBLISHED IN 1856.

PISTOL-ARMED HEAVY CAVALRY FROM A BOOK PUBLISHED IN 1640, DE GHEYN'S *EXERCISES DE L'HOMME DE CHEVAL DU 17ᵉ SIECLE*.

THE CAVALRY

FRENCH CUIRASSIER OF THE IMPERIAL GUARD, c. 1870. IN THE BACKGROUND, WEARING THE SASH, IS NAPOLEON III. FROM A CONTEMPORARY LITHOGRAPH.

SWORD DRILL

On the facing page are six plates illustrating sword drill as it was practised in the period immediately following the demise of Napoleon I. The book from which they are taken is entitled *Royal Prussian Cavalry*, and is by Messrs Lieder and Krüger; the superscription describes it as 'Showing the uniform of every regiment . . . and the position of the soldiers according to the latest regulation drill exercises'. It was published in Berlin in 1825.

PRUSSIAN UNDER-OFFICER OF THE 1ST REGIMENT OF HUSSARS CUTTING DOWNWARDS WHILE MOVING AT SPEED. NOTE THE FAMOUS DEATH'S HEAD BADGE IN THE FRONT OF HIS SHAKO. FROM LIEDER AND KRÜGER.

THE CAVALRY

TROOPER, 2ND CUIRASSIER REGIMENT, MARCHING WITH DRAWN SWORD.

TROOPER, 3RD CUIRASSIER REGIMENT, ON GUARD TO HIS FRONT.

TROOPER, 4TH CUIRASSIER REGIMENT, THRUSTING TO HIS FRONT.

TROOPER, 5TH CUIRASSIER REGIMENT, ON GUARD TO HIS REAR. THIS POSTURE, SPECTACULAR THOUGH IT IS, COULD NOT AND SHOULD NOT HAVE BEEN MAINTAINED FOR MORE THAN A FEW PACES.

TROOPER, 6TH CUIRASSIER REGIMENT, ON GUARD TO HIS RIGHT FLANK. FROM THIS POSITION A VARIETY OF THRUSTS, CUTS AND PARRIES WAS OPEN TO HIM.

TROOPER, 7TH CUIRASSIER REGIMENT, ON GUARD TO HIS LEFT FLANK. HE IS PROTECTING HIS BRIDLE ARM. IN A *MÊLÉE* THE ASSAILANT ALWAYS STROVE TO ATTACK HIS OPPONENT'S BRIDLE ARM, SO PUTTING HIM AT A CONSIDERABLE DISADVANTAGE.

THE LANCER

The lance declined in popularity with the decay of chivalry but did not altogether disappear. There were, for example, Scottish lancers at Marston Moor, while Polish and Cossack cavalry were normally armed with this weapon. In the Prussian Army under Frederick the Great we find that both Bosniak and Uhlan units were armed with the lance, though it was not until the Napoleonic Wars that it became generally adopted by the armies of Europe. In 1811 several French regiments were converted into lancers, and the Prussian Army had six regiments of Uhlans in the 1815 campaign. In addition, many of the Landwehr cavalry were armed with the lance. At Waterloo the French lancers distinguished themselves, and this persuaded the British to arm six regiments in similar fashion. In 1914 the British had a bamboo lance that was 9 feet long and weighed 4½ pounds. The Germans had a tubular steel lance 11 feet 9 inches long, weighing 4 pounds. The lance drill positions illustrated opposite are from *Royal Prussian Cavalry* by Lieder and Krüger (1825).

FRENCH LANCERS OF 1846. FROM A CONTEMPORARY LITHOGRAPH.

THE CAVALRY

PRUSSIAN TROOPER, 8TH REGIMENT OF UHLANS, CARRYING HIS LANCE.

TROOPER, 7TH REGIMENT OF UHLANS, CARRYING HIS LANCE AT THE OVERHEAD PARRY.

TROOPER, 2ND REGIMENT OF UHLANS, WITH HIS LANCE THRUST FORWARD.

TROOPER, 6TH REGIMENT OF UHLANS, WITH HIS LANCE TO THE LEFT REAR.

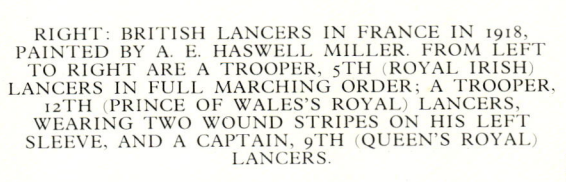

TROOPER, 5TH REGIMENT OF UHLANS, WITH HIS LANCE TO THE RIGHT REAR.

TROOPER, 4TH REGIMENT OF UHLANS, WITH HIS LANCE TO THE LEFT.

FAR LEFT: TROOPER, 3RD REGIMENT OF UHLANS, WITH HIS LANCE TO THE RIGHT.

LEFT: TROOPER, 1ST REGIMENT OF UHLANS, RIDING WITH HIS LANCE AT REST ON HIS RIGHT ARM.

RIGHT: BRITISH LANCERS IN FRANCE IN 1918, PAINTED BY A. E. HASWELL MILLER. FROM LEFT TO RIGHT ARE A TROOPER, 5TH (ROYAL IRISH) LANCERS IN FULL MARCHING ORDER; A TROOPER, 12TH (PRINCE OF WALES'S ROYAL) LANCERS, WEARING TWO WOUND STRIPES ON HIS LEFT SLEEVE, AND A CAPTAIN, 9TH (QUEEN'S ROYAL) LANCERS.

23

FIREARMS DRILL

The Prussian hussars illustrated here are also from Lieder and Krüger's book of 1825 (see previous pages). They are armed with flintlock smooth-bore pistols and carbines, both of which were essentially short-range weapons. This was especially true of the pistol, which to be effective needed to be fired at virtually point-blank range. The effective range of the carbine was about 50–60 yards.

TROOPER, 2ND REGIMENT OF HUSSARS, WITH HIS CARBINE ON HIS HIP, PRESUMABLY ON OUTPOST DUTY.

TROOPER, 3RD REGIMENT OF HUSSARS, RELOADING HIS CARBINE. HE APPEARS TO BE TAKING THINGS COOLLY, AS WOULD BEFIT A VETERAN OF THE NAPOLEONIC WARS (HIS MEDAL WOULD ALMOST CERTAINLY HAVE BEEN WON IN 1815 WHEN HIS REGIMENT WAS IN THE PRUSSIAN II CORPS, COMMANDED BY GENERAL VON PIRCH I). NOTE THAT HE KEEPS HIS RAMROD ON A CORD SO THAT IT WILL NOT GET LOST IN THE HEAT OF ACTION.

TROOPER, 4TH REGIMENT OF HUSSARS, FIRING HIS CARBINE; HIS HORSE REMAINS FIRM AND UNMOVING. AT WATERLOO THIS REGIMENT WAS IN I CORPS (VON ZIETHEN).

ABOVE LEFT: TROOPER, 5TH REGIMENT OF HUSSARS, HOLDING A PISTOL. HE IS EVIDENTLY ON OUTPOST DUTY, AND WOULD PROBABLY WARN HIS SUPPORTS OF THE APPROACH OF THE ENEMY BY FIRING HIS PISTOL INTO THE GROUND.
ABOVE RIGHT: TROOPER, 6TH REGIMENT OF HUSSARS, FIRING HIS PISTOL. HE IS SHOWN GALLOPING TO THE REAR AND, IT MAY BE ASSUMED, IS DISCHARGING HIS PISTOL EITHER AT A FOOT SOLDIER OR AT THE HORSE OF A PURSUING CAVALRYMAN. IN ACCORDANCE WITH THE RULES OF AIMING, HE HAS CLOSED HIS DISENGAGED EYE.

THE DRAGOON

The earliest dragoons, of the late 16th and 17th centuries, were mounted infantry armed with a kind of carbine called the *Dragon*. They were organized and trained as foot soldiers, and were mounted on horses which, generally speaking, would not have passed muster in the cavalry. Like the British Mounted Infantry of the Boer War (1899-1902), they dismounted to fight. But dragoons always tended to better themselves, improving their horsemanship and armament so that, in the British service for example, such regiments as the 1st Royals, 2nd Scots Greys and 6th Inniskillings became famous as cavalry, and by the time of Waterloo would sooner have been damned than go into action on foot!

AUSTRIAN DRAGOON, c. 1806. FROM *MILITARY COSTUMES OF THE IMPERIAL AUSTRIAN ARMY UNDER THE ARCHDUKE FERDINAND CHARLES, 1800-1812*, BY J. AND H. MANSFELD.

LIGHT CAVALRY

From the time of the first standing armies in the 17th century, the heavy cavalry were usually regular soldiers, whereas the light cavalry were often, though not invariably, irregulars of one sort or another. Cossacks, Bashkirs, Spahis, Hussars, the Plains Indians of North America – their range was broad and varied. By definition light troops, they were nevertheless expected to take their place in the line of battle, and when skilfully handled were capable of holding their own with heavy cavalry. Their main strength, however, was their suitability for outpost duty. Light cavalrymen were the eyes and ears of their commander, who depended on them to report to him the movements of the enemy, and to protect him from surprise. Patrols, scouting, raids and ambushes were their everyday work.

COSSACKS FROM THE CORPS OF THE CAUCASUS. FROM *LES UNIFORMES DE L'ARMÉE RUSSE EN 1843*.

LIGHT CAVALRY IN THE SERVICE OF LOUIS XIV, 1692. BY THE FEROCITY OF THEIR ATTITUDE, THESE MEN WERE CLEARLY IRREGULARS RECRUITED FROM BEYOND THE BORDERS OF THE FRENCH HOMELAND. FROM *COSTUMES MILITAIRES FRANÇAIS DE 1439 À 1789*. BY D. DE NOIRMONT AND ALFRED DE MARBOT.

FRENCH HUSSAR IN 1870.

THE CAVALRY

TWO HANDSOME PRINTS BY THOMAS ROWLANDSON ILLUSTRATING SABRE DRILL IN 1798.

TROOPER OF A MAHOMEDAN REGIMENT ON PATROL. FROM *COSTUMES MILITAIRES DE L'ARMÉE DE L'EMPEREUR DE TOUTES LES RUSSIES*, BY H. A. ECKERT AND CHEVALIER WEISS.

FORMATIONS FOR MANOEUVRE

In battle it is a good deal easier and safer to attack an adversary from behind, particularly when he is looking the other way. Most battle formations in properly disciplined and organized armies were designed to avoid conceding such an advantage. Until the latter end of the 19th century, when the magazine rifle and machine-gun radically altered all tactics, soldiers fought in some sort of line, each man keeping as close to his neighbour as he could without cramping the use of his weapons. The line had to be solid enough to repel a frontal assault and stretch far enough to make it difficult for an opponent to go round its end, or outflank it, without dangerously thinning his own line. The depth of the line therefore varied from age to age depending on the weapons of the time and the tactical doctrine, if any, then current.

Although armies fought in some form of line, when moving any considerable distance they usually marched in a long, thin column. Troops on the line of march were vulnerable and most drills were concerned with protecting them and enabling them to change rapidly from a formation suitable for movement to one suitable for combat. Two further considerations specifically affected the cavalry: first, horses in line tend to lean inwards, building up a pressure in the centre; second, because a horse is longer than it is wide, in close order it cannot execute individual turns in the same way as an infantryman. In the 18th century it was generally considered that not more than 60 horses should move close together in a continuous line.

For simplicity, the formations depicted here are those which were generally accepted and codified in most European armies towards the end of the 18th century. It can be assumed that the manoeuvres of all organized cavalry through the ages conformed to these in principle, although differing in detail; early cavalry were exceptional in that they fought in a line composed of more ranks than became customary later.

On the assumption that a continuous rank should not number more than 60 horsemen, the squadron, under various names, became the basic unit for manoeuvre. Where it was customary to deploy it in three ranks, its present strength numbered not more than 180, where in two ranks, not much more than 120; to allow for wastage, sick men and horses, and absentees, the authorized strength of squadrons varied between about 250 and 160 men *and* horses. In all formations troopers might ride in close order, that is, with each man's boots touching those of his neighbours; in loose files with six inches between boots, or open order with a horse's length (about three paces) between each man. Normally, for ease of control, manoeuvring was carried out in close order, the more open orders being employed only when tactically necessary. On the battlefield, formations tended to be less rigid than those advocated in the drill books. Irregular cavalry, whose duties required a more flexible approach, used less formal manoeuvres and looser formations. Control was exercised by the voice of the leader, often supplemented by trumpet calls, his gestures and example.

THE COMMANDER IS IN FRONT, THERE IS AN OFFICER COVERED BY A SERGEANT ON EITHER FLANK, AND SPARE OFFICERS AND SERGEANTS OCCUPY A SUPERNUMERARY RANK, OR SERRE FILE, BEHIND. THE POSITIONS OCCUPIED BY THE OFFICERS AND SERGEANTS VARIED FROM TIME TO TIME AND FROM ARMY TO ARMY.

A SQUADRON IN LINE (WITH TWO RANKS)

THE CAVALRY

A SQUADRON IN COLUMN (WITH FOUR DIVISIONS)

A SQUADRON WAS GENERALLY DIVIDED INTO A NUMBER OF SUB-UNITS CALLED, ACCORDING TO TASTE, HALF SQUADRONS, QUARTER SQUADRONS, DIVISIONS, SECTIONS OR SUB-SECTIONS; NOMENCLATURE WAS FAR FROM STANDARDIZED, AND IN THE 19TH CENTURY THESE SUB-UNITS WERE OFTEN CALLED TROOPS. AS IT WAS IMPORTANT THAT THEY SHOULD BE OF EQUAL SIZE, THEY WERE OFTEN DETAILED OFF AFTER THE SQUADRON HAD FALLEN IN FOR THE FIRST TIME THAT DAY. THE DISTANCE BETWEEN SUB-UNITS WOULD BE EQUAL TO THEIR FRONT SO THAT THEY COULD FORM LINE BY A SIMPLE WHEEL TO RIGHT OR LEFT.

A SQUADRON IN COLUMN OF ROUTE (SIXES)

THIS FORMATION WAS FOR LONG MOVES, E.G. OVER ROADS. FROM A POSITION IN LINE, THREE MEN OF THE FRONT RANK WOULD WHEEL TO THEIR RIGHT (OR LEFT) TO FORM A RANK WITH THREE MEN FROM THE REAR RANK WHO HAD EXECUTED A SIMILAR WHEEL; THUS THE SQUADRON WOULD MOVE WITH A HORSE'S LENGTH BETWEEN RANKS, AND ON A SINGLE ORDER THE THREES COULD WHEEL INDIVIDUALLY RIGHT OR LEFT AND THE SQUADRON WOULD BE ONCE MORE IN LINE. IF NEED BE, THE FRONT COULD BE REDUCED TO FOUR MEN, TWO OR EVEN SINGLE FILE; BUT IT WAS AN AXIOM THAT WHEREVER POSSIBLE THE LENGTH OF THE COLUMN SHOULD NOT EXCEED THE FRONT OF THE SQUADRON IN LINE.

THE COMMANDING OFFICER RIDES TWO HORSES' LENGTHS IN FRONT OF THE CENTRE OF HIS REGIMENT, THE SQUADRON COMMANDERS ONE HORSE'S LENGTH IN FRONT OF THE CENTRE OF THEIR SQUADRONS. THE OTHER OFFICERS AND THE SUPERNUMERARY RANK HAVE NOT BEEN SHOWN. THIS WAS THE NORMAL FORMATION FOR CHARGING CAVALRY, BUT THE PRUDENT COMMANDING OFFICER WOULD NORMALLY DETACH ONE SQUADRON FROM THE LINE TO ACT AS A RESERVE.

A REGIMENT OF FOUR SQUADRONS IN LINE

FORMATIONS FOR MANOEUVRE

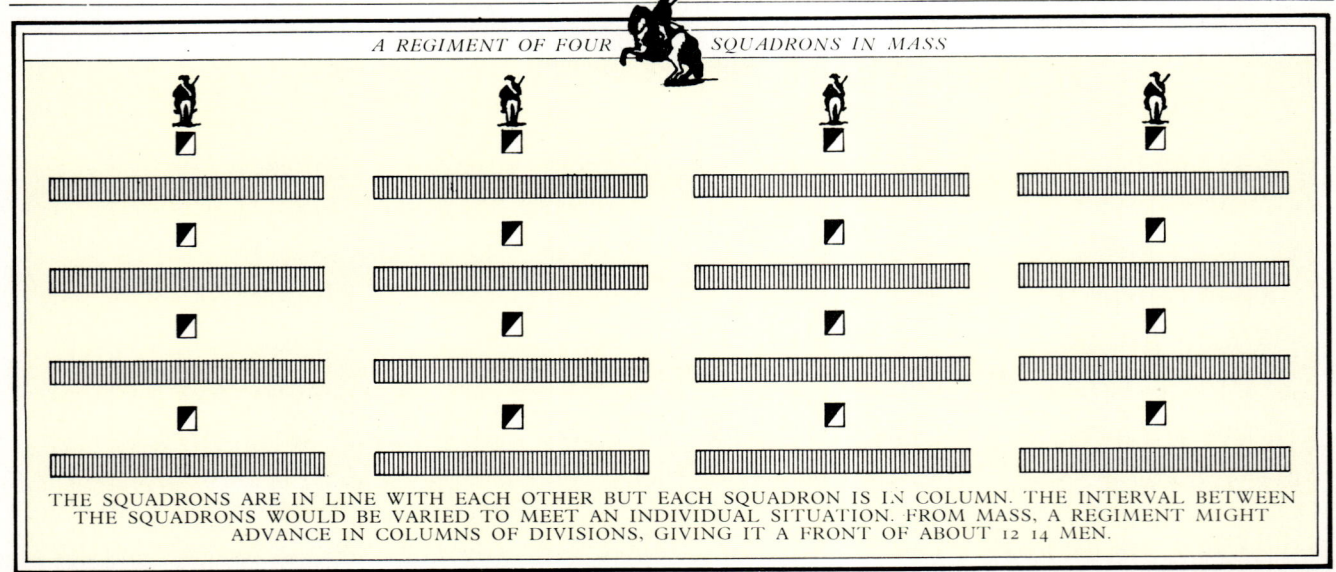

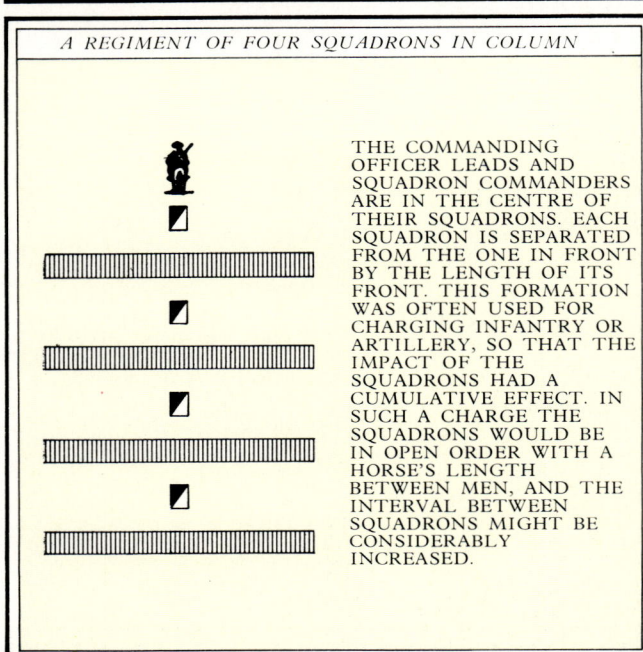

A REGIMENT OF FOUR SQUADRONS IN MASS

THE SQUADRONS ARE IN LINE WITH EACH OTHER BUT EACH SQUADRON IS IN COLUMN. THE INTERVAL BETWEEN THE SQUADRONS WOULD BE VARIED TO MEET AN INDIVIDUAL SITUATION. FROM MASS, A REGIMENT MIGHT ADVANCE IN COLUMNS OF DIVISIONS, GIVING IT A FRONT OF ABOUT 12-14 MEN.

A REGIMENT OF FOUR SQUADRONS IN COLUMN

THE COMMANDING OFFICER LEADS AND SQUADRON COMMANDERS ARE IN THE CENTRE OF THEIR SQUADRONS. EACH SQUADRON IS SEPARATED FROM THE ONE IN FRONT BY THE LENGTH OF ITS FRONT. THIS FORMATION WAS OFTEN USED FOR CHARGING INFANTRY OR ARTILLERY, SO THAT THE IMPACT OF THE SQUADRONS HAD A CUMULATIVE EFFECT. IN SUCH A CHARGE THE SQUADRONS WOULD BE IN OPEN ORDER WITH A HORSE'S LENGTH BETWEEN MEN, AND THE INTERVAL BETWEEN SQUADRONS MIGHT BE CONSIDERABLY INCREASED.

A DETACHMENT OF 12 TROOPERS ON OUTPOST DUTY COVERING THE MOVEMENTS OF THE ARMY AND BRINGING INFORMATION ABOUT THE ENEMY WERE TWO OF THE MOST IMPORTANT FUNCTIONS OF THE LIGHT CAVALRY. HERE EIGHT TROOPERS ARE SHOWN HELD CENTRALLY AS A RESERVE AND TO FURNISH RELIEFS FOR THE MOUNTED SENTRIES, KNOWN AS VEDETTES. PROVIDED THE LATTER OCCUPIED GOOD VIEWPOINTS, AND WERE REASONABLY ALERT, THEY WERE EXPECTED TO HAVE NO DIFFICULTY IN ELUDING ENEMY PATROLS, WHICH WOULD HESITATE TO LOSE FORMATION BY GALLOPING TOO FAST IN ENEMY-HELD TERRITORY.

THE CARACOLE: This was a manoeuvre in vogue towards the end of the 16th century, whereby cavalry in a series of ranks rode up to their enemy, discharged their pistols or carbines at them, then rode away to reload while another rank took their place. Pistol fire on horseback was inaccurate and largely ineffective; the caracole was probably the only manoeuvre open to cavalry confronted by infantry in a tight hedgehog of long pikes. With the development of the musket and artillery the need for this type of manoeuvre disappeared, and it was discontinued in the course of the 17th century.

THE CHARGE: This might be delivered at all speeds from a slow amble to an all-out gallop, depending on the weight carried by the horse and the tactics of the day. Galloping over a long distance was frowned on, particularly against enemy cavalry, for it was fatal to engage in a *mêlée*, the hand-to-hand combat that often followed the charge, with blown horses. Against infantry or guns in the 18th and 19th centuries, cavalry broke into a gallop when they came under effective fire. After a charge, ranks would be disordered and it would be necessary to halt and reform, or rally. When men and horses were excited and there was an inviting prospect of plunder this was by no means easy and required a high standard of discipline. It was generally thought that to receive an enemy cavalry charge at a standstill invited disaster.

PART 2
THE STORY
OF THE CAVALRY

THE CAVALRY

ASSYRIAN MOUNTED ARCHER OF THE 7TH CENTURY BC. THE HORSE HAS BEEN TRAINED TO REMAIN STILL WHILE THE ARCHER DISCHARGES HIS BOW. ILLUSTRATION BY DAVID POCKNELL.

ORIGINS by JAMES LAWFORD

THE first man to mount a horse probably fell off shortly afterwards; no less probably, he was discouraged. To other would-be horsemen it became apparent that an animal harnessed to a vehicle lost some of its freedom of movement, and so could be better controlled; besides, the floor of a vehicle must have seemed steadier and more comfortable than the bare back of a steed. Perhaps for these reasons it appears that horses first went into battle harnessed to chariots. At the time fighting in chariots must have seemed a daring innovation: in practice they were expensive to make, clumsy to manoeuvre, and useless on anything but an open, flat plain. Chariots, not least those with scythes fitted to their wheels, may have looked formidable enough, but they frequently proved an asset of doubtful value.

ASSYRIAN WAR CHARIOTS. THEY ARE DRAWN BY THREE HORSES, WHICH SUGGESTS A HIGH DEGREE OF HORSE MANAGEMENT ON THE PART OF THE DRIVER. CHARIOTS CARRIED TWO TO FOUR MEN—A DRIVER AND AN ARCHER PLUS, ON OCCASION, SUPPORTING INFANTRY. RELIEF DEPICTING THE CAMPAIGNS OF ASSURNASIRPAL (REIGNED 9TH CENTURY BC).

However, once the horse had been harnessed to a vehicle, bit and bridle grew progressively more efficient and, as the animal became easier to control, inevitably someone again clambered on its back and this time found his perch not unreasonably insecure. Probably some herdsman in the grassland regions of southern Russia or central Asia first succeeded in sitting on a horse, and then found his mount exceedingly useful for looking after his cattle. Once it was known that horses could be ridden with relative impunity, the practice undoubtedly spread rapidly.

The Assyrians, living in the region that is now northern Iraq, in a country without well-defined borders, created one of the first properly organized armies in order to deter the more predatory of their neighbours. In the palace at Nineveh, one of their capital cities, is a relief dated about 750 BC showing a mounted soldier drawing a bow while his well-drilled mount stands motionless to avoid disturbing his aim. Obviously by this time mounted archers formed an established part of the Assyrian army.

Although the chariot remained a weapon of war for some centuries to come, particularly in militarily backward countries such as Ancient Britain, the horseman, able to move more rapidly and freely over difficult country, clearly made the chariot obsolescent. In accounts of the Siege of Troy, which took place in the late 12th century BC, there is no mention of warriors riding into battle. It seems fair to assume, therefore, that the first cavalryman came on the battlefield at some later date, possibly in the 10th century BC.

Apart from stories of the mythical centaurs, as likely as not derived from highly coloured travellers' tales about some early tribe of horsemen, the first written accounts of cavalry actions refer to the Persian drive westwards. When Cyrus the Great (reigned 550–530 BC) thrust towards the eastern shores of the Mediterranean, he possessed a considerable force of cavalry; even so, he held in some awe the noted horsemen of Lydia. And when Croesus, King of Lydia, encouraged by a Delphic prophecy saying that if he fought, an empire would be lost—without specifying the empire—barred the way forward and offered battle near Sardis, Cyrus felt obliged to adopt an ingenious and unusual strategem. As Herodotus tells us, he deployed all his baggage camels ahead of his battle line, where the sight of these unprepossessing animals and their rank smell so affrighted the horses of the Lydian cavalry that, despite the desperate efforts of their riders, they turned and bolted, fatally disordering the ranks of their own army. The incident, besides suggesting that horse management

33

THE CAVALRY

still left something to be desired, brings to light one enduring characteristic of the cavalry, that horses as well as men have wills of their own and the two may conflict with unfortunate results. One needs also to remember that at this time the cavalryman rode bareback or on a cloth thrown across the back of his mount; some 10 centuries were to elapse before saddles and stirrups came into use.

Perhaps it was owing to a certain unsteadiness on their mounts that the early Persian cavalry remained largely mounted archers, reluctant to come to close quarters. This reluctance was to cost them dear when the westward march of the Persians brought them into conflict with the Greek city states. By this time the cavalry were the principal arm in the Persian army and as a result the infantry, gallant enough individually, were poorly trained and worse equipped. The Greeks,

In the spring of 479, Mardonius raided Athens; the Greeks, led by Pausanias, one of the Kings of Sparta, advanced to expel the intruders. For the first time the Greeks met an army with a considerable number of cavalry and Pausanias, acting with great caution, kept to the hills. The Persian cavalry harassed the Greek army cruelly, but at the Battle of Plataea the ill-equipped Persian infantry, although superior in numbers, could not match the Spartan hoplites, and the Persian cavalry, unwilling to charge into the mass of struggling infantry, failed to save the day. The defeat at Plataea ended Persian dreams of conquest in Europe, and the Greeks, unimpressed by the performance of the Persian cavalry and somewhat contemptuous of archers who killed the enemy from a distance instead of standing up to them man-to-man, did little to repair their weakness in

THE CAMEL, TO JUDGE BY THE DIRECTION OF THE ARCHER'S AIM, IS LEAVING THE BATTLEFIELD AT HIGH SPEED. IT HAS AN AIR OF SINGULAR FEROCITY, AND IT IS EASY TO UNDERSTAND WHY THE LYDIAN CAVALRY REFUSED TO FACE THE CAMELS OF CYRUS. ASSYRIAN RELIEF, *c.*7TH CENTURY BC.

on the other hand, living in a hilly country deficient in pastureland, possessed few horses, and developed highly trained, armoured heavy infantry, the hoplites, who fought in a formation known as the phalanx, in essence a pike-fringed wedge of heavy infantry in close order, numbering about 4,000 and ranged from 12 to 16 ranks deep. The war, therefore, was between one army in which cavalry were predominant, and one composed almost entirely of infantry.

In the first great clash, at Marathon in 490 BC, the Greeks had the advantage for the invading Persians came by sea and were unable to bring with them their horses. The Greek hoplites, fighting unarmoured Persian infantry protected only by flimsy wicker shields, tore their enemy apart despite being outnumbered by nearly two to one. In 480 BC Xerxes the 'Great King', as the Persian monarch was called, determined to make full use of his cavalry, and invaded Greece overland; he outflanked and destroyed a Greek army at Thermopylae, ravaged Attica and burnt Athens. The Greek navy, however, utterly defeated the Persian fleet at Salamis. Xerxes, worried that a Greek fleet in the Dardanelles might cut him off from Asia, returned to his vast dominions in that continent leaving Mardonius, one of his ablest generals, with a strong army to winter in northern Greece.

this arm. They could argue that in war a cavalryman with his horse probably cost twice as much as an infantryman yet did not appear to be twice as effective. By now, however, most of the wealthier among the Greeks rode, and in northern Greece, particularly in Thessaly, some cavalry units were raised.

When in 401 BC the Athenian Xenophon joined a mercenary Greek army of 10,000 Greeks hired by Cyrus, the brother of the Persian King, Artaxerxes, ostensibly to keep order in his dominions, the core of the army was still the hoplites accompanied by a due proportion of peltasts (lightly armed skirmishers), slingers and bowmen. Cyrus, having assembled his army at Sardis and added a strong contingent of Persian horse and infantry, wandered south-eastwards with it across the rugged mountains of modern Turkey. En route it became evident to the Greeks that Cyrus had duped them and intended to use them to overthrow his brother. When faced with this, Cyrus promised them rich rewards if his rebellion succeeded, and after long discussion among themselves the Greeks agreed to continue with him.

From the vicinity of Aleppo, well outside the boundaries of his own provinces, Cyrus marched east to the upper reaches of the Euphrates; he crossed to the far bank then followed the course of

ORIGINS

the river towards Babylon. Up to this time Artaxerxes had done nothing, but now some 2,000 Royal Persian horsemen appeared who fell back slowly before the rebel army. Of Artaxerxes himself, however, nothing was known. Then near the village of Cunaxa, some 50 miles from Babylon, Artaxerxes struck. Now Cyrus paid the penalty for not deploying his cavalry well forward. His army was strung out on the line of march in a long straggling column when at noon, just as its head was reaching the camping place appointed for the day, a horseman on a lathered horse galloped down its length, shouting out in Persian and Greek that Artaxerxes with a huge army in order of battle was upon them. In some confusion the leading units hurriedly deployed. However, it was not until early in the hot afternoon that a white cloud of dust in the distance heralded the approach of the enemy; the white cloud dissipated to reveal thick, dark columns filling the flat sandy waste, with sudden pinpoints of light flickering here and there on a spearpoint or a cuirass.

The Greeks, leading the advance of Cyrus's army, formed their phalanx with their right resting on the river. On their left Cyrus himself took station with 600 picked cavalrymen, armed, so Xenophon informs us, with helmet, breast-plate and thigh-piece and carrying 'Greek' sabres. The foreheads and chests of their horses also were protected by armour.

These and the Greek mercenaries succeeded in deploying, but much of Cyrus's army was still marching up when the enemy columns, coming forward steadily and in silence, closed to about 600 yards and the battle began. At this moment the Greek phalanx surged forward, the soldiers first singing the paean, their battle chant, then shouting out their war cry. As they neared the Persians, the Greeks in their eagerness began to run forward, endangering the regularity of the phalanx. The Persians opposed to them did not wait, but panicked and fled; some empty Persian chariots bolted through the Greek line, the files opening out to let them pass; many more galloped away from the gleaming spears and shields to scythe down their own troops.

As the Greeks pressed exultantly forward, their open left flank became exposed to a counter-stroke from a body of 6,000 cavalry that Artaxerxes had stationed in his centre. Cyrus, recognizing the peril and fancying moreover that he could see his elder brother lurking beyond them, charged impetuously forward. His 600 men crashed through the stationary Royal Persian horse scattering them to the winds, and he himself is credited with slaying their commander, Artagerses. But then the triumphant rebel cavalry, in chasing after their routed opponents, in Xenophon's words 'lost their order in the heat of the pursuit'. Cyrus with a handful of men cut his way to where he could see his brother surrounded by his bodyguard; but the odds were too great and Cyrus himself died from a javelin thrust in the face.

Deprived of its head, the rebellion collapsed. The Greek mercenaries, however, refused to give up their arms and surrender. Now their lack of cavalry came to be felt. The Greek generals discussed the situation, and their chances of fighting their way home. Clearchus, a Spartan and the accepted leader, said bluntly that in the Persian army the cavalry was the most numerous and efficient of their arms. If the Greeks defeated the cavalry, they could not pursue men on horses and exploit their victory whereas if they themselves were defeated, none would survive. The statement was incontrovertible, although at a later stage Xenophon himself pointed out that 10,000 horsemen were still only 10,000 men; insecurely seated on his mount the cavalryman could not strike such sure and powerful blows as the infantryman standing sturdily on the ground; the only advantage the cavalryman possessed over his infantry colleague was that he could retreat faster.

At first it appeared that Artaxerxes intended to allow the Greeks to go unharmed. They marched up the Tigris escorted by a Persian army under Tissaphernes. Near Nineveh, however, the Persian enticed the Greek generals into his tent, treacherously seized them and shortly afterwards Artaxerxes had them executed. The Greeks, dismayed but stubbornly determined not to surrender, pushed on up the Tigris towards the hills of Armenia. But now the Persians became actively hostile; seeing that his cavalry feared to charge the hoplites, instead Tissaphernes harassed the Greek column with large numbers of archers who showered them with arrows from a distance. When the hoplites charged their tormentors, the lightly armed archers had little difficulty in eluding them; then when the hoplites attempted to resume their march the archers once more closed in. The Greeks, however, were never at a loss for long. They improvised slingers who outranged the Persian slingers and

THE CAVALRY

bowmen, and mounted 50 of their number on horses to chase them. These tactics proved successful and the Persians ceased pressing an unprofitable pursuit. After many vicissitudes Xenophon led the army back to Europe after one of the most remarkable marches in history.

In this campaign were revealed most of the salient features of cavalry warfare through the ages. Artaxerxes, by deploying a large number of his cavalry well forward, disguised the movements of his own army while making certain he was fully informed about those of his adversary; as a result he gained an initial advantage that almost guaranteed victory. At Cunaxa the Persian cavalry appeared to have abandoned the use of missiles in favour of shock action, perhaps as a consequence of their failures in Greece. However, by receiving Cyrus's charge when stationary, the Persians were broken by a force numbering only a tenth of their own, the incident demonstrating how potent cavalry were in attack, how weak in defence.

Then, after his triumph, Cyrus failed to rally his men, never an easy thing to do when men and horses are excited by battle and the men not immune to the attractions of plundering the enemy's baggage. Their failure to rally cost him the battle, as similar failures were to ruin other armies time and again in the future. Lastly, the campaign showed clearly the interdependence of cavalry and infantry; without good infantry the Persians dared not attack a force of hoplites less than a quarter of their number; while, as Clearchus so cogently pointed out, the Greeks, with no cavalry of their own, could not contemplate attacking the Persians. One of the greatest of generals, Alexander III of Macedon (356–323 BC), was shortly to demonstrate how almost irresistible an army would be when cavalry and infantry were treated with equal respect, and combined so that each could use its own particular capabilities to the full.

Alexander's father, King Philip II of Macedonia (382–336 BC), ruled a state the inhabitants of which, Greek by extraction, were arrogantly regarded by the Athenians as little more than barbarians. Philip organized a splendid army; his son moulded it into one without peer. The striking power, the mailed fist of Alexander's army, was a corps of choice heavy cavalry and heavy infantry, an early Imperial Guard, certain of triumphing on whatever part of the battlefield they fought. The cavalry of the Guard, the *hetairoi*, he organized in eight squadrons 200–300 strong, including his bodyguard squadron, the choicest of the choice; these he recruited from the leading young men in his kingdom. He balanced them by his *hypaspists*, his infantry of the Guard, organized in three battalions each 1,000 strong. These were heavy infantry, possibly less heavily armoured than the hoplites

EARLY GREEK CAVALRYMEN, EACH ARMED WITH TWO THROWING JAVELINS. THEIR UNPROTECTED LEGS WOULD BE VERY VULNERABLE IN CLOSE-QUARTER FIGHTING. ATTIC VASE, 5TH CENTURY BC.

ABOVE: HELMETED GREEK HORSEMAN FROM GRUMENTUM. BRONZE STATUE. c.550 BC.

RIGHT: RELIEF OF A GREEK INFANTRYMAN, ERECTED ON THE SITE OF THE BATTLE OF MARATHON (490 BC).

ORIGINS

but so skilled and well trained that they could execute almost any infantry manoeuvre.

While the Guard was the backbone of his army, Alexander fully recognized the importance of numbers, and he bulked out his army with less highly skilled troops. The ordinary citizens of Macedonia and other Greeks he enrolled in an orthodox phalanx which he used as the anchor of his battle line. He added to them numerous unarmoured light infantry equipped with bows and slings, darts and javelins, whose function was to clear the way forward for the phalanx; these he recruited from his allies. For his ordinary cavalry he obtained 2,000 heavy cavalry from Thessaly and supplemented them with unarmoured light cavalry carrying bows and spears and a regiment with long pikes – the first lancers; the light cavalry he used to harass and reconnoitre the movements of the enemy; in battle their tasks were to drive in the enemy light troops and protect the flanks of the infantry phalanx. So catholic was his outlook that he even organized soldiers mounted on horseback but trained to fight on foot, who foreshadowed the dragoons and mounted infantry of the future. It could be said that Alexander anticipated almost every organization and function of the cavalry, and his employment of that arm was to be the foundation of his astounding series of victories.

His father had established his authority over all Greece, but when he died by the hand of an assassin in 336 BC, the Greek city states revolted. The young Alexander, 20 years old, trampled ruthlessly on Thebes and the revolt abruptly subsided; then in 334, perhaps to emphasize to the Greeks their common identity, he crossed the Dardanelles to deal a mortal blow to the ancient enemy, Persia, at that time ruled by Darius III.

While his army consisting of 30,000 foot and 5,000 horse reassembled after the crossings near the town of Canakhale, Alexander visited the ruined site of Troy. He returned to learn that his light cavalry had discovered a Persian army of 10,000 cavalry and 5,000 Greek mercenary hoplites encamped on the banks of the River Granicus, a few miles inland from the Sea of Marmora and about 60 to his east. He had planned to move south on Sardis, but now at once marched to deal with this small army impudently threatening his line of communications; he welcomed, besides, so excellent an opportunity to score an early success. He came on the Persians in a strong position protected by the river; they lined its far bank with their cavalry, but for some inexplicable reason placed their Greek infantry well back in reserve. The Granicus was everywhere fordable, but scrambling up the far bank in the face of the Persians seemed a hazardous business. His most experienced general, Parmenion, counselled delay. Alexander rejected with scorn his suggestion. He drew up his army in the traditional manner with the infantry in the centre and the cavalry on the flanks. He commanded on the right with the infantry and cavalry of the Guard, while Parmenion commanded on the left with the ordinary phalanx and the Thessalian heavy cavalry. As his wing advanced to the attack, Alexander abruptly altered its dispositions; he kept back his heavy cavalry and swung across its front a mixed

ALEXANDER THE GREAT, PROBABLY MOUNTED ON HIS FAMOUS CHARGER BUCEPHALUS, WHICH ONLY HE COULD RIDE. GRAECO-ROMAN BRONZE, POSSIBLY AFTER A FIGURE IN THE GROUP DEDICATED BY ALEXANDER TO COMMEMORATE HIS VICTORY AT GRANICUS (334 BC).

37

THE CAVALRY

force of light cavalry and infantry of the Guard to assault the Persian left.

A fierce struggle broke out as the Macedonians strove to force their way up the far bank of the river. The Persians weakened their centre to aid their threatened flank. It was the mistake Alexander was looking for. With the white plumes of his helmet waving proudly over his head, he led the Bodyguard squadron forward followed by the remainder of the cavalry of the Guard in column of squadrons.

The Bodyguard splashed over the river and up the far side; they thrust the Persians in front of them back, while the remaining squadrons poured over into the bridgehead they had created. For a brief period a violent hand-to-hand combat erupted. Alexander himself speared the Persian commander, Mithridates, and saw him fall. A Persian struck him from behind, sheering off some of his plumes and part of his helmet; unhurt, Alexander wheeled and cut down his assailant. By now the cavalry were over the river and elements of the infantry were beginning to form their phalanx in the bridgehead. Persian resistance suddenly ceased. As the cavalry in their centre streamed away, those on the two wings joined in their flight. Alexander did not pursue. Ahead of him stood a forest of steady spears and shields. The Greek mercenaries, knowing retreat to be useless, dourly stood their ground. Alexander attacked them in front with his heavy infantry and in the flanks and rear with his cavalry. They fought with their habitual courage but without hope. When nearly half their number had fallen the remainder ceased resistance and threw down their arms.

Again and again in future battles Alexander used his heavy cavalry of the Guard to execute the stroke that decided the issue. He proved that, although unable directly to assault unshaken heavy infantry, cavalry, correctly handled, could be the arbiters of the battlefield. Yet in Italy the Romans, confident in their own military prowess, paid little heed to what happened in faraway Asia.

Possibly because their earliest campaigns were fought in mountainous country, possibly because good horses were scarce and expensive, the Romans never valued cavalry to the full or used them to the best advantage. This strange error resulted in them suffering some of their most calamitous defeats, and when in the Second Punic War (219–202 BC) they fought against Hannibal, who handled his cavalry with something of the genius of Alexander, it nearly led to the ruin of Rome.

Hannibal was one of the great generals of all time. Livy, no admirer of the Carthaginians, wrote of him that he was equally ready to obey or command; heat and cold he endured with indifference; he ate and drank only to satisfy his physical needs; he was happy to sleep on the ground covered only by his mantle; the quality of his arms marked him out, never that of his dress. Such was the great Carthaginian who was to shake Rome to its very foundations.

His infantry, mercenaries drawn from Spain, Gaul and Africa, still fought in the phalanx, a tactical formation inferior to the looser and more flexible one practised by the Roman legions. Apart from his personal genius, Hannibal's superiority lay in his cavalry. His heavy cavalry, recruited from Spain and Gaul, differed little from that of Macedonia; his light came from Numidia. The Numidians, unarmoured and nearly naked, carried a light shield, a lance, two javelins and a sword. Such was their mastery of their desert ponies that they are reputed to have ridden them bareback without bit or bridle; they were one with their mounts, able to guide them by no more than a light touch with a staff. They avoided close combat, depending on baffling their opponents by their speed and agility. Tireless in pursuit, clever as a hunting leopard in the use of ground, expert in ambushes, they were the finest of light, irregular cavalry, the first of a tradition continued by the hussars of the Hungarian plains and the cossacks of the steppes.

The strength of the Roman Army lay in its legions composed of 4–5,000 heavy infantry organized in 10 cohorts with a light infantry component that included slingers and archers. But the organization of the cavalry was defective. It was founded on the *ala*, a squadron of unarmoured horse at this time about 300 strong, which formed part of the legion, in effect making the cavalry no more than an adjunct of the infantry; moreover the *ala* was split up into 10 troops or *turmae*, each of 30 troopers, and these were allotted one to each cohort. Thus the cavalry, although drawn from the 'knights', that is from the wealthier of the Romans, had no corporate identity, nor much practice in working together as a separate arm; on occasion they were known to dismount to fight on foot. Their functions were scouting and foraging and in battle to cover the flanks of the infantry.

In war the Roman Army, the 'State in Arms', was commanded by the two consuls currently at the head of the Roman senate; when serving together they commanded on alternate days – the Romans always mistrusted placing too much power in the hands of one man. In times of crisis, however,

A THRACIAN HEAVY CAVALRYMAN OF THE 3RD CENTURY BC. HE IS VERY LIKELY A SENIOR OFFICER, AND IS SHOWN GRASPING A PIKE OR LANCE IN THE OVERHEAD GRIP. A CENTURY EARLIER, ALEXANDER THE GREAT HAD ENLISTED THRACIAN LANCERS – ALTHOUGH THE LATTER WERE LIGHT CAVALRY. THE ILLUSTRATION IS A DETAIL FROM A THRACIAN HELMET.

ORIGINS

a single dictator could be appointed with a Master of Horse as his second-in-command (despite his title the latter was the deputy of the dictator and not a cavalry commander). Such was the Roman Army when in 218 BC Hannibal invaded Italy. The Romans staggered from defeat to defeat, culminating in a shattering disaster by the shores of Lake Trasimene; facing a threat to their very existence they appointed Quintus Fabius dictator. He pursued the 'Fabian' strategy associated with his name, avoiding battle and seeking at all costs to keep his army intact. Rome, far superior to the Carthaginians in resources and with a short line of communication, was bound to win a war of attrition. As the war dragged on, however, the Roman people wearied of a general who, with an army outnumbering that of his adversary, appeared frightened to fight him. When Fabius's term of office ran out he was replaced by two consuls, Aemilius Paulus and Terentius Varro, and these were sent to join the army with orders to put an end to the delays and bring the Carthaginian to battle.

Hannibal, frustrated by Fabius, had been compelled to remain on the east coast of Italy and watch helplessly as the balance of power inexorably tilted towards Rome. He needed urgently a victory that might cause Rome's allies to forsake that tottering giant. Before the two new consuls arrived, by a skilful march he slipped past the Roman army watching him into the rich plains of Apulia, and snatched the well-stocked Roman base at Cannae which, by an inexcusable oversight, had been neither adequately fortified nor garrisoned. Here in open country he waited for the Roman army to gather themselves before advancing to avenge the insult.

about seven miles distant. A little to the north of both armies flowed the River Aufidus, at this time of year fordable in most places; it was to have some significance in the actions that followed.

The day after their arrival, Varro led his army towards the Carthaginians and formed order of battle about three miles from Cannae. Hannibal saw the Romans leave the high ground with some satisfaction. He made as if to give battle but did not commit his army. A partial engagement ensued, at the end of which the Carthaginians retired to their camp by Cannae, while the Romans remained the apparent masters of the battlefield. Varro at once pitched his camp on the field where, as he thought, he had triumphed.

Next day Paulus took command. He disliked the situation and mistrusted the ability of the Romans to meet Hannibal in country which favoured the Carthaginian cavalry. He could not retreat from a victorious battlefield without making a mortal enemy of his fellow commander and exciting the contempt of his soldiers. Yet he was loath to fight on ground he deemed disadvantageous. He compromised, and built a subsidiary camp north of the Aufidus and west of the Carthaginians, from which he proposed to harry Hannibal's communications with the north and thus compel him to withdraw. Next day Varro muzzled his ardour sufficiently to consolidate the position without attempting any large-scale manoeuvre, while Hannibal prepared his men for the decisive battle he knew the Romans could no longer avoid. The following day with Paulus commanding, and part of the Roman army in the subsidiary camp north of the river, Hannibal marched his army out and offered battle. Paulus declined the invitation; in the afternoon Hannibal sent his Numidians over the river to harass the subsidiary Roman camp. The Numidians rode up to its palisades, jeering at the garrison and cutting them off from the river, their only source of water.

PORTRAIT OF HANNIBAL, THE GREAT CARTHAGINIAN GENERAL WHO TOOK THE ARMIES OF ROME TO THE BRINK OF DESTRUCTION. FROM A LATE 18TH-CENTURY ENGRAVING BY J. CHAPMAN.

Hannibal had with him about 40,000 infantry and 10,000 cavalry, the Romans 16 legions amounting to 80,000 infantry and 6,000 cavalry. Varro, a loud-voiced bull-like plebeian, wanted immediate action; his fellow-consul, the experienced patrician Paulus, favoured a more cautious approach, while the Roman soldiers as a whole, conscious of their superiority in numbers, burned for action. And so with their commanders divided, they marched on Cannae. Early in June 216 BC Hannibal waiting at Cannae saw the long, orderly columns of Romans appear, and watched them erect their customary fortified camp on some high ground at Canusium

Early next morning Varro resolved to show his timid colleague how the Romans should wage war. Leaving two legions to hold his camp, he marched the remainder of his army over the river, drove in the Numidian patrols, and formed line of battle with 2,000 Roman horse on his right by the river, his infantry in the centre stretching away to the north, and the cavalry of his Italian allies

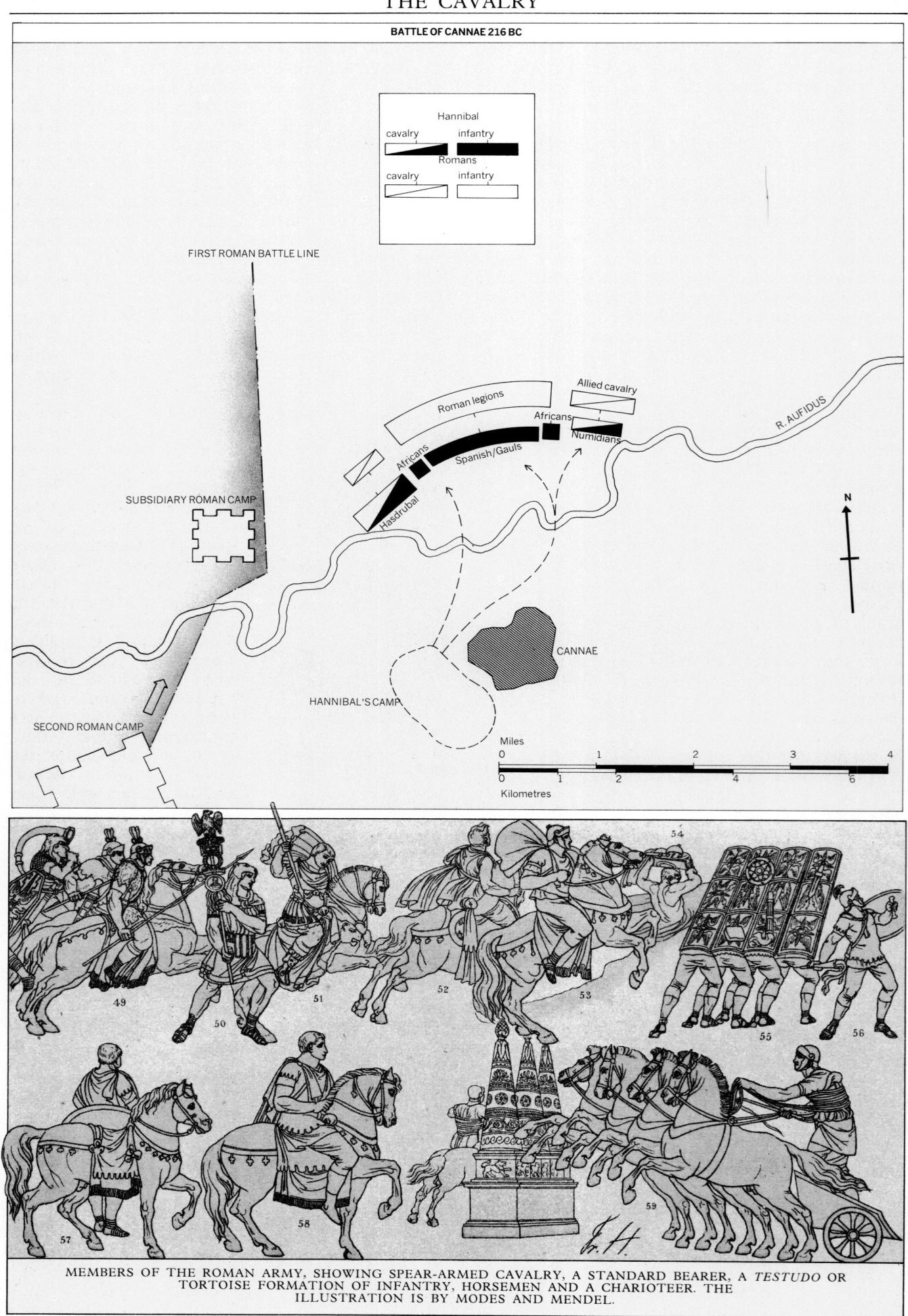

THE CAVALRY

BATTLE OF CANNAE 216 BC

MEMBERS OF THE ROMAN ARMY, SHOWING SPEAR-ARMED CAVALRY, A STANDARD BEARER, A *TESTUDO* OR TORTOISE FORMATION OF INFANTRY, HORSEMEN AND A CHARIOTEER. THE ILLUSTRATION IS BY MODES AND MENDEL.

who numbered 4,000 covering his open left flank.

When he saw the Romans marching out Hannibal knew the moment of decision had arrived. He crossed the river on a wide front about a mile to the north-east of the Romans, but then he halted with the river at his back and formed his battle line in a shallow arc of about 4,000 yards with the river as its chord. It was an unusual position to adopt, and a very dangerous one if the battle developed unfavourably, but for Hannibal it had two great advantages: the river protected both his flanks if the Romans tried to overlap him, and the ground in front was flat and open, well suited to his cavalry. He stationed his infantry in the centre of the line. Outnumbered two to one by the Roman infantry, he considered it essential to stretch his battle line so as to enable his cavalry to operate freely without either being confronted by Roman infantry or constrained by the need to safeguard the flanks of their own. He therefore deployed his Spanish and Gaulish infantry in only 10 ranks, but placed on their flanks his African infantry, 16 ranks deep, to act as pillars to constrict a Roman drive forward and form a base round which his own cavalry could manoeuvre. He placed his 8,000 heavy cavalry under his brother Hasdrubal opposite the Roman cavalry, and the Numidians on his right to keep the cavalry of the Italian allies in play. By this means he concentrated all his heavy cavalry in a solid mass against the weaker flank of his enemy, gaining a huge tactical advantage.

Varro swung his army round, pivoting on the Roman cavalry, so that his battle line enclosed that of his enemy. But instead of using infantry to strengthen his cavalry wings, as a Caesar would have done, he concentrated them into a mighty sledgehammer of steel with which to crush the Carthaginian centre; in doing so he deployed his legions in a close order unfamiliar to the soldiers. When his dispositions were completed the trumpets blared; bellowing their war cries, the legions advanced across the grassy plain towards the waiting Carthaginians. The sun glared down out of a hot blue sky, and as the Roman infantry strode forward the wind began to whip up sand and dust in their faces. The light troops loosed their missiles and withdrew, then the long line of shields crashed into the Carthaginian infantry.

Yet even before that blow was struck, Hasdrubal at the head of his cavalry had charged and broken the Roman knights after a brief but ferocious struggle in which Paulus, commanding on that wing, was wounded. With admirable precision the Carthaginian cavalry reformed. Then the mass of cavalry swept in a great loop behind the centre, already wreathed in dust, where the heavy infantry were locked in a grapple to the death. On the Carthaginian right the Numidians, outnumbered two to one by the cavalry of the Italian allies, contrived to keep their heavy, clumsy opponents in check. Then out of the dust rising behind the Italians, Hasdrubal's heavy squadrons came thundering down. The result was instantaneous; the ranks of the allied cavalry shattered into fragments. Varro, commanding on this wing, fled with the survivors. Again Hasdrubal rallied his victorious squadrons. Leaving the vengeful Numidians chasing the fugitives, he wheeled his cavalry round behind the embattled Roman infantry.

Here the Romans had driven the centre of the Carthaginian infantry nearly back to the river; but the flanks had held firm and the Romans, compressed into a shallow salient, had fallen into disorder, the legionaries jostling each other and unable to handle their weapons effectively. At that moment the heavy cavalry of Hasdrubal smashed down on the unsuspecting Roman rear, driving it headlong into the disordered ranks ahead. Now the Roman army was little more than an enormous, confused mob of soldiers enclosed in a ring of steel which remorselessly tightened about them. Paulus, despite his wounds, strove desperately to restore some form of order; he fell buried under a mound of corpses. Most of the Romans fought and died where they stood; some 17,000 managed to cut their way out, many taking refuge in their camps which surrendered next day. Out of the Roman army of 86,000 perhaps 14,000 rejoined the Eagles within the next few days. Hannibal had won his greatest victory, and although his infantry had fought well it was his cavalry who had gained the day.[1] The control and discipline that enabled a great mass of 8,000 horsemen to charge, reform, change front and charge twice again can rarely have been excelled.

---

[1] It has been suggested that Hannibal led the Romans into a trap in the infantry battle and that the African infantry, hitherto unengaged, swung round on the flanks of the Roman legions to destroy them by a double envelopment. Although there is historical evidence for this point of view, arithmetically it seems highly unlikely. Taking into account detachments, camp guards and sick, probably about 60,000 Romans organized in 14 legions confronted 30,000 Carthaginian infantry. Here some assumptions must be made. Assuming the Carthaginians had 3,000 light troops, they would have had 27,000 heavy infantry; assuming further that these numbers were spread more or less equally between the Spanish and the Gauls in the centre and the Africans on the flanks, each contingent would number about 9,000. Hannibal's centre would then consist of 18,000 men ranged in 10 ranks; at a yard per man, the normal distance in a phalanx, its front would cover 1,800 yards; the Africans ranged in 16 ranks would cover 600 yards, giving a total Carthaginian infantry front of 2,400 yards.

The Roman legions at this time fought on a front of 10 maniples each separated by a maniple's front, the gap being covered by a maniple in the second line. Each maniple operated on a front of 12 files, five feet being allowed for each man, making a total front of 60 feet, or 20 yards for each maniple. Thus the front of a legion, without its cavalry, would extend for 200 yards for the maniples plus 180 yards for the gaps between them, giving a total front per legion of 380 yards; in battle this would probably average 400 yards. The front occupied by 14 legions therefore would be 400 × 14 = 5,600 yards, more than twice that of the Carthaginians. It is recorded that Varro fought in an unusually close order, but even if he halved that front it would still be longer than that of the Carthaginians. In the circumstances it seems almost impossible that the African flank troops were not engaged at the outset, and that such envelopment as occurred was caused by the failure of the Romans to drive these flanks in.

That Hasdrubal should be able to move round behind the Roman army and first surprise the Italian cavalry from the rear and then repeat the same operation against the Roman infantry, with nothing being done to hinder him, seems inconceivable – if the Carthaginian cavalry could be seen. It must, therefore, be assumed that the Romans were not able to see them. It has been stated that the wind was blowing in the faces of the Romans and also that they were nearly blinded by the dust. Hasdrubal may thus have triumphed because the dust kicked up by 90,000 struggling infantrymen blew behind the Romans to hang in low clouds, veiling their rear.

THE CAVALRY

STATUE OF A ROMAN HEAVY CAVALRYMAN IN ACTION.

ORIGINS

EVEN IN ANTIQUITY WOMEN COULD MAKE THEIR VIEWS FELT: HERE AN AMAZON IS PORTRAYED FIRING A 'PARTHIAN SHOT'. SHE IS ONE OF FOUR FIGURES CIRCLING THE RIM OF AN ETRUSCAN LEBES OR CAULDRON.

In the end the superior resources of Rome proved too much for Hannibal and at last, the flower of his army destroyed in 14 years of unremitting strife, at Zama in Africa he met with defeat. The Romans drove the poor remnants of the Carthaginian cavalry from the field and Scipio Africanus won a Cannae in reverse. Carthage collapsed, although it was to be another 50 years before the final epitaph, *Carthago delenda est*, was pronounced.

Despite these experiences, the Romans never efficiently organized their cavalry; and curiously enough it was to be a race of mounted archers that showed how cavalry, in certain circumstances, could annihilate the famous legions unaided. In 54 BC Crassus, Proconsul of Syria, with an army of 40,000 invaded Parthia. He crossed the Euphrates and at Carrhae (Haran) met the Parthian mounted archers under the command of Surenas. In the open plains of Mesopotamia they ringed the legions at a distance and poured down on them a steady rain of arrows. If the Romans charged they galloped away, easily outwitting their heavy opponents; then when their baffled enemy withdrew, they closed in again and the deluge of arrows recommenced. Outranged and outridden, the Romans were helpless; they lacked the inspired resourcefulness of Xenophon and his 10,000. Crassus was treacherously murdered trying to negotiate a truce, and less than 5,000 Roman soldiers regained Syria. In 36 BC Mark Antony, leading a Roman army once again into Parthia, narrowly escaped a similar fate. Thereafter Rome treated the Parthians with the greatest respect.

It was ironic that after the failure 400 years earlier of the Persian mounted bowmen against the Greeks, it should be cavalry using missiles who destroyed the heavy infantry of Rome. The debate whether cavalry should use shock action or missiles was to continue down the centuries.

A RECONSTRUCTION OF THE OPENING STAGES OF THE BATTLE OF ZAMA (202 BC). THE CARTHAGINIAN ELEPHANTS ARE CHARGING THE ROMAN SKIRMISHERS, THE VELITES. THE ILLUSTRATION IS BY HENRI MOTTE.

DESPITE Cannae and Carrhae, the Romans continued to place their faith in the heavy infantry of the legions, and never sought to achieve the balanced armies that had made Alexander and Hannibal all but invincible. However, in the 1st and 2nd centuries AD that faith appeared to be far from misplaced. From Augustus onwards the frontiers of the Empire scarcely advanced, owing to the danger of that mighty edifice collapsing from its own enormous size. In consequence Roman strategy became defensive. The Roman legionaries dealt with such Barbarians as they met without undue difficulty; it seemed neither necessary nor desirable fundamentally to alter the structure of the army; in consequence Rome never produced a cavalry formation comparable to the infantry-based legion.

In the east beyond the borders of the Empire, cavalry began to play a more dominant role on the battlefield; yet still the Romans preferred to hire Barbarian horse rather than to raise adequate cavalry units of their own. Then the Huns, a race of horsemen, started their drive westwards from the heart of central Asia. Tacitus once said ironically of the Romans, 'They create a desolation and they call it peace.' His remark applied more justly to the Huns. They created a desolation wherever they went, but the word peace had no place in their vocabulary.

Their fatal effect on the Roman Empire and on the civilization of the ancient world at first was indirect. They assailed the Gothic Empire east of the Roman border, and the desperate Ostrogoths and Vizigoths eventually sought asylum within the apparently still formidable borders of Rome. The Roman Emperor in the east, Valens, reluctantly admitted them across the Danube. Once within the Empire, already distracted by civil wars and incursions by Germanic tribes, the Goths revolted against their Roman hosts. They had powerful mounted forces, and at the Battle of Adrianople (AD 378) they annihilated a great legionary army under Valens. The day of the legions was nearly over. The Empire now began to disintegrate while the Huns stood poised on the Danube, ready to give the *coup-de-grâce*.

J.P.L.

ALARIC, KING OF THE VIZIGOTHS, LEADS HIS BARBARIC FOLLOWERS TO THE SACK OF ROME IN AD 410. THE MAIDENS WATCHING THEIR ARRIVAL SEEM CERTAIN TO BE RAVISHED.

THE HUNS by R. CROSBIE-WESTON

A Roman soldier and historian, Ammianus Marcellinus, writing between AD 378 and 395, has left us a graphic description of the Huns.

'They never shelter themselves under roofed houses, but avoid them as people ordinarily avoid sepulchres, as things not fitted for common use. Nor indeed is there even to be found among them a cabin thatched with reeds, but they wander about, roaming over the mountains and woods, and accustom themselves to bear frost and hunger and thirst from their very cradles. They wear linen clothes, or else garments made of the skins of field mice, but after a tunic is once put round their necks, however it becomes worn, it is never taken off or changed till, from long decay, it becomes actually so ragged as to fall to pieces.

'They cover their heads with round caps and their shaggy legs with the skins of kids; their shoes are not made on any lasts but are so unshapely as to hinder them from walking with a free gait. And for this reason they are not well suited to infantry battles but are nearly always on horseback, their horses being ill-shaped but hardy. There is not a person in the whole nation who cannot remain on his horse day and night. On horseback they buy and sell, they take their meat and drink and there they recline on the narrow neck of their steed and yield to sleep so deep as to indulge in every variety of dream.

'Sometimes, when provoked, they fight, and when they go into battle form in a solid body and utter all kinds of terrific yells. They are very quick in their operation, of exceeding speed, and fond of surprising their enemies. With a view to this they suddenly disperse, then reunite, and again, after having inflicted vast loss upon the enemy, scatter themselves over the whole plain in irregular formations, always avoiding a fort or an entrenchment.

'And in one respect you may pronounce them the most formidable of all warriors, for when fighting at a distance they use missiles of various kinds tipped with sharpened bones instead of the usual points of javelins, and these bones are admirably fastened into the shaft of a javelin or arrow. But when they are at close-quarters they fight with the sword, without any regard for their own safety; and often while their antagonists are warding off their blows they entangle them with twisted cords so that their hands being fettered they lose all power of riding or walking.

'None of them ploughs or even touches a plough handle, for they have no settled abode but are homeless and lawless, perpetually wandering with their wagons. . . . Nor, if asked, can any one of them tell you where he was born as he was conceived in one place, born in another at a great distance and brought up in another still more remote.'

Such was the sober description of a Roman historian. It lacks some detail which those unfortunate enough to be in the path of the Huns could have supplied. Ammianus said elsewhere that they were like two-legged deformed beasts and others painted an even more lurid picture. Everyone agreed that their repulsive appearance, their huge, flat faces, their inability to walk, the fact that they ate, slept, conferred, and performed virtually every function from horseback made it seem unlikely that they could be genuinely human. According to such reputable authorities as the ecclesiastics Jerome, a contemporary, and Jordanes, who in 551 wrote a history of the Goths, even the Roman soldiers were terrified by their mere appearance. Their sunken eyes were those of wild animals. The linen garments they wore till they fell off were captured from others, for the Huns had no agriculture, could not grow flax and could not weave. When they first set out on their path of conquest and devastation they had no swords, for they had no means of making them; instead they used lassoes which were just as effective. But, as Ammianus ruefully wrote, once they had captured swords they were soon using them with a dexterity and skill equal to the best of their opponents. Initially too they relied on their own pasture-fed horses, which were good enough to defeat their early opponents. Later they acquired Roman horses which had been

PORTRAIT OF A HUN WARRIOR.
WOODCUT BY LARS HOKANSON.

fed on hay and grain and were even more formidable. Like other primitive warriors they seemed to make themselves at one with their mounts and exercised absolute control on their wide tactical sweeps, thrusts and withdrawals. A Hun charge was executed with such speed and suddenness that it usually overwhelmed everyone and everything in its path.

But horsemanship and devastating close-quarter fighting were not the principal threat from the Huns. Their most staggering accomplishment was their ability with their bows. These were short and made of horn and small pieces of spliced wood. One source speaks of the Huns having long bows, but if so the practice was probably limited to one tribe for the steppe was treeless, even though horn was plentiful. This compound bow – possibly not unlike the modern competition bow in appearance – seems to have had unprecedented power. Both Greeks and Romans commented with astonishment on its range and accuracy. Used by the Huns it was a weapon of unsurpassed power and accuracy, even when drawn from galloping or wheeling horses. Small wonder that this remote Asian tribe, whose empire briefly rose and fell over 1,500 years ago, left a name which symbolizes the epitome of swift, merciless destruction.

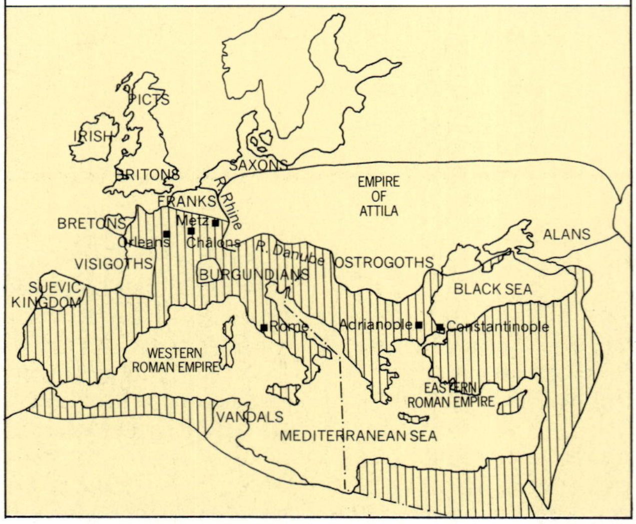

When in 409 the Huns eventually crossed the Danube they were heavily defeated, whereupon they withdrew and made little effort to push further west for nearly 50 years. There are various explanations for this inactivity. One is that they thought the country beyond was unsuited to their tactics, another that their leaders probably thought it was time to consolidate their already vast gains; another, and more likely, reason is that they were bought off by Roman gold. The speed at which they acquired a semi-civilized form of existence and organization was only equalled by the rapidity with which they learned to profit from their new status. Meanwhile they moved their main headquarters to the Black Sea area and diverted themselves by fighting the German tribes to the north. On occasion they fought as allies of the Romans.

During the first half of the 5th century the Huns became a much more coherent force. Instead of having minor independent leaders they gradually drew together under a single king, Rua. The Romans by this time were paying the Huns an annual tribute of 300 pounds of gold. This payment would soon be doubled. The Romans also gave the Huns hostages, and in return the Huns provided frequent assistance to the Romans in various provinces and even in Italy itself.

We are able to take up the Hun story in detail from 434, for that was the year Priscus, the Byzantine historian, began his chronicle. It was also the year in which Attila and his elder brother, Bleda, succeeded jointly as rulers. Four years later Attila murdered his brother Bleda and became sole ruler. The brothers were quite unlike and had always hated each other. Attila, however vile, had the attributes of greatness, whereas Bleda's principal occupation was laughing at his resident clown, a grotesque little Moorish dwarf. Roman ambassadors who tried to negotiate with Attila noted that even when gold was freely available Attila himself still wore plain clothes, ate off wooden plates and never touched bread. His followers did not always imitate his austere example. The ambassadors found Attila sullen, capricious and arrogant, but as he was confronted with potential treachery on all sides this moodiness is hardly surprising.

PORTRAIT OF ATTILA, THE 'SCOURGE OF GOD' MEDALLION ON THE FACADE OF THE CHARTERHOUSE AT PAVIA.

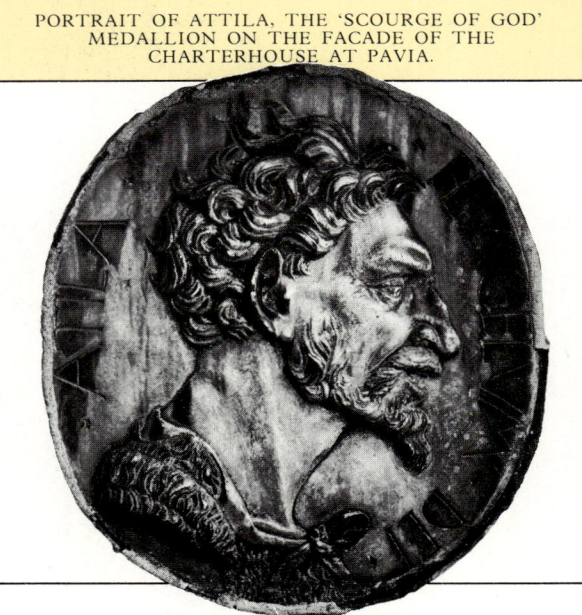

THE HUN EMPIRE IN AD 450

By now the Hun Empire under Attila occupied an impressive area. In the north it extended to the Baltic where, according to Priscus, 'he ruled all the islands'. It did not quite extend to the Rhine, for the Burgundians and Franks lay in between, but he was said to rule 'all Scythia'. Until then the Romans with some success had bought off their formidable neighbours, but now injudiciously allowed their payments of tribute to fall into arrears. In 441 and 443 Attila invaded the Eastern Roman Empire, defeating the Roman armies with deplorable ease; but his swarms of wild horsemen were ill-equipped to deal with strongly fortified cities and he refrained from attacking its capital, Constantinople.

However in 447, favoured by earthquakes which devastated Asia Minor almost as thoroughly as the Huns could have done, he marched on Constantinople, the walls of which had suffered severe damage. Fortunately for the Eastern Empire the fortifications were repaired just before the

THE HUNS

arrival of Attila's army. The latter turned aside from Constantinople, but drove on into Greece and were only checked at Thermopylae. Even though the Huns had now been in contact with more civilized nations for some time it had apparently had little effect on their behaviour. Seventy cities were sacked with brutal thoroughness, monks and nuns were slaughtered, and rape and pillage were everywhere. (It is from this campaign that Attila may well have earned his title 'The Scourge of God'.)

In 451 Attila decided to add fresh territories to his empire by invading Gaul. Having captured Metz and a number of minor towns he headed for Orleans, which occupied a valuable strategic position on the Loire. He was now acting in conjunction with allies and had to modify his tactics accordingly; but his army appears to have been as barbaric as ever, massacring men, women and children and indulging in various forms of wanton destruction on its path of conquest. Orleans had been expected to fall through treachery but this plan went awry and instead the town was vigorously defended. Before the Huns could do more than penetrate the outskirts of the town a large Imperial army came to its relief. This force was partly composed of Vizogoths, mostly cavalry under their ruler, Theodoric, and partly of Roman legions under Aetius. Attila withdrew, making for open plains where he could use his cavalry to best advantage. The withdrawal was not easy; the route was complicated and his rearguard was under constant attack from his opponents. Contemporary chronicles say that 90,000 Huns were slain in this retreat, but this is clearly a typical medieval exaggeration; no reliable figures are available for the armies of this era.

There is general agreement that the subsequent battle was fought in Champagne but there is much disagreement over the site. Gibbon in *Decline and Fall of the Roman Empire* thinks it was Châlons-sur-Marne, which was formerly called Catalauni. However, as the whole of the area of Champagne was known as the Catalaunian Plains there are plenty of other possible sites, including the frequently mentioned one of Maurica. This was said to lie five miles from Troyes, the present capital of Champagne, but no place of this name can now be identified. Whichever it was, the site was a flat open plain, admirably suited to the cavalry of the Huns. Attila commanded in the centre of his army, placing his allies on the flanks. The Imperial army was drawn up with the Vizigoths on the right and the Romans on the left. The centre was occupied by the Alans, a tribe whose loyalty to any cause but their own preservation was considered highly doubtful.

Authentic details of the battle are lacking. Theodoric apparently dispatched his son Thorismund to occupy some high ground overlooking the left flank of the Huns. Attila, detaching some troops to drive away Thorismund and casting aside the usual Hun guerilla tactics, launched the rest of his army straight at the enemy. A ferocious and bloody hand-to-hand combat ensued which lasted for most of the day, but at its end the Imperial army stood firm and although Theodoric had been killed, Thorismund still kept possession of his heights. As night fell, Attila drew back his confused and broken army to his laager of wagons and prepared for a battle to the death next day.

But Aetius, fearing his allies the Vizigoths scarcely less than the Huns, forbore from destroying a possible counter-poise to their power; he allowed Attila to withdraw unmolested. The battle saved France, and perhaps Christendom, although it could not save the ancient civilization of Rome. Next year Attila again ravaged Italy, and was compelled to withdraw only by a combination of famine and disease. In 453 he incautiously married a young girl and died in the course of the marital festivities. The Hun Empire broke up and disappeared, leaving behind it nothing but a name, a synonym for cruelty unsurpassed in the world.

ATTILA INSIDE HIS WAGON LAAGER AFTER THE DEFEAT AT CHÂLONS (451). DETERMINED NOT TO BE CAPTURED, HE MADE HIS FOLLOWERS ERECT A FUNERAL PYRE ON WHICH HE THEN STOOD WHILE TORCHES WERE HELD READY TO FIRE IT SHOULD THE ROMANS ATTACK.

THE HUNS SURGE INTO EUROPE. THE HORSEMAN IN THE FOREGROUND IS SHOWN USING STIRRUPS.

AT Châlons the Roman legionary performed his last service to civilization. It was at about this period too that the saddle and stirrup came to Europe: although their origin is obscure, there is little doubt that their arrival made the cavalry supreme for nearly the next 1,000 years. Now the horseman on his charger was as firmly based as the infantryman on the ground; moreover he had the advantage of height and could move wearing heavier armour than the infantryman could carry; not only therefore could he travel faster than his adversary on foot, he could go into battle better armed and equipped. It was the deathknell of the legions.

Rome's Western Empire vanished before a horde of Barbarians, but the Eastern or Byzantine Empire fared better. Here some of the old Roman skills survived. The Byzantines recognized that the heavy foot-soldier of the legions could no longer bear the brunt of the battle. They mounted him on a horse and produced an armoured horseman called a cataphract who still practised on horseback some of the old legionary tactics. The cataphract wore a helmet, a suit of chain-mail reaching to his thighs and armoured boots to protect his ankles and shins; he was equipped with a small shield, a spear and a sword, and many carried bows-and-arrows besides. They trained and fought in properly organized units, and aided by the tortuous type of diplomacy to which the Byzantines were to lend their name, they enabled that Empire to outlive its counterpart in the West, only finally to disappear after the fall of Constantinople 10 centuries later.

In the West, armies degenerated into mobs composed of illiterate tribal leaders at the head of their fierce and ignorant followers. The power of the infantry, except in mountainous regions, was virtually extinguished, and the horseman became sovereign of the battlefield. In Asia there arose a new religion, Islam; inspired by its fighting creed, waves of Moslem warriors broke against the southern and eastern borders of Europe. They were mainly light horsemen, lightly armoured, if armoured at all, making up for their lack of organization by the fanatical zeal with which they fought. They could outride their clumsier European opponents, but in close combat the heavier arms and equipment of the Europeans were apt to tell.

Spain fell to the invaders, but perhaps their menace impelled some sort of unity into the warring chaos of Europe. At the Battle of Toulouse (721) the Franks under Charles Martel overthrew a great Moslem army under Abd-er-Rahman. In this battle, Charles dismounted his heavy cavalry to form a wall of steel that utterly baffled Abd-er-Rahman's light horse. Charles's son Pepin III drove the Moslems back behind the Pyrenees. Charlemagne (742–814) succeeded him to promote a European hegemony which, despite its collapse after his death, by the strength of its components enabled Europe to withstand the invader. J.P.L.

BELISARIUS LEADS A ROMAN ARMY AGAINST THE GOTHS. IN THE SERVICE OF JUSTINIAN, THE GREAT 6TH-CENTURY RULER OF THE EASTERN EMPIRE, BELISARIUS WON MANY VICTORIES AGAINST THE BARBARIANS, IN PARTICULAR THE SLAVS AND BULGARS.

CHARLEMAGNE AND THE DAWN OF CHIVALRY by R. CROSBIE-WESTON

Charlemagne recognized that enduring military power depended on properly organized and disciplined armies sustained by an effective administrative system. He decided that the backbone of his army must be heavy cavalry: he planned to thicken the protection of the horseman, to give him at least two weapons, and also to mount him on a horse which would be strong enough not only to carry all this weight but also to smash a way through the centre of any opposition. At this period in Europe there was nothing to check a heavy cavalry charge; the methods used in the ancient world had apparently all been forgotten, and pikes, crossbows, longbows, and obstacles such as caltraps and *chevaux-de-frise* were not to be discovered – or rediscovered – for many centuries.

Charlemagne's plans created considerable problems. A horse suitable for his purposes needed to be specially bred and selected. Armour adequate to withstand arrows must be designed, manufactured and paid for. The last item soon became the most important and led directly to feudalism and the dawn of chivalry. For warfare was now acquiring a characteristic it has never lost: it was rapidly becoming more expensive. After the cavalryman had faced the initial expense of providing himself with a horse and armour, with a lance and a sword, he soon found that the armour needed modification, that weapons bent or broke on impact, and that to maintain and convey all this material to the battlefield he needed an assistant.

Feudalism solved the financial problem very simply. All land was held to belong to the monarch – or in Charlemagne's case the emperor – and it was leased out in estates to leading supporters. They in turn sub-leased. The 'rent' was military service, and military service meant the provision by the feudal vassal of however many armed followers he was assessed to bring. The holder of a large estate might be required to provide 100 knights and attendant men-at-arms. These would only be required for limited periods, for the campaigning season was short. Two factors made it so. One was that winter weather usually made trackways impassable and the other was that peasants – from whom foot soldiers were drawn – were needed for spring sowing and autumn reaping. Any campaign which interfered with these two vital activities would unavoidably be followed by starvation in the winter.

PORTRAIT OF CHARLEMAGNE, RULER OF ALL THE FRANKS FROM 771. THE WORK, A BRONZE STATUETTE, IS IN THE CLASSICAL TRADITION; THE EMPEROR IS SHOWN RIDING WITHOUT SADDLE OR STIRRUPS AND WITH A RUDIMENTARY BRIDLE.

However, among the layers of this apparently rigid social and economic pyramid there was some degree of mobility. The feudal baron might lose his position by personal treachery against his monarch, or by treachery from those below. Enterprising and intrepid peasants might so distinguish themselves in battle that they would be rewarded by land and a knighthood. A superior form of knight was a 'banneret' (no connection with the later creation of baronet) who had some 20 or 30 knights under his command. Some lived out their miserable existences ill-fed, barely clothed and with scant comfort but others contrived to claw their way to a better life by stealing or trading sufficiently to buy a plot of land and eventual freedom. Once on the feudal ladder the way up – or down – could be quite rapid. In the later stages of medievalism a swift path to riches was the capture of a prisoner whose unfortunate relations and tenants would have to toil for years to pay off his ransom. Many a fine English building was raised from the ransoms of French knights knocked from their chargers and captured on the field of Agincourt.

Once he had overcome the problem of raising his armies, Charlemagne conquered a great span

THE CAVALRY

of Europe between the Elbe and the Pyrenees. By the time of his death in 814 the knight in armour, accompanied by his esquires and usually by a number of mounted men-at-arms, had become the basis of all Western armies. And because cavalry was believed to play the leading part in securing victory, morale on the battlefield was greatly influenced by the numbers of cavalry present.

For nearly 700 years heavy cavalry enjoyed an immense prestige that perhaps was not wholly justified. In the Battle of Muret in 1213 Simon de Montfort defeated an army from Aragon by a lucky cavalry charge at the critical moment. At Bouvines in 1214, when the infantry of Otto of Saxony had seemed to be gaining the ascendancy, they were charged by a squadron of French cavalry and sent reeling. In both these battles it was their impact on enemy morale that carried the day for the heavy cavalry. On the other hand, the Battle of Lewes (1264) produced a spectacular demonstration of how cavalry could lose a battle while apparently winning it. Prince Edward, the future Edward I, was commanding the right wing of an army confronting a rebel force under Simon de Montfort (descendant of the victor of Muret). The rebel left wing was composed of ill-equipped and untrained troops and young Edward had no difficulty in sweeping them before him, although the ground was by no means suited to cavalry. However, like many other impetuous cavalry commanders after him, he carried on the pursuit for too long, riding far away from the battlefield. When he returned with horses blown to celebrate his victory, he was surprised to find that his side had lost the battle and that he himself was a hostage.

Cavalry was nevertheless to undergo worse setbacks than Lewes with no great loss of prestige. In effect, however, the writing was already on the wall for heavy cavalry as early as the beginning of the 12th century, for by that time the crossbow had been developed to the point at which it was more than a match for a knight. A force of crossbowmen, other things being equal, could upset a charge long before it reached its objective. Worse was to come. The crossbow was a slow weapon: with luck it could send off two bolts a minute. But there was already in existence an even more devastating weapon—the longbow. In the 12th century a Norman knight on a pacification mission in Wales was surprised by a falling arrow which penetrated his mailed skirt, his leg and his wooden saddle and finally wounded the horse. As he turned sharply to ride out of range, another arrow came out of the sky and apparently, allowing for medieval exaggeration, did precisely the same to the other leg. In 1182, on another occasion, an arrow was observed to have penetrated four inches of an oak door at Abergavenny.

These developments were to be of great significance in the Hundred Years' War soon to break out between England and France. At the same time, while the knight in armour continued to enjoy a reputation for being almost invulnerable, the idea grew up, perhaps in some curious way by reason of this very invulnerability, that he should refrain from exploiting his superiority too grossly; thus the mystique known as chivalry was born. The growth of chivalry and the rise of the knight from being a capable soldier of no particular breeding to the status of a minor aristocrat all occurred in the 12th and 13th centuries.

The Crusades undoubtedly played a large part in the development of knighthood and chivalry. There were in all eight main Crusades and a number of minor ventures which scarcely deserve the title. The first, which captured Jerusalem in July 1099, was the most successful. Its victory was celebrated by a massacre of Jews and Moslems which made the Holy Places run ankle-deep in blood. Yet, in spite of excesses, the Crusades undoubtedly refined the concept of knighthood. Although in an emergency any man with a horse and sufficient money to equip himself with arms could be, and frequently was, ordered to become a knight, the usual aspirant to that position followed a much longer route. He began as a page, and developed to an esquire. An esquire had to supply his knight with arms on the battlefield and on occasion was charged with contriving his escape. The normal process of becoming a knight was enshrined in religious ceremony. It usually included an all-night vigil of prayer and the taking of special vows. The robing of the new knight was an impressive ceremonial. Unfortunately in practice the knight's chivalric responsibilities only seemed to apply to those of his own social class. Inferiors usually received short shrift and scant courtesy. But there were exceptions. There are records of knights who fought bravely in the field and were compassionate to a defeated enemy, whatever his social class. There were knightly landowners who, by the standards of the day, were kind to their tenants. There were orders of chivalry such as the Knights Hospitallers, who devoted themselves to caring for the sick and wounded, and the Knights Templars whose aim was to protect pilgrims while themselves living

A FRENCH KNIGHT ON HORSEBACK WEARING SPURS OF THE ROWEL TYPE AND USING STIRRUPS. THE SADDLE IS HELD IN POSITION BY A BROAD SINGLE GIRTH; EVEN ALLOWING FOR THE OBVIOUS DISPROPORTION BETWEEN THE KNIGHT'S OVER-LONG BODY AND THE LOWER HALF OF THE WORK (INCLUDING THE HORSE), THE POMMEL OF HIS SADDLE SEEMS REMARKABLY LOW. FROM THE CLUNY MUSEUM.

CHARLEMAGNE AND THE DAWN OF CHIVALRY

almost as modestly. The fact that the Templars rapidly became inordinately wealthy, leading to the dissolution of the order, has tarnished a reputation for doing good deeds which in their early days was wholly justified.

The apotheosis of knightly chivalry, in theory at least, was the Crusader. The aim of all Crusades was to clear the infidel from the Holy Lands. The cause was represented as the battle of Good against Evil – even though in practice the Saracens were often more chivalrous than their Christian opponents. The Crusades lasted for 350 years: they stimulated trade and a valuable exchange of ideas between East and West. Strategically they were a disaster because the early Crusaders failed to secure the key points when these were readily available, and tactically they were chaotic because there were no maps and the Crusaders, lacking all knowledge of military geography, set themselves impossible tasks. Yet for all that they were a triumph of human endurance and persistence. In terms of logistics, the effort required was enormous. For example, among his other stores on the Third Crusade (begun in 1189) Richard I is said to have taken 50,000 horseshoes, and quantities of specially hard stones for use in catapults.

The Crusades were a particularly difficult military assignment for not only did they involve open warfare but also the siege of cities. Conditions would have been difficult enough with such predictable hazards as the heat, disease and monotony, but the Crusaders considerably amplified their discomforts by the armour and clothing they wore. Armour at the time of Richard's Crusade consisted mainly of chain-mail and a pot helmet. Chainmail was manufactured by hammering together hundreds of small links. It was worn over a leather tunic and extended over the legs, feet, arms and

NORMAN CAVALRY IN 1066, AS DEPICTED ON THE BAYEUX TAPESTRY. THEY ARE WEARING COMPLETE SETS OF CHAIN-MAIL, CONICAL HELMETS – DEEMED THE BEST SHAPE FOR RESISTING A DOWNWARD BLOW – AND 'NASALS' TO PROTECT THE NOSE. BISHOP ODO, HALF-BROTHER OF WILLIAM OF NORMANDY, IS ENCOURAGING HIS MEN BY WAVING HIS MACE IN THE AIR.

A MAN-AT-ARMS WEARING A *POT-DE-FER*, OR POT HELMET, WITH A LARGE NASAL, ABOVE A HAUBERK OF CHAIN-MAIL PROTECTING HIS CHEEKS AND NECK. AFTER AN ILLUSTRATION IN AN 11TH-CENTURY FRENCH MANUSCRIPT.

51

THE CAVALRY

hands. Scale armour might be worn over the top as additional protection. The pot helmet was a large circular form of headgear which fitted right over the head and rested on the shoulders. The Crusader knight also carried a shield, a long sword and a lance. The weight of all this on man and horse may be imagined. Another major drawback was that the armour took so long to put on or take off that for safety reasons it was worn for days on end. All this occurred in temperatures which could vary between 100°F by day to almost freezing point by night.

Not least of the Crusaders' problems was that of feeding their armies. Richard's army on the Third Crusade was probably about 7,000 strong (though contemporary accounts put it at 700,000!), the horsemen making up about one-seventh of this total. In addition to the fighting men and their attendants, a motley collection of camp-followers attended the progress of the Crusader armies, so straining further the meagre resources available in that hostile territory.

By contrast, the Saracen opponents of the Crusader knights were lightly armed and mounted on swift horses. Fortunately for the Crusaders, Saracen tactics consisted almost entirely of wheeling and harassing; if possible they tried to draw out the Crusaders to pursue them, and would then turn to cut off detachments. Within these limitations they were nevertheless a constant menace. If they could be brought to battle, on the other hand, the Saracens were particularly vulnerable to a cavalry charge.

The Battle of Arsouf on 7 September 1191 was a striking example of Richard I's tactical ability. Having captured Acre, Richard realized that he could not move directly towards Jerusalem owing to the mountain barrier which lay in between. He decided to march south along the coast road to

ABOVE LEFT: WILLIAM MARSHAL, FIRST EARL OF PEMBROKE (1146–1219); FROM HIS MEMORIAL BRASS. HE WEARS A COMPLETE SUIT OF CHAIN-MAIL WITH A PLAIN SURCOAT ON TOP (THIS BEING BEFORE THE PRACTICE OF EMBROIDERING AN EMBLEM ON THE SURCOAT HAD COME IN). HE IS ARMED WITH AN ENORMOUS SWORD, COMMON AMONG THE CRUSADERS, AND A HEAVY SHIELD WITH A SHOULDER STRAP TO HELP HIM CARRY IT. MARSHAL ACTED AS REGENT WHILE RICHARD I WAS AWAY ON THE THIRD CRUSADE.

ABOVE RIGHT: A SARACEN WARRIOR, AS DEPICTED IN AN ARABIAN MANUSCRIPT.

Arsouf, thereby also keeping in touch with his fleet. Food could then be supplied from the sea; there was no food available on the land route, Saladin having thoughtfully destroyed all possible sources of supply.

The Saracens, typically, harassed them throughout the march. Richard spaced out the cavalry at intervals but ensured there were no gaps in his column which the Saracens could penetrate. There were 12 divisions of infantry and 12 of cavalry and all were fully alerted to the fact that they might have to turn from column to line at a moment's notice to fight off a Saracen attack. On alternate days Richard halted, and while on the march never covered more than 10 miles a day. However, the Crusaders needed all the rest they could take. The route was so broken and uneven that it was impossible at times for the column not to straggle, and the Saracens were always hovering ready to exploit gaps. Describing the Christian foe, a Saracen account stated that 'each foot soldier had a thick cassock of felt and under it a mail shirt so strong that our arrows made no impression on them. They meanwhile shot at us with crossbows which struck down horse and man among the Moslems. I noted among them men who had one to ten shafts sticking in their backs, yet trudged on at their ordinary pace and did not fall out of their ranks.'

Having failed to break the discipline of the column, Saladin tried a last desperate expedient. Concealing most of his army in woods on the road to Arsouf, at the critical moment he burst out and launched a ferocious attack on Richard's rearguard. Meanwhile other Saracens rode round to the enemy's front and yet others poured arrows into the flanks.

Richard remained cool. He planned to reply

A KNIGHT HOSPITALLER. HE IS WEARING PLATE ARMOUR AND HIS SWORD, ALTHOUGH STILL EXCESSIVELY LONG, IS BETTER BALANCED THAN WILLIAM MARSHAL'S. THE ORDER WAS ORIGINALLY DEDICATED TO CARING FOR THE SICK, BUT ITS MEMBERS OFTEN TOOK A MORE BELLIGERENT PART IN AFFAIRS.

DRAWING OF THE SEAL OF THE LORD OF CORBEIL, 1196.

ON THE THIRD CRUSADE. THE DRAWING, BY V. ADAM, SHOWS THE CRUSADER ARMY ON THE LINE OF MARCH ACROSS THE DESERT.

A SAVAGE COMBAT BETWEEN CRUSADER AND SARACEN, POSSIBLY AT ARSOUF AND SOMETIMES REPRESENTED AS A PERSONAL DUEL BETWEEN RICHARD I AND SALADIN—ALTHOUGH THERE IS NO DEPENDABLE EVIDENCE THAT SUCH A COMBAT EVER TOOK PLACE.

CHARLEMAGNE AND THE DAWN OF CHIVALRY

by ambushing the ambushers. The column plodded on, more slowly as horses fell and encumbered the ground. By the time the walls of Arsouf came in sight the Crusader column, particularly the rearguard which consisted mainly of Knights Hospitallers, was in a state of great pent-up fury, while the Saracens, becoming bolder, swarmed round their apparently timid foe. The rearguard begged leave to charge, but Richard said no, not yet. Finally, when it seemed the order would never come, the knights and a French division could wait no longer and wheeled and hurled themselves on their tormentors.

Richard saw that the time had come. He gave the signal, the trumpet blew and the whole column suddenly swung outwards to charge down on the astonished Saracens. The effect was devastating. After throwing back the Saracens for a mile Richard rallied the lines, re-formed and put in a second charge. This effectively dispersed the resistance which the Saracens were just beginning to make again. After one final charge, Richard called off the pursuit. The defeat of the Saracens had been so crushing that Saladin never again dared to confront the Crusaders in open conflict. From then onwards the Saracens restricted themselves to skirmishing, harrying and the cutting-off of detachments. Charlemagne, had he been at Arsouf, would have witnessed a superb demonstration, some 400 years after his own innovations, of what could still be achieved with heavy cavalry in the hands of a master tactician.

THE Crusades, by taking the war between the continents into Asia, offered a counter to the Moslem aggressors who were hammering at the gates of Constantinople and endeavouring to consolidate their rule in Spain; from the East, however, still the mounted hordes came. Charlemagne gave Europe a military framework that enabled it to survive, but it was to be severely tested. In the second half of the 9th century the Magyars, emerging from southern Russia, migrated to the central Danube basin and settled in what is now Hungary. Like the Huns, they were essentially light horsemen, mounted archers who disliked close-quarter fighting, preferring to encircle their enemy and shoot him down from a distance. They outrode the heavy European cavalry without difficulty and could harass them unmercifully, but they lacked the ability to overthrow them in the open field. During the first half of the 10th century, from their strongholds in the Danube basin they carried out far-reaching raids into eastern Germany and the Balkans, but the combination of heavy European cavalry and well-fortified castles prevented them from establishing themselves any great distance west of the Danube. In their greatest raids they penetrated into Italy and northern France, whereupon Europe for a space forgot its factions and united to resist the invader. By the middle of the century the raids petered out. In the 13th century the invaders were succeeded by a more formidable and better organized foe, the Mongols. J.P.L.

A MOUNTED COMBAT BETWEEN SLAVS AND BULGARS.
THE BULGARS ARE BEING ROUTED.
SLAVONIC MANUSCRIPT OF THE 10TH CENTURY.

THE MONGOLS by R. CROSBIE-WESTON

The architect of the Mongol Empire was Jenghiz (or Chingis) Khan. His sons extended his already huge empire. Soon it ranged from Peking to Russia, Persia and the outskirts of Europe. Within approximately 200 years it had disintegrated, but component parts still continued to function with vigour.

Had the Mongols never become a great conquering nation their earlier history would have been of such little interest as to pass largely unnoticed, except perhaps by their closest neighbours. One of those neighbours, China, recorded that as early as 400 BC the Mongols had a cavalry army which was so effective as to cause the Chinese to develop cavalry themselves; previously they had depended on war chariots and infantry. The Chinese had good reason to hate and fear the Mongols, for they were frequently tyrannized by them. The Mongols demanded tribute of silk and corn; if these were not forthcoming in what the Mongols thought were adequate quantities, there would follow a short but venomous period of destruction. The Chinese noted that the men in Mongolia formed an *élite* military caste: in their nomadic life they never needed to work but amused themselves by riding and shooting. The Chinese, on the other hand, spent their days bent in agricultural toil, and had no time for warlike games. As might be expected, when battle came, the Chinese were defeated. Chinese historians also noted that the Mongols were much addicted to feigned retreats and recorded that when unwise opponents pursued them they were drawn into ambushes and slaughtered. This tactic was successfully practised in the Mongolian heyday 1,700 years later.

Even Mongolian organization varied little from patterns set in ancient times. The basic unit was 10. A division consisted of 10,000. In that basic ten every man was held responsible not only for his own actions but also for his neighbour's, and for those of men in the adjoining tens. If a man did not fight hard enough or retreated a step (except by tactical order) he was instantly put to death. If a man saw such an offence and did not immediately punish it, he too must be killed. Behind this ferocious code Mongol society had an unusual homogeneity. If a man was killed a son would marry his mother and a brother marry a widow. The custom seemed to promote harmony. Women had little time or energy to think of complaining: they worked incessantly at making, mending and milking, at camp administration and the chores which went with the preparation and preservation of food. The one labour they never performed was washing, neither of clothes nor utensils. But they too learned to ride and shoot, and could be as dangerous as their menfolk in battle.

PORTRAIT OF JENGHIZ KHAN.

The birth date of Jenghiz Khan is not known. He was the son of an obscure Mongolian chieftain and nobody troubled to remember the year in which he had been born. By the time he died it was a very different story. The year of his death was 1227; the world had good cause to note it. He was considered to be in his mid-60s when he died, perhaps even as old as 70.

It is, of course, almost impossible to disentangle fact from heroic legend in early chronicles, but it seems that the young Jenghiz had a difficult early life. His original name was Temujin; his father was poisoned by a Tartar tribe and his family nearly starved. Temujin took service with a powerful Khan and at his *ordu* (camp) met other Mongol leaders. The word *ordu* became the origin of 'the (Golden) Horde', the term by which the Mongols were widely known. Temujin soon displayed the qualities which would take him to fame. One was ruthless determination linked with flexibility; another was a magnetic personality combined with strength of mind and body; yet another was a sense of mission. Even those living in his time and close to him found Jenghiz difficult to understand. He was utterly ruthless and untrustworthy in war, and yet he appreciated loyalty and had no truck

THE CAVALRY

with men who behaved treacherously to gain favour with him.

By 1206 Jenghiz had disposed of his immediate enemies, both real and potential, and united Mongolia. Among those he disposed of were numbers of Tartars (whose name later became attached to the Mongol forces as a whole). His method of ensuring that the Tartars would look to no one but himself for leadership was to kill any Tartar taller than the height of a cart axle.

Jenghiz codified the Mongol military system. The leader of any group, large or small, was a *noyan*. A man serving with a *noyan* stayed with him or faced immediate execution. These military leaders commanded either an *arban* (10 men), a *jegun* (100), a *mingan* (1,000) or a *tumen* (10,000). The Great Khan, it was said, had been appointed by God to rule Mongolia and conquer the earth. Resistance to his will was therefore not only futile but irreligious. Similarly, anyone questioning the hideous atrocities, massacres and pointless destruction perpetrated by Mongol armies was held to be dangerously unstable. Later in life, when Jenghiz came to realize that there were other methods of rule than by burning, slaughtering and destroying, his followers were so conditioned that they quickly adapted to his ideas. Discipline was so strict in Jenghiz's army that most offences were punishable by death, although a few merely attracted huge fines. Bathing in running water was a capital offence; this may seem bizarre to us, but since many endemic oriental diseases such as cholera and bubonic plague are spread by polluted water and its denizens, this particular edict can be seen to have had at least a basis in reason. Stepping on the threshold of a military chief's tent was also punishable by death. This was probably a necessary precaution against assassination. In all military societies, even those in the West today, the presence of the unbidden on the threshold of high-ranking officers is materially and psychologically dis-couraged. A similar shrewdness was applied in appointing leaders; for example, men of exceptional physical endurance were passed over because they would be unable to understand the physical limitations of men under their command.

The bow was their essential weapon. Most Mongol soldiers possessed two. Both were manufactured from the same materials, but one was short, for use on horseback, the other longer, for use on foot. Both were made of spliced wood, unlike Western bows, and both had a range of approximately 200 yards. The shorter bows had lighter arrows. The arrow-heads took a variety of forms: some had a concave cutting-edge which could be used against ropework, others were designed to slice widely, and yet others to penetrate deeply. There were incendiary arrows and a type of head which was not previously known in the West. This was the fluted or pierced head which could be used – like a screaming bomb with a fluted tail – to intimidate; it was also a valuable signalling device, used to indicate when to swerve, when to feign, when to encircle, and so on. Each archer carried at least 60 arrows of different kinds in various quivers. He also carried a sword, and often a lance. Armour tended to be light, consisting of conical steel caps and leather jerkins; this was traditional wear for archers, whether or not they were horsed.

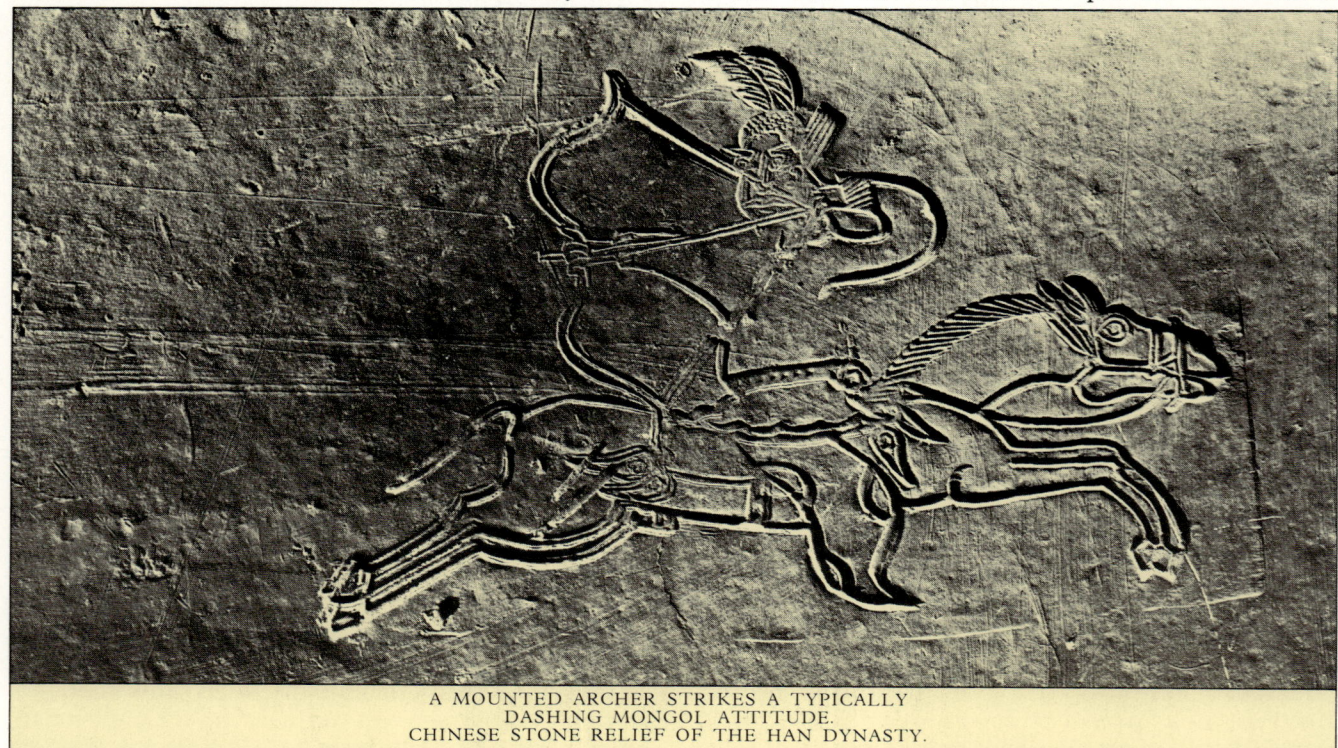

The fighting combination by which the Mongols established their empire depended on mobility allied to tactical cunning and accurate archery. Mongol mobility, naturally enough, depended on their horses. These were in fact ponies, usually less than 14 hands high (a 'hand' = 4 inches). They were carefully reared and not ridden until they were three years old; huge herds of such ponies were raised in the north of Mongolia. On a campaign each Mongol warrior had up to 20 ponies. Thus he always had a fresh mount, and if necessary could eat one; he also drank his mares' milk.

A MOUNTED ARCHER STRIKES A TYPICALLY DASHING MONGOL ATTITUDE. CHINESE STONE RELIEF OF THE HAN DYNASTY.

THE MONGOLS

A MOUNTED MONGOL ARCHER. IN REALITY HE
WOULD NOT HAVE BEEN AS BENEVOLENT
AS HE IS HERE MADE TO APPEAR.

THE CAVALRY

In addition to his basic weapons the Mongol carried a hatchet; fish hooks and lines; two leather bottles, one containing water, the other holding fermented mare's milk; a file for sharpening arrows, and a coil of rope. In colder regions he carried extra warm clothing. He also equipped himself with a large waterproof leather bag into which he put all his weapons when crossing rivers; this was tied to the horse's tail, while he himself swam ahead leading the animal. Tents were carried and on later campaigns there was a baggage train carrying sophisticated siege equipment. Although the Mongols preferred open warfare, there were occasions when it was necessary to besiege and reduce towns. For such operations they used siege techniques borrowed from the Chinese, and were expert at assembling their ballistas, mangonels, siege towers and scaling ladders. Such machinery was said to be greased with fat made from boiling the bodies of their enemies. In view of some of their other activities, this is not overly difficult to believe.

Those of their opponents who were taken in by Mongol promises of clemency and honourable terms paid dearly for their innocence. To the Mongols promises were merely another way of obtaining an advantage; they were surprised and pleased that men should be foolish enough to believe them. Terror was a deliberate policy. Contemporary reports usually attributed vast and overwhelming numbers to the Mongols. In fact their numbers were far smaller than was believed at the time. This has only indirectly to do with the tendency, mentioned in the previous chapter, of medieval observers to exaggerate numbers. What the Mongols did was deliberately to create an impression of overwhelming strength. One tactic they employed was to send spies ahead to spread alarming rumours; another was to disperse their relatively small numbers of men over a wide area.

Internal communication was maintained by a complex system that used fast-riding messengers, flags, torches, drums and trumpets. A Mongol army could – and often did – cover 50 miles in a day, and it was obviously essential to maintain coherence and control. Iron discipline and careful co-ordination enabled them to execute precise manoeuvres which quite bewildered their opponents. One day the Mongols would be far away, heading in another direction; suddenly they were confronting their foe, moving incessantly and apparently without any overall plan, seeming not to want to give battle but only to survey and probe. Then, unless it was very alert, an enemy army could find itself trapped in the centre of a great V of Mongols. Their wings had reached far out to the sides, while remaining out of sight; from this position they could rapidly turn inwards, encircling their enemy and moving in for the kill. Attempts to break out would be headed off, usually by means of accurate arrow fire. In different circumstances a feigned withdrawal would be made to induce an enemy to break up his own formation. When this happened, the Mongols would then charge with their heaviest cavalry. Some of their opponents believed the Mongols were invincible – a reputation the Mongols were only too ready to foster. Partly this belief derived from the silk undershirts the Mongols wore, another idea they had adopted from the Chinese. Arrows hitting their bodies were enfolded by the silk and the arrow-head could then be pulled out; the damage, though painful, was not lethal. Witnesses of Mongols pulling arrow-heads from their bodies could scarcely believe that such men were human.

The course of the Mongols' conquests was vast and complicated. Jenghiz Khan's first task had been to unify his own country. As the area included 31 powerful groups spread over a vast plateau, it was not easy. It was accomplished by establishing a form of feudalism – a military hierarchy headed by Jenghiz. Laws were codified. Although Jenghiz was fully prepared to massacre those whom he thought unconvertible – or useless – he also knew how to unite, lead and organize. His first conquering sweep, into China, began in 1211. The total strength of his invading army was said to be nearly 200,000; virtually the whole nation took part. Advancing in three columns, all able to converge at short notice, they penetrated deep into China. Their gains were mainly in open country, however, for when the Chinese immured themselves in cities the Mongols could only lure them out by treacherous promises which were promptly broken. Peking withstood the Mongol threat for five years but then agreed to buy off Jenghiz. As a result the Great Khan now had money, technical expertise and further resources of manpower.

His next drive was to the south-west, where his objective was the conquest of the Khwarazmian Empire which lay south-east of the Caspian Sea. This meant traversing the Alatau mountains, and the Akkum desert. A diversion towards Tashkent and Samarkand drew the Shah of Khwarazmian's main force out of its best defensive position and soon columns under the notorious Mongol generals, Jugi and Jugatai, were linking up with Jenghiz, having turned the Shah's flank. Bokhara fell easily. Jenghiz pressed on westwards, openly declaring himself to be 'the scourge of God', the title formerly given to Attila, but which seemed no less true when taken up by Jenghiz. The wretched inhabitants of the former Khwarazmian Empire fought desperately for their lives but their efforts did not save the majority from slaughter. Jenghiz's lieutenants, Subotai and Chepenoyan, rode on through the Caucasus, but Jenghiz then recalled them. It seemed to him perhaps that he had already conquered the known world. He returned to his capital, Karakorum.

The Mongol Empire did not cease with Jenghiz's death (in 1227, while on a campaign against the Hsi-Jsia, to the south of Mongolia). His four sons, Jochi, Jugatai, Ogodai and Tolui, each inherited a vast tract of his huge empire; and Ogodai succeeded to the title of Great Khan. In 1237 Ogodai extended his Empire to include most of Russia, capturing Moscow. In 1241 his general, Subotai, with an army over 100,000 strong, invaded central Europe. Subotai advanced on a wide front driving all before him. He reunited his army in the plains of Hungary where Bela, King of Hungary, was assembling a large army at Pesth. The Mongols penetrated almost to the Danube, but in the face of Bela's host they retired about 100 miles to take up a position on the far bank of the River Sajo. The Hungarian king, following up his adversary with some caution, came upon the Mongols lining the

THE MONGOLS

river. Acting with a speed and audacity that surprised the Mongols, Bela established a bridgehead across the river. Then in the dark hours before dawn the Mongols struck back. A storm of arrows descended on the garrison holding the bridgehead accompanied, it appears, by showers of Chinese crackers which greatly alarmed them. They fled across the river pursued by their attackers. The main Hungarian army formed to repel the attackers, only to find themselves duped by a typical Mongol strategem. Subotai with a large part of his army, under cover of the diversion, had crossed the Sajo undetected by the Hungarians. He swung up the river and Bela, mistakenly believing he had the Mongol army in front of him saw to his horror Mongol columns in the early-morning light bearing down on his flank and rear. A ferocious battle raged, then the Hungarians broke, trying to escape by their open flank. The Mongol horsemen ruthlessly hunted them down and the Hungarian army perished almost to a man.

It was a brilliant victory, won by tactics typical of the Mongols. By their rapid initial withdrawal they had drawn the Hungarians on, filling them with a false self-confidence. Then, using a surprise attack to deceive them further as to their intentions, they crushed them by a totally unexpected assault from the flank and rear.

Now a panic-stricken Europe lay at the mercy of the savage invaders; but Providence intervened. Ogadai died on 11 December 1241 and the Mongols withdrew while the succession was decided. For another century and more the Mongols were to retain their hold on Russia, but to the Danube and the vulnerable lands of central Europe they never returned.

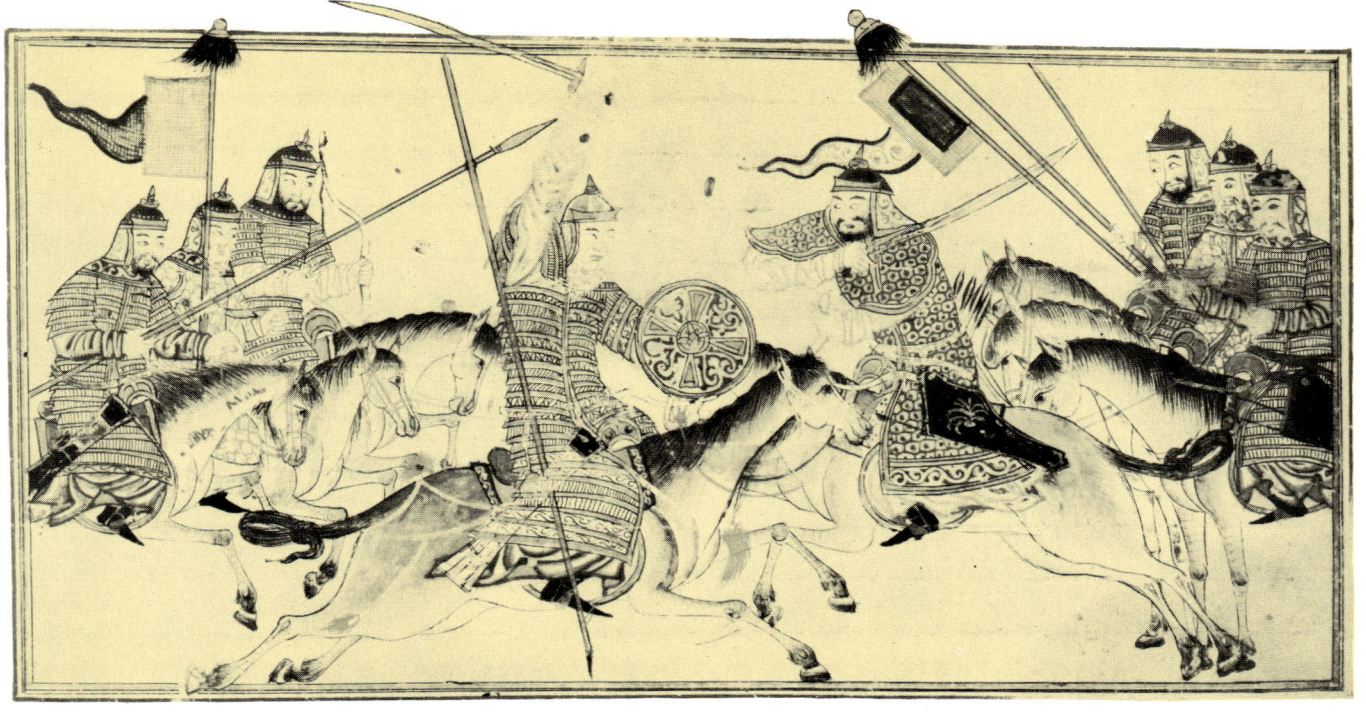

ORIENTAL CAVALRY, VARIOUSLY ARMED WITH SWORDS, BOWS AND LANCES.

T HE battlefield supremacy of the heavily armoured cavalryman was not seriously challenged in the century after the Battle of Arsouf. The role of infantry, and military science as a whole, remained subservient to the uncomplicated bravado of the knight, whose driving instinct was to close with his enemy and engage him in single combat. Not surprisingly, the battles of this epoch were, for the most part, massive brawls, and the commanders could form little more than rudimentary plans, certain in the knowledge that they would lose what little control they had the moment the action commenced. The infantry, meanwhile, huddled together in formless masses like the Asiatic multitudes of ancient Persia. Undisciplined, rudely armed, fundamentally leaderless, and too poor to provide themselves with protective armour, they presented an easy prey to the mounted knight. J.P.L.

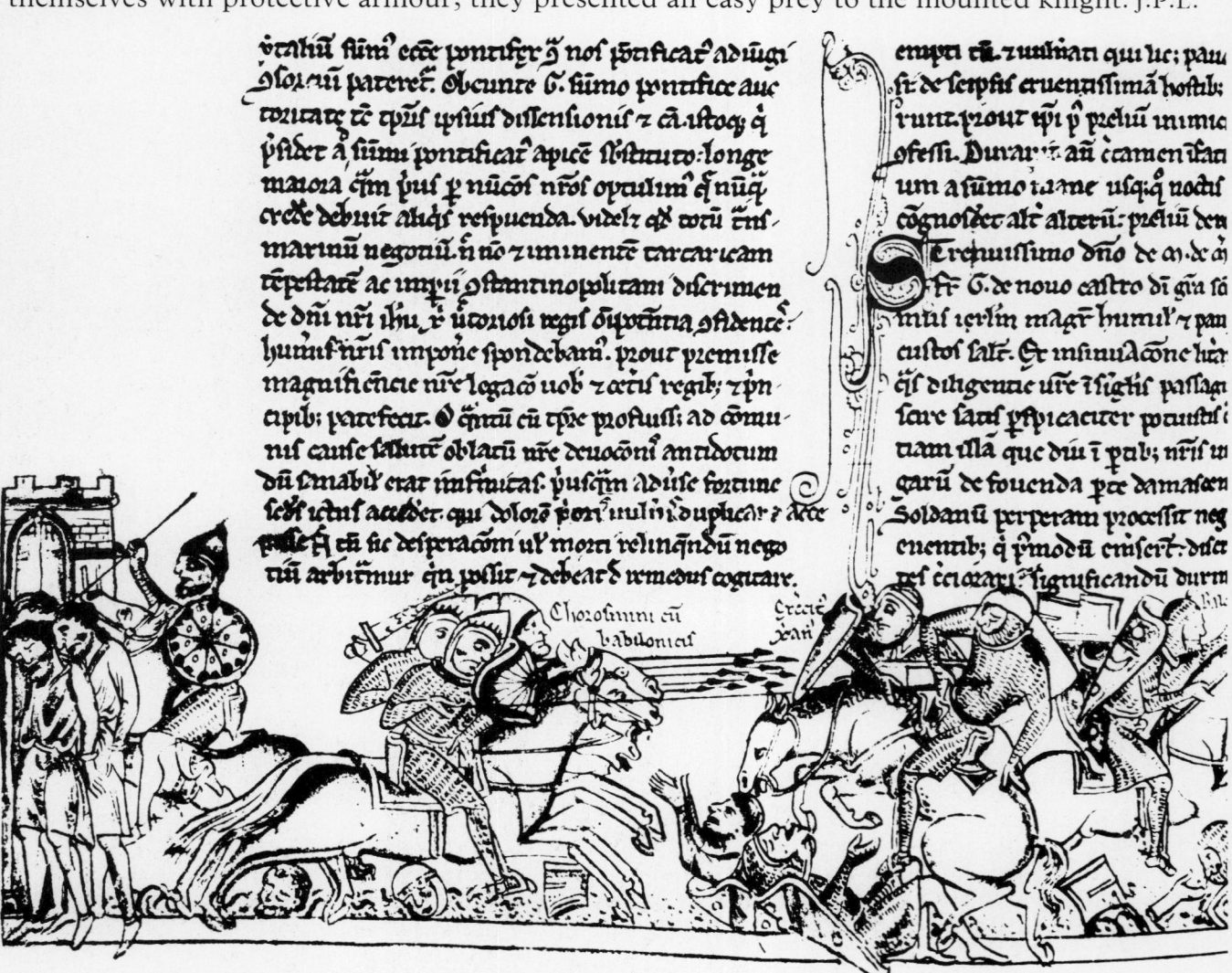

EUROPEAN KNIGHTS OF THE CHAIN-MAIL PERIOD. FROM A MEDIEVAL MANUSCRIPT.

DECLINE OF THE KNIGHT by CURT JOHNSON

The Hundred Years' War between England and France marked the eclipse and progressive decline of knightly cavalry. At its beginning, in 1337, the medieval knight, superbly armed and armoured, still dominated the battlefields of Europe. Marvellously skilled in the use of the lance and the straight-bladed, double-edged sword, and brave to the point of recklessness, and often far beyond, the knight's deficiencies as a soldier – his lack of discipline and fundamental inefficiency – though already apparent, had not begun seriously to work against him. The signs of his imminent demise were, however, clearly evident; harsh reality would soon be upon him.

Because for centuries the feudal system had prevented the humbler classes from acquiring skills in combat or the use of serviceable weapons, the eventual challenge to the domination of the medieval knight originated among the hardy races on the periphery of European feudalism. The Welsh, for example, who were known to 'expose their naked bodies to the attack of mail-clad knights . . . engage without weapons fully armed men and rush on foot against masses of heavy cavalry', developed the longbow, a fearsome missile weapon, capable of creating havoc among bodies of heavy cavalry. The Anglo-Norman barons, after they had largely subdued the Welsh, integrated Welsh bowmen and spearmen into their armies and used them with telling effect against the Irish and the Scots. In time, English yeomen adopted the longbow, their skill increasing as relations with France grew worse.

On the Continent, the Swiss and the Flemings revived the use of the pike, the ancient weapon of the Greek phalanxes. The Flemings were anything but warlike, yet their citizen militia, armed with pikes and pole arms, managed to inflict a serious defeat on the chivalry of northern France at Courtrai (1302) in the famous 'Battle of the Spurs'. The effect of Courtrai, though stunning at the time, was only temporary. The Flemish infantry, preferring to avoid the offensive, used the pike as a defensive weapon. Such passive tactics were easily countered, and in 1328 Philippe de Valois avenged Courtrai by overpowering the Flemish hedgehogs at Cassel, and so regaining control of Flanders.

The reversal at Courtrai did not therefore greatly disturb the ascendancy of the knight. It remained for the Swiss to re-establish the place of infantry by combining the pike with truly aggressive tactics. Unlike the relatively supine Flemings, the Swiss invariably took the initiative and, by attacking briskly, brought the battle to the enemy. Unless forced to assume the defensive the Swiss generally formed for battle in three columns. The first column or vanguard advanced vigorously and 'fixed' the enemy line of battle. The second, sometimes referred to as the 'battle', followed the van at a distance and pitched into another part of the enemy's line. The third column formed the rearguard and acted as a general reserve – a prudent measure rarely seen in a medieval order of battle; it advanced to a position from which it could support either one of the two attacking columns and halted. Deployed in this manner it could move to the assistance of a beleaguered attacking column or add its weight to the attack at the most opportune moment. If the attacking columns were defeated or repulsed, the rearguard covered their retreat from the field.

Significantly, too, the Swiss were more mobile and better disciplined than any of the armies they faced. Because of their poverty, few Swiss could afford complete armour. Instead, they relied on their weapons and rapidity of movement on the battlefield. The great columns of pikemen and halberdiers often moved faster even than the opposing cavalry – a remarkable speed made possible because the Swiss soldier was unencumbered by much protective armour.

A SWISS PIKEMAN. THE LONG PIKES MUST HAVE BEEN DIFFICULT TO CARRY ON THE LINE OF MARCH. ENGRAVING BY JACOB DE GHEYN AFTER HENDRIK GOLTZINS.

THE CAVALRY

The most significant factor in the Swiss formula for success, however, was the morale of the ordinary soldier. He marched and fought with a fierce, unshakeable determination. In 1291 the three forest cantons (Schwyz, Uri and Unterwalden) had formed a perpetual pact for the defence of their liberties against Hapsburg Austria. This was the beginning of the Swiss nation. Like all men fighting for freedom, the Swiss seemed to be infused with a fanatical spirit. The most ruthless soldiers in a ruthless age, they refused to observe the code of chivalry and neither proffered nor accepted quarter. Facing an attack by such a grim, determined people, the best soldiers were shaken and the worst demoralized.

The Swiss League was first tested at Morgarten (1315), where to the surprise of all Europe the peasantry of the forest cantons destroyed a large army of Austrian knights. Following Morgarten, the Swiss won a succession of victories, each one marked by the complete or near-complete destruction of the opposing force. At Sempach (1386) the Austrian Duke Leopold III dismounted his knights and tried to oppose the Swiss pikemen with a wall of lances. Undaunted, the Swiss advanced in massive wedge formations. Led by the heroic Arnold von Winkerlreid, who sacrificed himself to effect a gap in the Austrian line, they broke into the enemy's position and put the Austrian knights, overburdened with armour, to rout.

The Swiss record of success continued unbroken for 200 years until Marignano (1515). There, after two days of fighting, the furiously sustained attacks of the Swiss were blunted and brought to a halt by the charges of the French *gendarmes*, and the magnificent French artillery galled the pike columns to such an extent that they finally withdrew. The Swiss suffered 12,000 casualties out of their 22,000-man force. The French king, filled with admiration, allowed the survivors to withdraw unmolested. Shortly thereafter the Swiss made a perpetual peace and alliance with the French, and thousands of Swiss soldiers were taken into the French Army as mercenary troops.

Impressive as was the fighting record of the Swiss, the most remarkable victory in this period dominated by the resurgence of infantry was that gained by the English over the French at Crécy in 1346. The English army was strangely unlike other armies of the time. It had, to be sure, the appearance of a feudal host, but there similarities ended. Certainly, compared with that of his antagonist, Philippe VI, Edward III's army was less feudal – and therefore better disciplined and organized. Most of the English soldiers who fought at Crécy were paid professionals, men who contracted to serve for a specified period of time under a leader, called a captain, who acted as their commander and as a broker for their services. This factor, in itself, was enough to elevate the English army above its contemporaries. The spirited independence of the knight and the grudging, half-hearted obedience of the peasant levy had no place in the English army. All men, high and low, submitted to a comparatively rigorous discipline and fought for the king's wages.

A possibly more significant factor was the high proportion of longbowmen in the English army. At least 50 per cent of the army's manpower (fully 60–70 per cent of the available infantry) consisted of archers. The longbow carried by these men was by far the most effective and efficient missile weapon of the day. It had a maximum effective range of about 220 yards, and a skilled bowman

SCENES FROM THE BATTLE OF MARIGNANO, 1515. THE BATTLEFIELD IS DOMINATED BY PIKES AND MOST POSITIONS OF THE WEAPON ARE SHOWN. THEY WERE HELD VERTICALLY AT THE HALT: IN THE CENTRE FOREGROUND

could loose four or five aimed shafts per minute. Against such firepower the medieval knight was virtually defenceless. At extreme range the archers aimed high into the air, directing their fire at the gaily caparisoned horses of their enemy. The most devastating fire, however, was loosed when the attacking knights had close to within 100 yards or less of the defending archers. At this point the longbowmen began to shoot 'fore-hand shafts': the steel-tipped, 36-inch shafts were shot horizontally and with a velocity well capable of penetrating the armour (mail reinforced with plate) of the period. Should any of the attacking horsemen survive this veritable sleet of arrows and break into the English line, he would have to contend with the dismounted men-at-arms of the 'battle'. In most encounters, however, the issue was decided by the archers' firepower.

Two other factors accrued to the advantage of the English. One was the splendid leadership provided by the king, Edward III, a tactician of the first order. The second was the presence of a train of artillery with the English army – the first appearance of field artillery in warfare. There is no hard evidence that these few crude cannon materially affected the course of the battle, but several contemporary narratives state that the roar of the gunfire demoralized the crossbowmen of the Gen-

DECLINE OF THE KNIGHT

oese contingent forming the French vanguard.

The French army of King Philippe VI was numerically much the stronger; the English, with about 20,000 were outnumbered three to one by the French who totalled some 60,000. However, instead of being a single, cohesive force, the French army was composed of several independent feudal armies. The King and his marshals exercised nominal command, but predictably lost control at an early stage; the chief contribution of the marshals, in fact, seems to have been the vain one of appealing to their headstrong barons *not* to engage.

The battle came about as the invading English army, having ravaged the country round Paris, was retreating northwards to Flanders, pursued by the vastly more numerous French. Then, on 26 August 1346, Edward III decided to turn and face the enemy near the market town of Crécy. He had ample time to select a position and he chose well. The army was posted on a ridge to the north-west of the town. Crécy itself, and the River Maye which flows through the town, prevented the line from being turned by its right flank. From there the line ranged some 2,000 yards along the ridge to the village of Wadicourt, which, like Crécy on the right, formed a flank guard for the dangerously exposed left flank.

As was their custom the English dismounted their men-at-arms, conducted the horses to the rear, and formed for battle in three divisions. The vanguard, commanded by the king's son, Edward, Prince of Wales (the Black Prince), took the post of honour on the right. The young Prince was assisted by two veterans, the Earls of Warwick and Oxford, who, in reality, exercised command. The Earl of Northampton's division (the rearguard) was placed on the left. The centre was weakly held because three terraced strips of cultivated land presented an effective barrier to movement on horseback in the area. The King's division, which constituted the army's reserve, took position in the centre by a windmill about 700 yards from Crécy and to the left and rear of the Prince's division. Thus posted, the King could move to reinforce his left or right should the occasion demand it.

The English position overlookd a funnel-shaped valley formed by the watershed of the River Maye. This valley, subsequently called the Vallée aux Clercs, begins as a faint depression near Wadicourt but attains a depth of about 100 feet below Crécy. It is nowhere very steep, nor is it much of an obstacle, but its gentle slope was just enough of a hindrance seriously to impede the movement of the French men-at-arms towards the English line.

The French army approached from the south-east: it was late in the afternoon after a long day's march when they came upon the English position. King Philippe wished to halt for the night, but his knights angrily refused to wait. No idea of manoeuvre crossed their minds; intent only on coming to grips with the English, they wheeled down from the roads and prepared to descend into the Vallée aux Clercs before pressing towards the English line ranged along the ridge above. Philippe managed to restrain his knights sufficiently to order his Genoese crossbowmen to lead the attack. The Genoese, who numbered some 6,000, were good troops, the only reliable infantry in the French army. But they, like their comrades, were fatigued by the day's march – part of it through a shower which had saturated their bowstrings – and their leaders, Antonio Doria and Carlo Grimaldi, protested against the order. For this they were roundly abused by the French

SOLDIERS ARE AT 'PUSH OF PIKE'. ON THE RIGHT AND IN THE CENTRE BACKGROUND BATTERIES OF CANNON TAKE PART IN THE ACTION. BASED ON A RELIEF ON THE TOMB OF THE FRENCH KING, FRANCOIS I, AT ST DENIS.

AN ENGLISH MAN-AT-ARMS AND AN ARCHER, FROM THE LATTER HALF OF THE HUNDRED YEARS' WAR PERIOD. THEIR ARMOUR IS OF A HIGHLY EVOLVED KIND, WITH PLATE PREDOMINATING OVER CHAIN-MAIL.

THE CAVALRY

knights jostling round them, and eventually the Genoese went forward. In view of the relative chaos in their rear, the orderly advance of the Genoese was remarkable. Three times, in the course of their descent into the valley, they halted and corrected their alignment. At the third halt, about 300 yards from the English line, they raised their crossbows to their chests, gave a shout and discharged their bolts.

The English archers, deployed in large wedge-like 'herce' formations, looked on impassively as the iron darts of the Genoese fell far short of their position. Undeterred, the Genoese laboriously reloaded their ungainly weapons and advanced still closer. The English remained silent, but on receiving the word of command the mass of archers strode one step forward, raised their longbows high into the air, and loosed a powerful volley. Then, quicker than it takes to relate, the longbowmen began a devastating independent fire, so rapid that 'it seemed as if it snowed'. The Genoese were quite unprepared for this galling fire. Leaderless (Doria and Grimaldi fell in the first discharge), unable to reply, their formation riddled, they began to hesitate and mill about. This sudden turn of events disturbed Philippe, who cried out, 'Away with this faint-hearted rabble who do but hinder our advance!' The Comte d'Alençon, leading the first division of men-at-arms, needed no encouragement. He and his men fell on their allies and proceeded to hack them to pieces. The English, as yet unhurt, continued to fire, plying the bizarre fracas at the bottom of the valley with arrows.

The butchery of the Genoese contingent was quickly finished, and the battle entered its second phase as column after column of French men-at-arms pushed into the valley and made directly for the English line. On the left, in the valley of the Maye, the division of the Comte de Flandre advanced on the Black Prince's battle. In the centre, Jacques de Bourbon's division pressed hard on the rear of Alençon's force, which was busy extricating itself from the shambles on the valley floor, while, on the right, Jean de Hainault led a band of men towards Wadicourt. Farther back other columns, led by the King of Bohemia and the Comte de Blois, struggled towards the valley. All around these columns surged the peasant infantry of the communes, a confused rabble in arms, excited by the prospect of bloodshed, shouting, 'Kill! Kill! Death to the English traitors!'

The English surveyed this sprawling, boiling mass of humanity with remarkable equanimity. The sight of thousands of French men-at-arms urging their great destriers up the slippery incline of the ridge, their banners and standards snapping in the brisk sea-breeze wafting in from the coast, might have demoralized most medieval infantry, but the English were veteran soldiers who knew from past experience the terrible potential of their bows. Battles at Falkirk (1298), Dupplin Moor (1332), and Halidon Hill (1333) had been won by the longbow in similar circumstances; thus they remained confident.

Now, with the sun setting in their faces and the long red and orange rays bathing their armour and glinting from their swords, lances and shields, the French horsemen attempted to drive their attack home. The English held their fire, allowing the French to close the gap between the rival lines. Then, at very close range, each English archer 'laid his body into his bow' and, drawing the bowstring with all his strength, loosed his arrow. This process was repeated again and again in rapid succession. The French columns, raked and torn by this deadly fire, were staggered and began to break up. Knots of survivors continued forward, veering away from the herces of archers towards the men-at-arms. A handful, led by the Comte d'Alençon, actually broke into the English line, but these few were easily defeated. In a matter of minutes, the crisis had passed, and the first French wave had been utterly destroyed. The slope in front of the English position was littered with the corpses of hundreds, perhaps thousands, of men and horses. Of the high nobility the Comtes d'Alençon and Flandre had perished, while Louis le Mâle, the son of Flandre, and Jacques de Bourbon were severely wounded.

DECLINE OF THE KNIGHT

THE BLACK PRINCE COUNTER-ATTACKS AT CRÉCY. THE WINDMILL FROM WHICH HIS FATHER WATCHED THE BATTLE CAN BE SEEN TO HIS RIGHT REAR.
CLOSER TO THE PRINCE, AN ENGLISH LONGBOWMAN DRAWS HIS BOW. DRAWING BY PAGET.

The English archers, however, were not permitted to savour their victory, for a few moments after the first onslaught had receded, a fresh wave of mounted men trotted up from the valley. This new attack, led by the Duc de Lorraine and Jean de Hainault, washed up to and around the heroes, ebbing as once again the archery of the defenders took its toll. Then, just as suddenly, a new crisis occurred.

A third offensive, led by Johann, the blind King of Bohemia, and consisting almost entirely of Germans and Luxemburgers, loomed in the half-light just in front of the Black Prince's division. These German knights had benefited from the archers' preoccupation with the second attack and were already crowding in upon young Edward's men-at-arms before they could be subjected to fire. The blind king himself, guided by his companions, Alard de Baseille and Heinrich von Klingenberg, led the rush into the English right, but he and his knights were cut off and overwhelmed when the archers shifted their fire to the rear of the German column.

Johann, who was later eulogized by King Edward as 'the crown of chivalry', was knocked from his horse and killed. All those who followed him into the English line suffered a similar fate. Most of the Germans, however, failed to make contact and were driven off in disorder. Some, like the Markgraf of Moravia and Karl of Luxemburg, were so thoroughly discouraged that they quit the field in a panic. Despite this success, the work of the Prince's division had not ended. A new phalanx of horsemen, headed by the Comtes de Blois and St Pol, dashed at the embattled Englishmen even as the débris of King Johann's attack trailed away in the opposite direction. The pace of the battle again quickened.

This thrust, as it developed, was the most serious attack the English faced all evening. The Frenchmen goaded their chargers up the slope with the same bravery and reckless abandon they had exhibited before, and several of the divisions managed to arrive before the English line at the same time. Though galled terribly by the English archery, columns led by at least six counts broke into the line of the Prince's division and engaged the English men-at-arms in bitter hand-to-hand combat. The Prince, fighting in his first battle, feared the worst and applied to the King, his father, for reinforcements. Sir Thomas Norwich carried the Prince's plea for assistance to the King, who was watching the action from the windmill. Edward, with characteristic detachment, denied his son's request and dispatched Sir Thomas back

BELOW: A FRENCH ARCHER AND TWO CROSSBOWMEN OF THE *COMPAGNIE D'ORDONNANCE*, c.1448. FROM *COSTUMES MILITAIRES FRANCAIS DE 1439 À 1789*, BY D. DE NOIRMONT AND ALFRED DE MARBOT, c.1859. BOTTOM: KNIGHTS IN BATTLE DURING THE FIRST HALF OF THE 14TH CENTURY.

DECLINE OF THE KNIGHT

to the Earl of Oxford with the admonition to 'let the boy win his spurs'. But, just moments after Norwich's departure, the King relented and sent a token reinforcement of 30 horsemen to the Prince. More important, he then ordered Northampton's division to advance a short distance and so relieve some of the pressure on the Prince's beleaguered men. The French were unable to exploit their breakthrough, and despite the anxiety and confusion their attack produced in the darkness, they were soon defeated.

The ground in front of the English position was by now so choked with dead and wounded men and horses that it had become a horrific shambles and was, in places, impassable. Even so, more French attacks, perhaps as many as a dozen, shouldered through the wreckage of previous onslaughts and attempted to storm the English line. The archers were dog-tired, but each new attack was lashed and raked by a furiously sustained fire. Finally, about six hours after it had begun, the fighting abruptly ceased. The English remained under arms all night, unaware that the battle had ended. Philippe's army was routed, having suffered a defeat unparalleled in French history to that time. The infantry of the communes, however, continued to wander aimlessly onto the battlefield, ignorant of the extent of the disaster. The next morning was foggy, and Edward sent out a strong force of men-at-arms and archers to discover the whereabouts of the French. This party ran into the communal infantry and slew 2,000 of them before the field was cleared.

It was only when the fog had lifted that the magnitude of the English victory became apparent. Edward sent his clerks and heralds into the valley (hence Vallée aux Clercs) to count and identify the French dead. Among the slain were the King of Bohemia, the Duc de Lorraine, 12 counts, 80 bannerets, 1,200 knights and uncounted thousands of men-at-arms and infantrymen. Edward's own losses were inconsequential, amounting to less than 100 men-at-arms and infantry altogether.

Aside from its political results, Crécy was a truly significant battle because it was the first permanent defeat of knightly cavalry by infantry. More than any other battle of the era, it ended the dominance of feudal cavalry and helped to usher in the new age of infantry. The pattern established by Edward's archers at Crécy was repeated at Poitiers (1357) and Agincourt (1415). Knightly cavalry never regained the stature it had enjoyed before these defeats, which shattered beyond repair the mystique of the armoured horseman.

THE BATTLE OF AURET (1364) BETWEEN CHARLES DE BLOIS AND JEAN DE MONTFORT. AS A RESULT OF EXPERIENCES AT CRÉCY AND POITIERS, BOTH SIDES ARE FIGHTING MORE ON FOOT THAN FORMERLY. COPIED FROM A WOODCUT IN THE *CHRONIQUES DE BRÉTAGNE*, WRITTEN BY ALAIN BOUCHARD AND PUBLISHED IN 1514.

During the Hundred Years' War the crossbow, the longbow and the pike dealt near-mortal blows to the knight in armour. Puzzled and alarmed, as we have already seen, he descended from his charger and struggled forward on foot only to meet with fresh disaster. Then came an effective gunpowder, and as a result shot of various kinds could now penetrate not only his armour but the walls of his castle as well. It was too much: the knight took his leave of a battlefield become exceedingly complex and thorny, to be replaced to a large extent by professional soldiers of fortune among whom the *Landsknechte* and *Reiter* of Germany were perhaps the most famous. When not actively engaged in fighting these mercenary soldiers occupied their leisure hours by plundering the countryside and towns around them and murdering any who opposed them. However useful they might be in war, they were certainly intolerable in peacetime; yet to disband them might only result in strengthening an enemy or adding to the bands of brigands who infested the more desolate areas. In 1439 Charles VII of France took a momentous decision. He paid some carefully selected captains to recruit companies of French soldiers to be called the *Compagnies d'Ordonnance*, each composed either of a hundred 'lances' or a hundred 'archers'; these were the *Gendarmes*. The number of these companies fluctuated between 12 and 20; they were stationed at important strongholds near the frontiers and soon proved their worth. In a further decree Charles forbade any of his subjects to raise any troops without his express orders. It was the end of the old feudal levies and the beginning of the modern standing army.

During the 15th and 16th centuries the design of both handguns and cannon was steadily refined. The French in particular developed an artillery arm which, from the point of view of the English at least, was sensationally effective, the French gunners playing a major part in their expulsion from France. The matchlock, whereby a trigger depressed the match, a length of burning fuse, into the priming pan, exploding the charge in the barrel of the gun, made possible a firearm that one man could load and fire. At first the range of the ball was short, a bare 100 yards, the rate of fire was slow and misfires common. A curved butt was given to this weapon so that it could fit into the shoulder of the firer, and the weapon, in view of its hacked-out butt, became known as the hackbutt, or, more commonly, the arquebus.

With cannon and arquebuses added to the hazards of the battlefield, it began to seem no place for a man on the back of a horse. The horsemen in turn discarded their lances and frantic efforts were made to adapt a weapon for firing on horseback. It then became clear that a horseman could not hope to shoot as accurately as a man on the ground, nor could he pierce a steady line of pikes. There appeared to be little use at that stage for cavalry except for foraging for provisions or pursuing an already beaten foe. However, towards the end of the 16th century, partly as a result of his studies of the military methods of Antiquity, now rediscovered, Maurice of Nassau, followed shortly by Gustavus Adolphus of Sweden, was to demonstrate that properly handled and organized cavalry could still dominate the battlefield. J.P.L.

ABOVE: EARLY ATTEMPTS AT HAND ARTILLERY, CARRIED BOTH ON FOOT AND ON HORSEBACK. THE PROBLEM OF APPLYING THE BURNING MATCH WHILE AIMING THE WEAPON IS CLEAR TO SEE. THE EXAMPLES ARE FRENCH, c.1488.

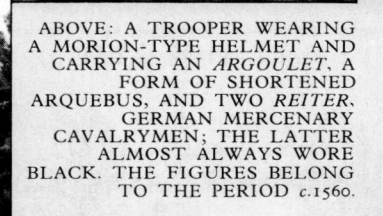

ABOVE: A TROOPER WEARING A MORION-TYPE HELMET AND CARRYING AN *ARGOULET*, A FORM OF SHORTENED ARQUEBUS, AND TWO *REITER*, GERMAN MERCENARY CAVALRYMEN; THE LATTER ALMOST ALWAYS WORE BLACK. THE FIGURES BELONG TO THE PERIOD c.1560.

ABOVE: CROSSBOWMAN AND SOLDIER WITH A HACKBUTT. THE MATCH IS NOW APPLIED TO THE FIRING PAN BY A TRIGGER MECHANISM, AND THE WEAPON IS AIMED WITH GREATER PRECISION.
BELOW: ARTILLERY IN THE REIGN OF FRANCOIS I, c.1520. THE SKILL OF THE FRENCH GUNNERS BECAME A BATTLE-WINNING FACTOR TOWARDS THE END OF THE HUNDRED YEARS' WAR. ALL THE ILLUSTRATIONS ON THIS PAGE ARE FROM DE NOIRMONT AND DE MARBOT.

GUSTAVUS ADOLPHUS, THE LION OF THE NORTH, BY P. SOUTMAN.

THE THIRTY YEARS' WAR by ALAN SHEPPERD

The onset of the Thirty Years' War in 1618 brought to central Europe an era of devastation and misery almost unparalleled since the days of Barbarism. By 1630 two Catholic Imperialist armies had subjugated all Germany up to the shores of the Baltic. Then in July of that year Gustavus Adolphus, the soldier-king of Sweden, landed in Pomerania with a national army (the first in Europe) of around 13,000 men. The arrival of the 'Lion of the North' proved to be the turning-point in the struggle for the survival of Protestantism and by December his army in Germany had swollen to 42,000 men. Over the next two years large areas of Germany were liberated from the yoke of the Holy Roman Emperor, and at the time of Gustavus's death, in November 1632 in the Battle of Lützen, 149,000 men were serving under his standard.

Renowned in his lifetime as a fearless leader in battle, Gustavus was also an outstanding administrator, and a general whose innovations in organization and tactics set him above any of his contemporaries and led directly to the birth of the art of modern warfare. As Michael Roberts shows in his essay, *The Military Revolution 1560–1660*, it was the reforms of Maurice of Nassau and Gustavus Adolphus, and the return to linear formations, that 'solved the problem of how to combine missile weapons with close action: how to unite hitting power, mobility and defensive strength'. As for cavalry tactics, these were dramatically changed.

Nowadays a new weapon can be out of date almost before it is off the drawing-board, so it may seem something of a paradox that the introduction of firearms to the battlefield had a debilitating effect on offensive action for nearly two centuries. In the early part of the 17th century the arquebusiers or musketeers were still subordinate to the heavy infantry, the pikemen, whose proven worth was reflected in their better pay and equipment. Little had been done to lighten the weight of their weapon, now more commonly known as the musket, which had a painfully slow rate of fire, was wildly inaccurate and could only be properly fired from a rest. At close-quarters the musketeer was at a serious disadvantage while reloading, and if sent forward to close the range he became an easy prey to the enemy's cavalry. So the majority of the musketeers were held back in close support of the pikemen, whose massed formations, based on the deep Swiss column and the Spanish *tercio*, the latter consisting of 1,000 or more men densely packed in a square, were primarily adopted to counter the cavalry charge. Against the inert mass of the *tercio*, hedged around by tier upon tier of 18-foot pikes, neither sword nor lance was effective. In time more musketeers were brought in to the *tercios*: they were formed in some 10 or more ranks in front of and at the corner of the squares of heavy infantry. After each rank fired, the musketeers then countermarched to the rear to reload, and if hard-pressed they scuttled into the protection of the squares. But this slow spasmodic fire rarely achieved a sufficient breach in the enemy's lines to allow the cavalry to intervene.

It was the introduction of the wheel-lock pistol that at last gave the cavalry the opportunity to take part in the fire fight; thus armed, each rank rode forward to fire into the mass of the infantry before wheeling away to reload in the rear. This manoeuvre was known as the *caracole*. In the face of a determined body of musketeers, however, the troopers could well need an excess of zeal to close to some 10 paces (which was the effective range of their cavalry pistol) before firing. As Michael Roberts explains, 'The essential of cavalry tactics – the utilization of the impact of man and horse to disrupt the enemy's formation – was thus totally lost, except in Poland; and cavalry became a debilitated arm, fit only to snap its pistols at other horsemen as debilitated as themselves.' They could still sweep down on 'forlorn' musketeers skirmishing in the narrow no-man's-land between the battle lines and chase away artillerymen from their exposed positions in front of the infantry,

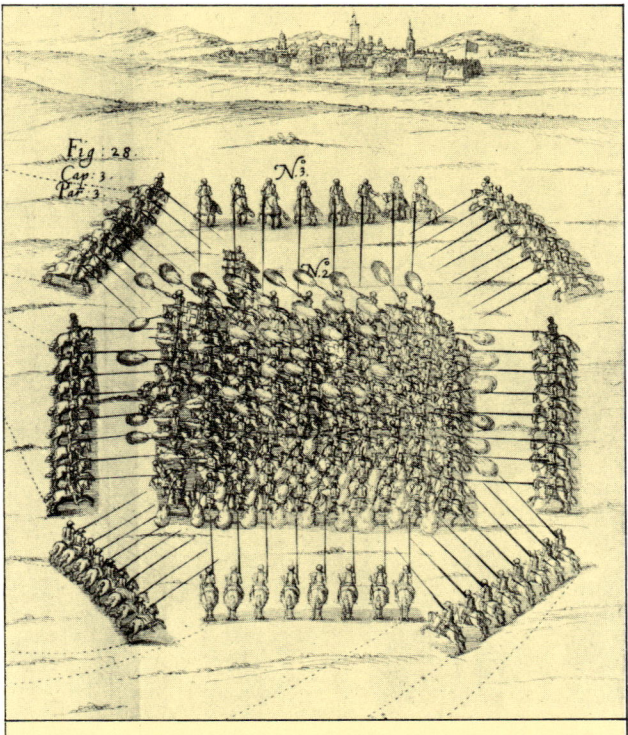

AN ILLUSTRATION OF HOW CAVALRY ARMED WITH THE LANCE SHOULD ATTACK A TERCIO OR SQUARE. UNFORTUNATELY IT DID NOT WORK, AND THE LANCE BEGAN TO DISAPPEAR FROM THE CAVALRY OF WESTERN EUROPE. FROM JACOBI'S INSTRUCTIONS ON THE PRINCIPLES OF THE CAVALRY, 1616.

THE CAVALRY

but otherwise they were kept to the flanks, restless spectators of the surging clash of the heavy infantry, ready to be launched only against a formation that had lost its cohesion or was in flight. As the proportion of shot to pike increased, the offensive powers of the latter diminished and both they and the horse were deprived of their individual powers of offensive action. Musketeers were becoming the arbiters of the battlefield.

In his long struggle against Spanish rule (between 1590 and 1609), Maurice of Nassau had sought to break this deadlock. His tactical reforms, clearly based on those of the Roman Legion, brought a return to smaller units and linear formations. The advantage of a shallower formation, where practically every man could bring his weapon to bear at the same time, was economy. Its drawback was that any over-rigid adherence to geometrical patterns had a stultifying effect, and opportunities for initiative and mobility, so necessary to any return to the doctrine of offensive action, were suppressed. Moreover, nothing was done for the cavalry. Thus we find in the opening years of the Thirty Years' War that the use of the lance was forbidden and the tactics of the *caracole* had become more formalized than ever before.

The reforms introduced by Gustavus went much further than those of Maurice—and as the monarch he could ensure that they were put into effect. By spending half the national budget on the army he ensured that his conscripts were regularly paid, properly clothed and provided with the most up-to-date weapons and equipment. As a soldier he was a brilliant cavalry leader whose personal courage and fine generalship brought him universal renown. Consequently the foreign mercenaries who flocked to serve under his flag willingly accepted his high standards of training and discipline. Under his direction the technology of his time was harnessed to improving missile weapons, and particularly the artillery. Here the introduction of the 4-pounder field-piece, which could be drawn by one horse or two to three men, was to prove an immediate success.

As an administrator Gustavus knew no equal: supply depots were set up and field hospitals introduced, all of which brought new standards of efficiency and morale. He had an iron will and, as T. A. Dodge in *Gustavus Adolphus* (1890) expressed it, a 'quick sensitive, almost touchy habit' coupled with 'a deep feeling for right, truth and religion'. These personal qualities were reflected in his *Articles of War*, which bound Swedish citizen and foreign mercenary alike to a rigid code of conduct in and out of battle.

The organization of the Imperialists' armies was firmly based on the battle tactics of the *tercio*, and their cavalry, especially the cuirassiers, were similarly used *en masse*. Johann Tilly, who commanded at the Battle of Breitenfeld (1631), could call on many different types of cavalry, some with distinctive national characteristics such as the Croats. The cuirassier regiments comprised between 2,000–2,500 men divided into either three or two squadrons of around 1,000 or 800 heavily armoured soldiers, wearing a cuirass both front and back and mounted on large and powerful horses. Their weapons were the inevitable pair of pistols and a broad edged sword. Carbineers were also employed, but in smaller units. These wore light armour and carried a short-barrelled firearm, evolved from the earlier arquebus, and a sword. Like the cuirassiers they were formed 10 deep and trained to fire by ranks in succession, which then retired to reload. These were the shock troops, if such a term can be used for cavalry which relied entirely on firearms. Dragoons were introduced shortly before the start of the Thirty Years' War, and although they were armed with the infantry musket and trained to fight on foot, they were on occasion used in a mounted role to increase the firepower of the heavy cavalry; they formed up in the same manner. As mounted musketeers they provided outposts and detachments to protect convoys from the otherwise customary depradations of that most violent period.

Lieutenant-Colonel George T. Denison in *A History of Cavalry* (1877) describes the light cavalry of the Imperialists as hussars and mentions their richly decorated uniforms and trappings. Military uniforms in the modern sense, however, were unknown at this period, although some regiments may have been provided at a later stage in the war with a form of tabard to wear over their battle-stained dress on special ceremonial parades. The light cavalry carried a sword and two pistols, wore no armour and were drawn up in shallow formations of six ranks, and later five under Wallenstein, the Austrian general who commanded at Lützen (16 November 1632). They were principally used, however, in surprise attacks on con-

JACOBI'S DIAGRAMS DEMONSTRATE CORRECT POSITIONS FOR THE LANCE WHEN USED AGAINST PISTOL OR LANCE, THE POINT CARRIED HIGH (1), RIGHT CENTRE (2) AND LOW (3).

THE THIRTY YEARS' WAR

voys and baggage parks and for cutting communications.

Before examining in detail the organization and tactics of the Swedish cavalry we should first see how these link up with the wide-ranging reforms made by Gustavus as a result of his experience in earlier campaigns and his close study of classical methods of warfare. His whole philosophy of war led towards a single aim—the destruction of the enemy forces. He constantly sought ways of restoring the power of offensive action through mobility, increased fire-power and shock action. The proportion of shot to pike was progressively increased and the pike itself was somewhat shortened, proving still effective against cavalry but deadly when his highly disciplined infantry charged the opposing foot soldiers. Armour was lightened and often dispensed with. Shallow linear formations gave more men the chance to use their weapons at the point of contact. The size of units was reduced but there were more of them and at each level the number of officers and non-commissioned officers was considerably increased, bringing a degree of control and flexibility hitherto unthought of. Under Gustavus the artillery became standardized, much increased (by 1630 there were about 9 guns per 1,000 men), more mobile and better served. The infantry guns, the regimental field-pieces using cartridged ammunition, were trained to the point where they could be attached to the cavalry as well as to the heavy infantry and could fire eight rounds of grape or canister to the musketeers' six. Accuracy of aim was insisted upon as a basic necessity and the use of weapons continually practised. Whether conscripted peasant or experienced mercenary, each and all were trained on identical lines, and when it came to the practical business of war the King who led the army was the first to pick up a shovel, lay a gun or lead a patrol deep into enemy territory.

Under his personal tuition the foot were organized into battle groups drawn up in what is best described as a wedge formation, with the attacking point consisting of pikemen flanked and supported in the rear by bodies of musketeers. The army formed up in two shallow lines about 300 paces apart; the infantry were in the centre and the cavalry on the flanks. Behind each line there was a strong reserve and between each regiment of horse there was a body of up to 200 'commanded musketeers'. This use of musketeers, and the attachment of light field-pieces in direct support of the cavalry, clearly demonstrated Gustavus's determination to restore the *arme blanche* to its former eminence on the battlefield. Yet these two particular tactical innovations would have been of little value if Gustavus's cavalry had not been completely revitalized. The *caracole* was forbidden. The squadrons were formed only four and later three ranks deep. The charge was made at a fast but steady pace, the first two ranks discharging their pistols in the very faces of their enemy and then engaging with the sword, while the remaining rank, swords drawn, followed close behind, reserving their fire for the *mêlée*. Some authorities claim the charge was delivered at the gallop, others at a fast trot. What mattered was that line upon line of well-disciplined and determined horsemen were trained to charge home with cold steel, and that the regiments were so placed that they could be instantly ordered forward to crash into any gap blown in the enemy's battle line by the concentrated fire of the guns and the heavy volleys of the musketeers.

Commenting on the military reforms of Gustavus, Michael Roberts notes how the Swedish cavalry were recruited. Under ancient obligations the noblemen of Sweden were responsible for filling their quota of heavy cavalry, but in 1611, the year

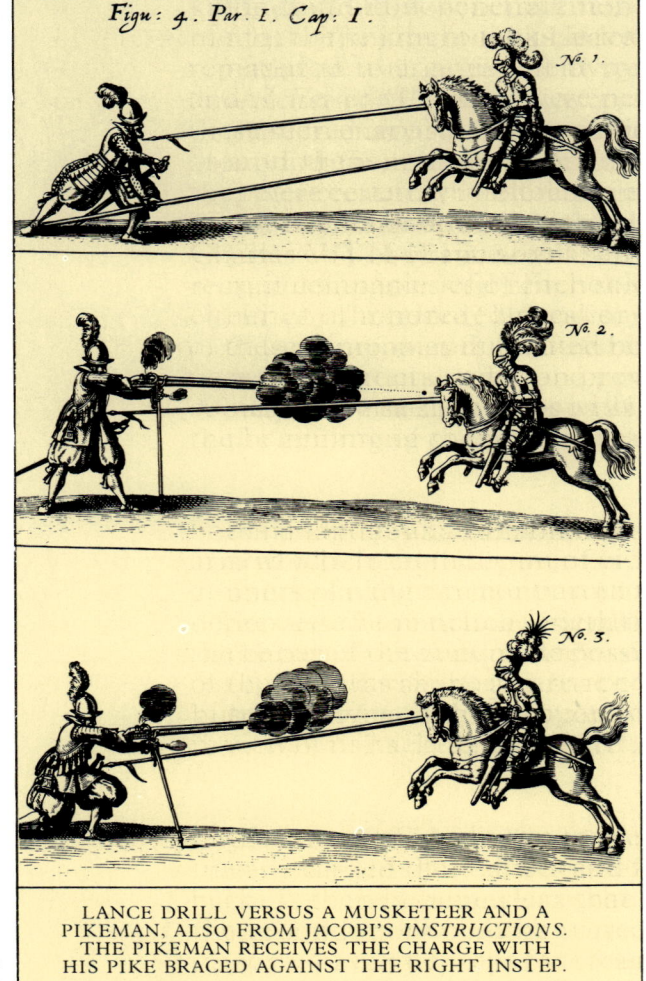

LANCE DRILL VERSUS A MUSKETEER AND A PIKEMAN, ALSO FROM JACOBI'S *INSTRUCTIONS*. THE PIKEMAN RECEIVES THE CHARGE WITH HIS PIKE BRACED AGAINST THE RIGHT INSTEP.

JACOBI: THE DRILL FOR FIRING ON HORSEBACK. THE EQUIPMENT, TOP LEFT, INCLUDES A BREASTPLATE (1), A BELT AND HOOK FOR AN ARQUEBUS (2), A SHORTENED ARQUEBUS (3), AND A POWDER FLASK (4).

THE CAVALRY

when Gustavus became King, such resistance to the system had been built up that only 30 horsemen were enrolled. While the infantry could be readily conscripted on a national scale, Gustavus never succeeded in compelling the nobility to do knightly service. Even in the peak year of 1630, for instance, only two squadrons were raised in this manner. 'He had therefore to fall back on inducements to volunteer, and this proved to be a better solution. The cavalry he obtained was light cavalry, and its horses were smaller than the great chargers of Germany; but by the time he had finished he made it the equal of any cavalry in Europe and the superior of most.'

In winter or summer, at home or overseas, his army was regularly paid. In peacetime the soldiers returned to the farms from which they had been recruited and their pay was offset against the farmer's taxes. Officers received grants of land for which the treasury dues were deducted from their pay. Recruiting areas coincided with the provincial administrative boundaries and the establishments of the provincial regiments reflected the new pattern of tactical formations used in the field. In 1620 the establishment of a squadron of horse was set at 175, and later (in 1628) two squadrons were formed into the first provincial cavalry regiment, the Västgöta, which has retained its identity to the present time.

In the early years of the King's reign a Swedish cavalry regiment on active service at full strength had an establishment of 974 men and 1,000 horses. It was organized with a small regimental headquarters and eight squadrons or cornets. Each of these squadrons mustered three officers and two non-commissioned officers, a quartermaster, muster-clerk, chaplain, provost, barber (who doubled as a medical orderly under the regimental surgeon) and a farrier, together with two trumpeters and 120 troopers. By the 1630s, however, Gustavus had not only perfected his famous wedge-shaped brigade, based on four battle groups of 400 pike and shot, he had also reduced the size of the cavalry regiments to 560 men. This new pattern of cavalry regiment was still divided into eight squadrons (of 70 men) and, by virtue of its small size and the shallow formations used, was both flexible and readily manoeuvred, as well as being

A REITER AND A FRENCH GENDARME, c.1587. FROM DE NOIRMONT AND DE MARBOT.

ONE OF THE OLDEST MILITARY PRACTICES, BREWING UP, PERFORMED BY FRENCH INFANTRY c.1494. FROM DE NOIRMONT AND DE MARBOT.

76

THE THIRTY YEARS' WAR

easy to control in the turmoil of the battlefield.

The clothing worn by the Swedish mounted troops, in common with the rest of the national army, was ordinary peasant dress. It consisted of a sleeveless tunic of coarse cloth worn over an undershirt that covered the arms, and loose knee-breeches with coarse woollen stockings. The cuirassiers wore high knee-boots with spurs, while the dragoons wore shoes and boots in winter. As winter campaigning was generally considered quite impracticable, the Imperialists' generals were often caught out and much confused when Gustavus carried on the war the year round. The King indeed went to great lengths to see that his soldiers were properly clothed against the cold and wet weather, and warm outer clothing was either sent out from Sweden or bought locally. The normal issue was a fur coat or cloak and fur gloves, together with fur-lined boots, some being of waterproof leather in the Russian style. The cuirassiers wore a helmet and breastplate, the dragoons a helmet only and the light cavalry no armour at all.

Mention has already been made of the weapons of the cuirassiers, the long sword and pair of pistols; the dragoons were armed with an infantry musket and a sword. The musket was shorter and lighter than those used by their opponents and this was a critical factor when it was fired from the saddle. Another of the King's innovations was the issue of cartridge pouches to replace the bandolier, which tended to become entangled during mounted action. In his *History of Gustavus Adolphus*, published in 1759, Walter Harte claims that the King 'was the first to alter the muskets of the cavalry to carbines', and in this connection he makes an interesting comment on the value of the latter when used against the enemy's irregular horse. 'The King, in frequent conflicts with the Croatians, a set of beings he mortally hated, as waylayers, robbers, and murderers, devised a new practice in the military art, for mixing dragoons, who then carried a shorter musquet, and not carbines, with his own light cavalry, either serving on foot, as occasion required, or doing great mischief on horseback, as their pieces discharged a heavier ball.'

In the winter of 1630–31, Count Johann Tilly, General of the League, was dispatched with a hastily assembled force to stem the advance of the Swedish invader. The Count, a Netherlander by birth, was a short, sparsely built, sharp-featured man in his early 70s. Educated in a Jesuit order, he had turned at an early age to the profession of arms, and by seeking service against the Turkish infidel and the Protestant heretic earned himself the sobriquet 'the monk in armour'. A hard ruthless man, he had shown in the past a flair for daring plans and incisive action. As a general he had never been beaten. Now his mercenary soldiers affectionately called him 'Father Tilly', but his subordinate commanders were conscious of his failing powers, and Gustavus disdainfully dubbed him 'the old corporal'. But his presence with an Imperialist army was not to be taken lightly. Frustrated in his initial moves, in November 1630 he turned against the city of Magdeburg, which by the following May was reduced to ashes and the entire population of some 30,000 souls massacred, an act of gross barbarism that endorsed the Count's already considerable reputation for cruelty.

In the autumn of 1631 Tilly invaded Saxony with the intention of dealing with Leipzig as he had with Magdeburg. Abandoning his neutrality, Johann Georg, the Elector of Saxony, now joined forces with Gustavus and the two Allies met at Düben some 25 miles north of Leipzig on 15 September. Both were determined to bring the Imperialists to battle with the least possible delay. In round terms the strengths of the opposing forces were slightly in favour of the Allies, although the state of training and morale of the Saxons could hardly be compared with that of the Swedish troops, as we shall later see. The Imperialists' army consisted of 21,000 infantry, 11,000 cavalry and 30 guns. The national archives give the number of troops in the Swedish army that took part in the Battle of Breitenfeld, or Leipzig as it is sometimes known, as 26,800. The true strength of the Saxon army is unrecorded, but probably brought the Allied total to between 34,000 and 38,000 men. Knowing that 12,000 reinforcements of veteran troops from Italy would shortly arrive, Count Tilly could well have played a waiting game and accepted a siege of Leipzig. His immediate subordinates, the two cavalry commanders Pappenheim and Fürstenberg, thought otherwise. By persistent argument, including a falsified reconnaissance report, they persuaded the Count to leave the shelter of the city and fight it out in the open.

A small garrison of 3,000 men was put into Leipzig and Tilly took up a position some five miles north of the city on a slight rise facing towards the village of Podelwitz and close to Breitenfeld itself. A low hill towards the right gave his guns a commanding position and away to the rear on the left there was a sizeable wood. Otherwise the ground is best described as a treeless and slightly undulating plain, admirably suited to the battle tactics of a 'past master in the Spanish tactics'. Tilly indeed had the advantage of ground, wind and sun. His infantry were formed in the traditional line of *tercios*, some 14 solid squares stretched across the centre of the position. On either flank was a strong force of cavalry, six regiments in each wing. The right wing was strengthened by two regiments of Croats and commanded by Fürstenberg, while Pappenheim commanded on the left. Colonel Munroe, who was serving with one of the Scottish regiments in the Swedish centre, remarked that the Imperialists occupied a front of two English miles. This breadth of line was important to Tilly, whose favourite tactic was to use his massed cavalry for flank attacks from an overlapping position and with a minimum of manoeuvring.

On 16 September the Allied armies advanced to within about two miles of Tilly's encampments. An attempt by the Swedish dragoons to seize part of the ridge where Tilly's heavy guns were later posted was beaten off, and after 36 hours of forced marching both Allied armies went into bivouac for the night. The following morning at dawn Gustavus ordered the advance to be sounded. He later wrote, 'Because between us and Leipzig there was no wood, but only great flat fields, I drew out my army in full battle array and marched towards the city. The march lasted a short hour and a half,

THE CAVALRY

when we came in sight of the advanced guard of the enemy with his artillery on a hill, and behind it the whole mass of his army.' It seems that Tilly was still reluctant to take the initiative and made little or no attempt to attack the Allies while crossing the Loder stream, although Malleson in *The Battle-Fields of Germany* comments that some of Pappenheim's horse were engaged against the Swedes and in retreat set fire to the village of Podelwitz, attempting to delay their advance.

In the Allied camp Gustavus plainly saw that he must look to his own protection at the junction-point with the Saxons on his left. The inter-army boundary, to use a modern term, was the Leipzig–Düben road, and Gustavus took care that there was room for his cavalry to operate in the gap between the two armies.

By noon the opposing lines were finally in position and a glance at the map will show how totally different was the tactical formation adopted by the King to that of Count Tilly and indeed to that of his ally the Elector of Saxony. Three points are worth underlining: Gustavus's use of over 2,000 musketeers in direct support of his cavalry; the careful placing of a cavalry reserve in the second line and behind the third line, and finally the employment of regimental guns in depth alongside their parent units, with a small artillery reserve in the rear.

After a little over two hours of cannonading, in which the better served and more numerous Swedish artillery had the advantage, Pappenheim could stand the fire no longer. Without waiting for orders he led an attack with some 5,000 horsemen against the Swedish right wing. Tilly was furious, exclaiming, 'They have robbed me of my honour and glory!' But at that moment he could hardly have foreseen the full consequences of Pappenheim's actions. As the massed ranks rode up to discharge their pistols they were met by volley upon volley of well-aimed musket fire, and repeated charges by the opposing regiments whenever they wavered. As General J. F. C. Fuller wrote, 'Seven times Pappenheim charged and each time he was repulsed; on the last occasion Baner hurled his reserve upon him and drove him in rout from the field.'[1]

On the other flank, however, the Imperialists had come very near to carrying the field. Following the example set by Pappenheim, Fürstenberg's cavalry, backed up by a number of *tercios*, had struck at the Saxons, who gave way and fled in panic, pausing only to plunder the Swedish baggage train. The Swedish left flank was now completely exposed and Field-Marshal Horn, its commander, was faced with some 18,000 foot and 5,000 horse. But the *tercios* needed time to reform and many of Fürstenberg's horse had to be stopped from pursuing the Saxons, while others were milling about in the gap by the road. Seeing hope only in attack during this temporary confusion, Horn threw himself on Fürstenberg's cavalry, driving them into the ranks of the *tercios*. Then he launched his reserve; by then the two reserve brigades of infantry from the second rank were also on the move; meanwhile, drawing on his right wing, the King ordered forward the West Gotland Horse. Slowly the tide began to turn. The Imperialists, unable to reform against the growing weight of the Swedish reserves, were tightly packed together. Units intermingled, confusion spread, and they became an easy prey to the disciplined volleys and the almost point-blank discharge of grape from the Swedish regimental guns, recently rushed forward.

The time was now about 6 pm. Pappenheim's cavalry had made their last effort and were in full flight. Collecting four regiments of horse, Gustavus placed himself at their head and, calling on the remaining infantry brigades from the centre, swept forward against Tilly's exposed flank. The battery on the hill was overrun and the cannon turned on the Imperialist troops; at the same moment the Swedish reserve artillery, wheeled forward from the rear, came into action to add to the destructive fire now cutting great gaps in the densely packed squares. As the light began to fail the victory was complete. Of all Tilly's veteran troops only four regiments of Walloons, the experienced Belgian foot, attempted a final stand. Rallying at the wood in the rear of their position they resisted all attacks, and 600 of them finally got away, carrying the wounded Count Tilly with them. The Swedish losses were just over 2,000 officers and men and the Saxons are believed to have lost about the same number. The Imperialists, however, lost 7,600 in killed and wounded and another 6,000 taken prisoner. A further 8,000 Imperialist troops surrendered to the Swedish cavalry during the pursuit that continued for four days under the personal direction of Gustavus, who entered Halle on 21 September.

In early November 1632 an Imperialist army commanded by Albert von Wallenstein, Duke of Friedland and Mecklenburg, was again near Leipzig and threatened to cut the line of communication between Gustavus and the Baltic ports. On 16 November Gustavus attacked the Imperialists near Lützen. After a ferocious struggle the Swedish army was victorious, and the irascible and gouty Wallenstein was hastily taken in his sedan chair from the battlefield. But Gustavus Adolphus himself was dead, shot down by a lone horseman.

The long war dragged on. By 1634 the politics of power had replaced the prejudices of religion and Cardinal Richelieu, more anxious to curb the power of the Hapsburgs than to stamp out the heresy of Protestantism, allied France with the Protestant princes of Germany, primarily aiming at ousting the Spanish from the Netherlands. He did not live to see France victorious, but his *protégé*, the Duc d'Enghien, putting into practice the offensive principles of Gustavus Adolphus, triumphed at the Battle of Rocroi, in 1643, and so ended for ever Spain's military supremacy.

Louis de Bourbon, Duc d'Enghien was born in 1621, the eldest son of the Prince and Princesse de Condé. As a child he was frail and delicate, with an ill temper and moodiness that only disappeared in the presence of his father. Under the Prince's personal direction he was educated at a Jesuit college, where he showed outstanding ability as a student and underwent a salutary toughening. By the age of 18 his conduct at Court, stewardship of

[1] *The Decisive Battles of the Western World*, Vol. 1 (1954).

THE THIRTY YEARS' WAR

THE BATTLE OF BREITENFELD OR LEIPZIG (1631), FROM A CONTEMPORARY ENGRAVING. THE ARTIST HAS BEEN SOMEWHAT LAX IN HIS GEOGRAPHY AND SHOWS THE BATTLE FOUGHT FROM EAST TO WEST INSTEAD OF SOUTH TO NORTH, AND THE SAXONS ARE SHOWN ON THE SWEDISH RIGHT NOT THEIR LEFT. AS AN IMPRESSION OF THE BATTLE, HOWEVER, IT HAS CONSIDERABLE MERIT. THE SWEDISH ARMY IS SHOWN ON THE RIGHT, THAT OF THE IMPERIALISTS ON THE LEFT. TO THE RIGHT OF GUSTAVUS ADOLPHUS (LEFT FOREGROUND) A FIELD-GUN IS BEING TOWED INTO ACTION, AND FURTHER TO THE RIGHT IS A GROUP OF HEAVY CAVALRY. IN THE CENTRE OF THE BATTLEFIELD CAN BE SEEN THE HEAVY INFANTRY *TERCIOS*.

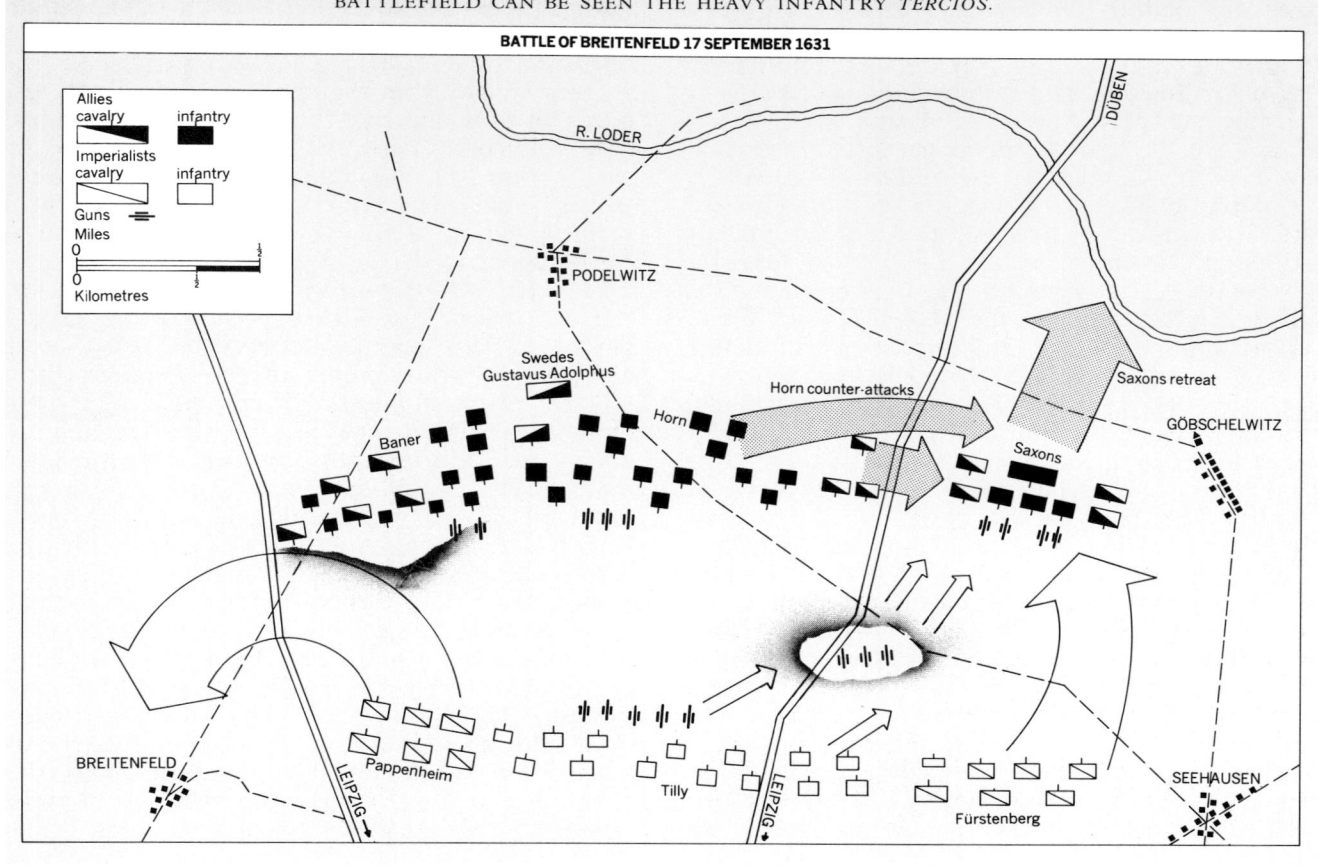

BATTLE OF BREITENFELD 17 SEPTEMBER 1631

THE CAVALRY

the Burgundy estates, and active services in the Flanders campaign, brought him to the attention of Richelieu. Under the Cardinal's patronage the young Duke, who showed a positive thirst for every kind of military knowledge, rose quickly to high command and in 1642 was appointed commander-in-chief of the French armies on the Flemish frontier.

In May 1643 a Spanish army of 20,000 experienced foot and 7,000 horse with 28 guns under Don Francisco de Melo laid siege to the frontier fortress of Rocroi. D'Enghien was advised by his elderly and cautious mentor, the veteran Maréchal de l'Hôpital, to attempt the relief of the fortress but to avoid a pitched battle. The youthful commander-in-chief, however, had just received news of the death of King Louis XIII, and considered that any sign of weakness could prejudice the throne of the child King and the safety of France herself. The forces immediately at his disposal were weaker in infantry and guns than those of de Melo, but with some 32 squadrons of cavalry (around 7,000 horse) the French total came to 23,000 men. Approaching Rocroi from the south-west, the French had to advance through broken wooded ground with many defiles. De Melo, meanwhile, chose to rely on his superior numbers, especially as reinforcements were on the way, and to play for time; his plan was to draw his opponent onto the open plain close to the fortress, there to be crushed by his ever-victorious *tercios*. Placing his right-hand cavalry wing under the Flemish Comte d'Isembourg, he formed his *tercios*, 20 in number, in one huge, almost solid, rectangle backed onto the fortress. The Duque d'Albuquerque and the remainder of his cavalry held the left flank. His guns took their usual place in front of the *tercios*, but in advance of the left flank he placed 1,000 musketeers in ambush, hidden in a neck of woodland protruding from the forest. De Melo's army, though predominantly Spanish, also contained Italian, Flemish, Walloon, German and mixed mercenary elements.

When the French drew clear of the woods on the morning of 18 May, the Spanish commander could hardly wait to spring the trap that he had laid. Soon, however, he was frantically sending out scouts and cavalry detachments to try to discover his opponent's strength and intentions, as d'Enghien had deployed his whole cavalry force to screen and disguise the deployment of his infantry as they emerged from the forest defiles and even until they were within 1,000 yards of the enemy. It was now about 6 pm and d'Enghien was just about to order the advance when he saw La Ferté Senneterre, the commander of his left wing of cavalry, lead out half his force in an apparent attempt to reach Rocroi and relieve the garrison. This foolhardy act was the work of de l'Hôpital, whose disregard of the prearranged plan could have led to disaster, had not the Spanish commander of that flank been told to avoid any serious engagement before the arrival of their German ally, General Beck, with 6,000 reinforcements. The opportunity for a concerted French attack, as originally planned, had been lost. La Ferté was intercepted by an aide-de-camp sent by the furious d'Enghien, who now had no option but to order his troops to hold their positions and get what rest they could. With the outposts nearly on top of each other, and the whole plain ablaze with camp fires, the soldiers of both armies settled down for the night.

For the French, there was to be little opportunity for sleep. A deserter from the enemy had been brought in who disclosed the news of Beck's expected arrival; at about the same time the presence of the musketeers hidden in the wood on the right wing was reported by a standing patrol. D'Enghien's plans were quickly changed. Assembly for the whole army was ordered for 3 am and the attack would start at first light. A little before dawn the Regiment of Picardy fell on the Spanish musketeers and cut them down to a man. As the sky lightened the Comte de Gassion, with half the horse of the French right wing, was seen moving fast in a wide arc with the evident aim of outflanking the Duque d'Albuquerque's position. The latter reacted as expected and formed to the flank. At this moment d'Enghien with the remainder of the wing broke into the gap; under attack from two directions d'Albuquerque's horse, after an hour's fighting, were routed and in flight, with d'Enghien's ferocious Croats hard behind them.

Meanwhile the impetuous La Ferté had again disobeyed his orders and launched an independent attack. This time d'Isembourg was placed well forward and was waiting for such a move. La Ferté's wing was scattered and his cannon captured. De l'Hôpital hastily mounted a counterattack and recovered some of the guns, only to lose them again to the Italian infantry. With at least 30 cannon turned against them, the French centre began to give way. Only the gallant Sirot, in command of the reserve, stood firm and, having succeeded in halting the withdrawal, prepared for a final stand. At this point d'Enghien was on his way back from defeating d'Albuquerque. Peering through the drifting smoke from the top of a low hill, he saw sufficient to realize that the crisis of the battle had come. Turning back with his whole force, he swept round at top speed behind the Spanish centre to charge straight into the rear of the German *tercios* in the third line, throwing them back on to the Walloons in the second line.

In the confusion all but the Spanish squares began to crumble and break, although the Italians fought on until completely overwhelmed. Seeing d'Enghien's white plume in the distance, Sirot called to his men, pointing it out, and with a great shout they surged forward. But the five Spanish *tercios* were still virtually untouched and in good order, 8,000 disciplined veterans well placed on a small hill. Their commander, General Fontaine, long disabled by old wounds, was carried forward in his chair to signal with his cane for the guns and musketeers to fire a terrible salvo as the French attack came in. D'Enghien's cavalry now joined in the charge, but three times the French were repulsed with heavy losses. The Duke himself was wounded and had a horse shot from under him. Both sides knew that Beck and his reinforcements must be very close. For the French time was running out and only de Gassion with two or three squadrons was left to watch the forest rides

THE THIRTY YEARS' WAR

TERCIOS ARE SEEN FORMED UP AND READY TO MOVE OFF IN THEIR USUAL CHEQUER FORMATION, THE MUSKETEERS IN FRONT. IN THE RIGHT FOREGROUND, TWO OFFICERS ARE PASSING THE TIME AT DICE WHILE A THIRD, PERHAPS BETTER EDUCATED, READS A LETTER. ON THE LEFT TWO MEN WITHOUT HATS ARE POSSIBLY RECEIVING A REPRIMAND ACROSS A DRUMHEAD. FROM JACQUES CALLOT'S *GRANDES MISERES DE LA GUERRE*.

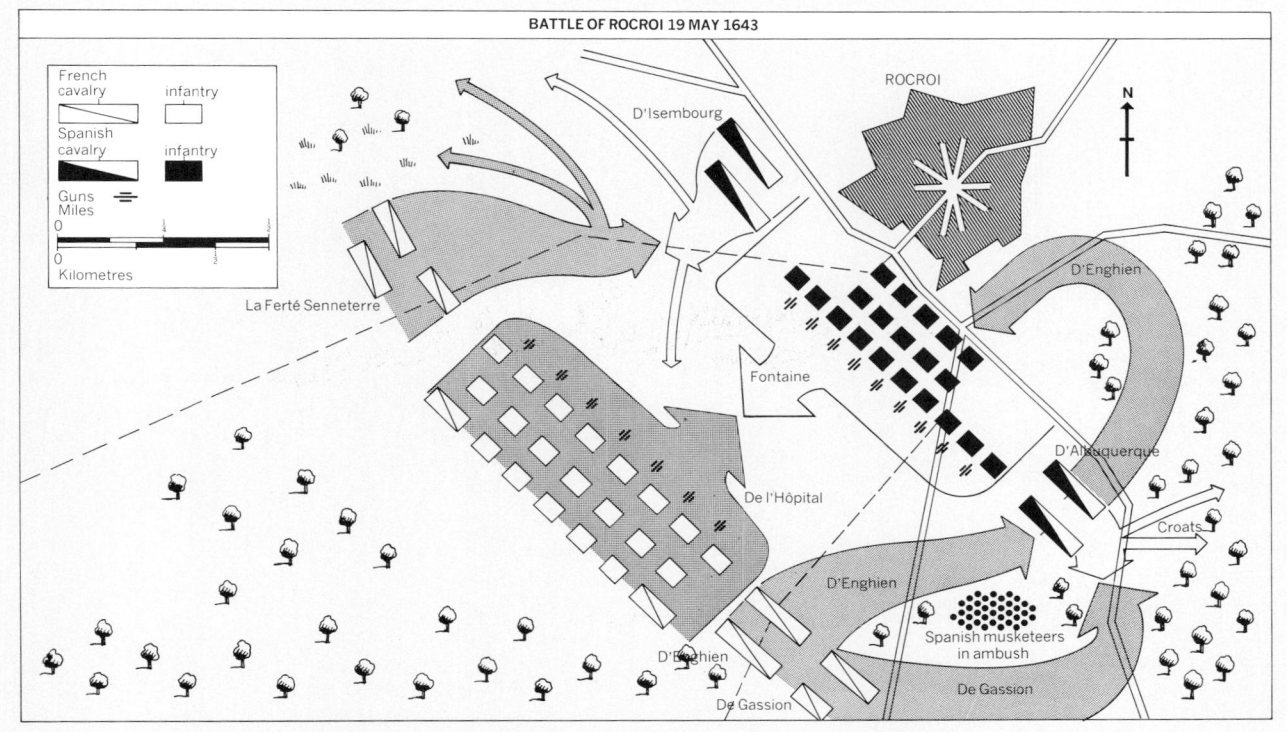

BATTLE OF ROCROI 19 MAY 1643

CALLOT'S VERSION OF SOLDIERS SACKING A TOWN DURING THE THIRTY YEARS' WAR.

THE CAVALRY

through which Beck would soon emerge. D'Enghien ordered every gun to be trained on an angle of the Spanish square and once again formed up his men ready to charge. The French opened a fierce bombardment but, with all their rounds expended, the Spanish guns made no reply. Fontaine, easily recognizable by his long white beard, was dead from a musket ball. The Spanish infantry, outnumbered and surrounded, could no longer face the concentrated gunfire and repeated charges. Waving their hats some officers signalled their surrender and the Duke rode to meet them, only to be met with a volley from nearby soldiers who feared that another assault had started. On the instant the French horse rode in, and only d'Enghien's intervention at great personal danger halted the killing. The Spanish army lost 200 colours and 21,000 men, including over 13,000 prisoners and missing. The French casualties were less than a fifth of this total. Of Rocroi the British historian Cyril Falls wrote in *Great Military Battles* (1964), 'The victory was won by sheer generalship. The calculated risk of the passage behind the Spanish centre, which might have turned about and virtually destroyed d'Enghien's horse by fire, can rarely have been paralleled.'

FRENCH CAVALRY AT ROCROI (1643), ARMED AFTER THE SWEDISH MODEL. ON THE LEFT ARE DRAGOONS WEARING NO ARMOUR EXCEPT THEIR HELMETS; IN FRONT OF THEM ARE CUIRASSIERS WITH HELMETS AND BREASTPLATES AND, ON THE RIGHT, LIGHT HORSEMEN WITHOUT ARMOUR. PAINTING BY A. LALAUZE.

FRENCH LIGHT-CAVALRY OFFICERS, c.1630. THE LIGHT-CAVALRY WERE ORGANIZED IN INDEPENDENT COMPANIES, EACH CONSISTING OF A CAPTAIN, A LIEUTENANT, A MARÉCHAL DES LOGIS (ROUGHLY EQUIVALENT TO A QUARTERMASTER SERGEANT), A FARRIER, A TRUMPETER AND 90 HORSEMEN. FROM DE NOIRMONT AND DE MARBOT.

THE CROATS

The old Roman custom of hiring irregular cavalry from savage border tribes of horsemen was revived in post-medieval Europe. These mounted brigands, born to the horse and utterly self-reliant, their initiative unimpaired by the rigid drills needed for the battlefield, were invaluable for scouting and harassing an enemy. Among them the Croats, ready to sell their services to any bidder, came into prominence, especially in the Imperialist armies. Troops of Croatian light horse were raised in large numbers from the region that is now Yugoslavia, and formed an irregular force of considerable value. Wild, undisciplined and volatile, they were mounted on small fast ponies, despised the use of firearms and relied on the speed of their attack and the sharp cutting edge of their sabre-like swords and long-handled battle-axes. Invariably they were employed in an independent role to screen and forage for the Imperialist and French armies; their treatment of the luckless villagers and peasants in their path was wholly savage, and they left a trail of murder, rape and pillage. As a result they were usually excluded from the terms of any capitulation or surrender, and in recompense for earlier atrocities were cut down as heathen barbarians.

A POLE AND A CROAT IN A FRENCH LIGHT-CAVALRY REGIMENT, c.1650. BY THIS DATE THE LIGHT-CAVALRY COMPANIES HAD BEEN GROUPED INTO REGIMENTS, AND THERE WERE 12 FOREIGN LIGHT-CAVALRY REGIMENTS IN THE FRENCH ARMY. FROM DE NOIRMONT AND DE MARBOT.

THE army reforms of Continental Europe were reflected in England, where the decisive battles of the Civil War (1642–49), Marston Moor and Naseby, were both decided by cavalry. Although effective regiments of horse had not previously existed in England, when war broke out in the summer of 1642 both Prince Rupert, for King Charles I, and Cromwell, for Parliament, formed regiments of horse trained and equipped much after the style of Gustavus Adolphus's Swedish cavalry. With the passage of time they evolved their own techniques which made them second to none, and as the wars progressed both sides, but especially the Cavaliers, included an ever-increasing proportion of cavalry. At Naseby, the Royalists may even have had more horse than foot. J.P.L.

OLIVER CROMWELL: THE 'RIGHT HONOURABLE AND UNDAUNTED WARRIOR' IS SHOWN IN A CONTEMPORARY ENGRAVING WEARING FULL ARMOUR.

THE ENGLISH CIVIL WAR by PETER YOUNG

England in the days before the Enclosure Acts lent itself to the movement of large bodies of cavalry. The mounted troops of the period included four principal types: cuirassiers, harquebusiers (arquebusiers), lancers and dragoons. Of these, the cuirassiers, or 'lobsters' as they were called after their jointed-tail 'pot' helmets, were already somewhat rare, while the lancers were even rarer, and seem to have been employed only in the Scots Army. The great majority of horse in all the English armies of the period were harquebusiers of one sort or another. The dragoons at this time were used as mounted infantry, and seldom fought on horseback, though they deserve some attention nonetheless.

To begin with the cuirassiers, their appearance and equipment may be deduced both from portraits and from a contemporary manual. The latter is John Cruso's *Militarie Instructions for the Cavallrie* (1632), which must have been widely used by officers of both sides, since no other equivalent of the modern *Cavalry Training* was available in those days. Particularly useful is the plate in which Cruso shows all the cuirassier's arms and armour (right).

For Parliament, Sir Arthur Hesilrige's Regiment must have been equipped after this fashion, though without the lance. It is likely that his men wore not a closed helmet but the triple-barred variety. Captain Richard Atkyns's pursuit of Sir Arthur Hesilrige at Roundway Down (13 July 1643) shows that it was no easy matter to overpower a cuirassier, even when he was in full flight.

In that encounter Hesilrige first missed Atkyns with his carbine; Atkyns then fired one of his pistols, touching his adversary before he discharged it. 'And I'm sure I hit him,' he wrote, 'for he staggered, and presently wheeled off from his party and ran.' Atkyns followed Hesilrige for about 100 yards and fired his other pistol. 'And I'm sure I hit his head, for I touched it before I gave fire, and it amazed him . . . but he was too well armed all over for a pistol bullet to do him any hurt, having a coat of mail over his arms and a headpiece (I am confident) musket proof, his sword had two edges and a ridge in the middle. . . .' Hesilrige rode down the side of the hill, going at three-quarters speed, and 'waving his sword on the right and left hand of his horse, not looking back [to see] whether he were pursued or not. . . .' Atkyns kept up with him

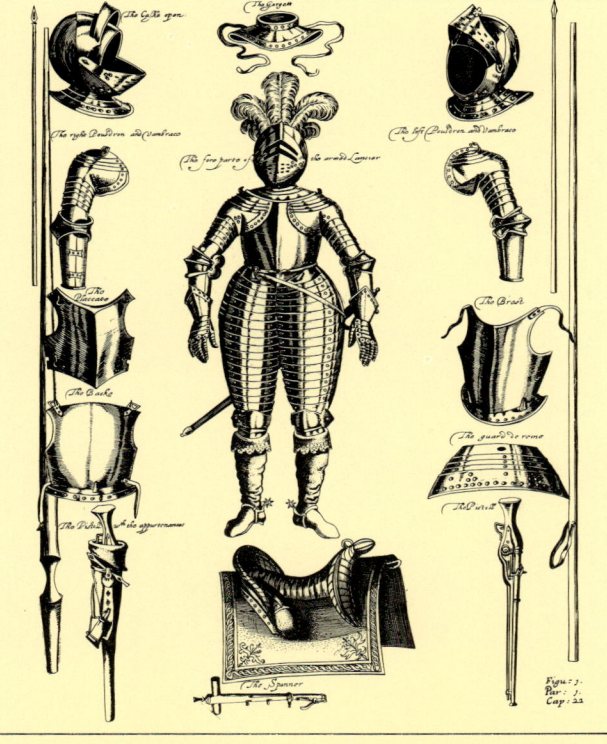

THE EQUIPMENT OF A HEAVY CAVALRYMAN, FROM JOHN CRUSO'S *MILITARIE INSTRUCTIONS FOR THE CAVALL'RIE*, 1632.

'and tried him from head to the saddle, and could not penetrate him, nor do him any hurt'. Hesilrige, for his part, managed to cut the nose of Atkyns's horse as well as giving him such a blow on his sword arm that he could scarcely hold his blade. Cornet Robert Holmes and a Captain Buck also set about the Roundhead general, who eventually pulled up his wounded steed. Atkyns had managed to prick him in the neck when 'upon the faltering of his horse his headpiece opened behind'. After all this Hesilrige was then rescued by a runaway troop of his own side. The episode provoked one of King Charles I's few jests, when he commented, 'Had he been victualled as well as fortified he might have endured a siege of seven years.'

The principal disadvantage of all this armour, quite apart from its weight, was the discomfort the cuirassier had to suffer. Edmund Ludlow, a Parliamentarian, tells us how at Edgehill (23 October 1642) 'being dismounted I could not without great difficulty recover on horse-back again, being loaded with cuirassier's arms, as the rest of the guard were also'. He spent an uncomfortable night after the battle too. 'No man nor horse got any meat that night . . . neither could I find my servant who had my cloak, so that having nothing to keep me warm but a suite of iron, I was obliged to walk about all night, which proved very cold by reason of a sharp frost.' Ludlow was as yet but a young soldier. He would have done better to have strapped his cloak to the back of his saddle, rather than trust to meeting his batman at the close of day.

As for their horses, it is not easy to explain what they were. Clearly they were weight-carriers,

THE CAVALRY

such as one sees in pictures by Albrecht Dürer or in *The Rout of San Romano* (1472) by Paolo Uccello. Possibly the best illustrations of the sort of horses used by the cavalrymen of the Civil War are to be found in the Marquis of Newcastle's *La Méthode et Invention Nouvelle de Dresser les Chevaux* (Antwerp, 1657). The plates show that they were not exactly the cart-horses of our own day; rather they were more like heavy hunters or the modern chargers of the Household Cavalry.

The harquebusiers of 1642 were not unlike the cuirassiers of Napoleon's Army. Cromwell's Ironsides wore back- and breastplates, a triple-barred helmet and a buff coat. They were armed with a good strong straight sword and a pair of pistols; some at least also had carbines. In addition to their other weapons the pole-axe was popular amongst the Cavaliers. Sir John Hinton in his *Memoirs* describes how at Edgehill he dismounted a Roundhead 'but being armed cap-a-pe, I could doe noe execution upon him with my sword, att which instant one Mr. Miles Matthewes, a Gentleman Pensioner, rides in, and with a pole-ax immediately decides the businesse....' Sir Richard Bulstrode, a Royalist, tells us that during Rupert's charge, he was 'wounded in the Head by a Person who turned upon me, and struck me with his Pole-axe....' It is evident that the Cavaliers wore pretty much what they pleased, or what they could lay their hands on. The Earl of Clarendon in his *History of the Rebellion and Civil War in England* tells us that at the outbreak of hostilities the Royalist cavalry officers 'had their full desire if they were able to procure old backs and breasts and pots, with pistols or carbines for their two or three first ranks, and swords for the rest; themselves (and some soldiers by their examples) having gotten besides their pistols and swords, a short pole-axe'. The cavalry of both sides wore sashes or scarves, and cloaks, in addition to their arms and armour. The sashes of the Royalists seem to have been of a rose-pink hue while the Roundheads wore the Earl of Essex's colours of 'orange-tawny'.

In the ordinary way, a Royalist colonel was commissioned 'to raise and entertayne a Regiment of 500 horse volunteers'. Normally this was organized in six troops, commanded by the three field officers (colonel, lieutenant-colonel and major) and three captains. By 1644 the strongest Royalist regiments numbered about 300, and the troops averaged about 40. Only Rupert, who had 10 troops in his regiment could muster 500 men, although, of course, his powers of leadership 'charisma' were quite exceptional. Parliamentarian regiments did not usually have lieutenant-colonels, unless, which was rare, they were double regiments. Otherwise units on either side were organized in much the same way. There were four officers in each troop: a field officer or captain; captain-lieutenant or lieutenant; cornet, and quartermaster, the latter being a commissioned officer. In addition a troop was supposed to have three corporals, two trumpeters, a sadler and a farrier. With 70 or so horses to shoe every four to six weeks the farrier must have been a busy individual, even though it must have been possible to rely to some extent upon the local blacksmith, wherever a troop was quartered. Each troop had a standard which was normally carried by the cornet; these usually measured two feet by two, and were sometimes of damask, but more often of painted taffeta. Colonels, at least on the Parliamentarian side, generally had plain damask standards; others had political motifs and some displayed their coats of arms or a device indicating their office.

In 1642 the dragoon was still a mounted musketeer, and the regiment in which he served was organized on the same establishment as a regiment of foot. For dragoons to make a charge on horseback was quite out of the ordinary. It is true that Colonel John Okey's Regiment charged into the flank and rear of the Royalist foot at the end of the Battle of Naseby, but that was exceptional. As Cruso

A PARLIAMENTARY PAMPHLET PUBLISHED IN 1643 WITH A NOT PARTICULARLY FLATTERING PORTRAIT OF PRINCE RUPERT WHO IS REFERRED TO AS THAT 'BLOODY PRINCE'.

A CAVALRYMAN, AFTER ALBRECHT DÜRER, SHOWING THE HEAVY TYPE OF HORSE. THE DOUR-LOOKING TROOPER WITH HIS LANCE DATES FROM THE 16TH CENTURY, AND IS PROBABLY A GERMAN MERCENARY.

THE ENGLISH CIVIL WAR

shows, they were expected to fire whilst mounted, and no doubt that was a useful accomplishment when they were on outpost duty. Sir James Turner, a contemporary, summed up the whole question very neatly. 'They ought to be taught to give fire on horseback ... but ... their service is on foot, and is no other than that of musketeers.' Accounts of the fighting confirm this view. At Marshall's Elm for example (4 August 1642) the Royalists hid their 14 dragoons in two gravel pits to their front, where they fired three volleys; then, when the enemy staggered, the Royalists charged with their 80 horse and routed 600 raw Roundhead foot.

The Battle of Naseby (14 June 1645), unequal though it was, may serve to illustrate the cavalry tactics of the period. The Royalist horse were organized in four brigades, and had in addition, Rupert had 12 squadrons to Ireton's 11, the latter's were far stronger. The strongest squadrons in the Prince's line did not exceed 150, whilst all Ireton's seem to have been well over 200 strong, and probably nearer 250.

The Royalist foot, under Lord Astley, were outnumbered by nearly two to one, and for this reason the Royalists gave close support to their centre with Colonel Thomas Howard's brigade of 880 horse, drawn up in three bodies. The Parliamentarians drew up no horse in their centre.

On the Royalist left, Sir Marmaduke Langdale had the two brigades of Northern horse, numbering 1,500 men. His squadrons may have averaged rather more than 100 apiece, and since his brigades contained the remnants of not less than 20 regiments it is likely that these 1,500 men, diehards who had carried on the struggle after the disaster at Marston Moor, mustered many officers and many of the gentry in their ranks. Even so, they were scarcely a match for Cromwell's 13 squadrons who outnumbered them by at least two to one. Cromwell's New Model cavalry regiments had no difficulty in filling their ranks with volunteers from the armies of Essex, Manchester and Waller.

The Royalists, who had learned the lesson of Edgehill, kept a reserve of both horse and foot: two bodies of horse and two regiments of foot. The Newark horse, 800 strong under Major-General Anthony Eyre, were in

A PLATE FROM THE MARQUIS OF NEWCASTLE'S *MÉTHODE ET INVENTION NOUVELLE DE DRESSER LES CHEVAUX*, PUBLISHED IN 1657. THE ILLUSTRATION STRESSES THE IMPORTANCE OF STABILITY IN THE SADDLE: THE STIRRUP LEATHERS ARE SO LONG THAT THE LEG IS STRAIGHT, WHILE THE HIGH POMMEL OF THE SADDLE HELPED TO KEEP THE RIDER STEADY AND OFFERED EXTRA PROTECTION TO THE LOWER PARTS OF HIS BODY.

certain unbrigaded units. They drew up their cavalry in more or less equal squadrons, despite the fact that their regiments and troops varied widely in strength. The Parliamentarian horse were not organized in brigades: they were simply divided into two wings under Lieutenant-General Oliver Cromwell and Commissary-General Henry Ireton.

The Royalist right wing under Prince Rupert was approximately 1,610 strong. It was drawn up in two lines, with seven squadrons in the first and five in the second. Rupert was opposed by Ireton with about 2,750 horse in 11 great squadrons, and flanked by Colonel John Okey's dragoons, lining Sulby Hedge, and numbering – if they were up to strength – some 1,000 men. Here, clearly, the dice were loaded against the Cavaliers, for though

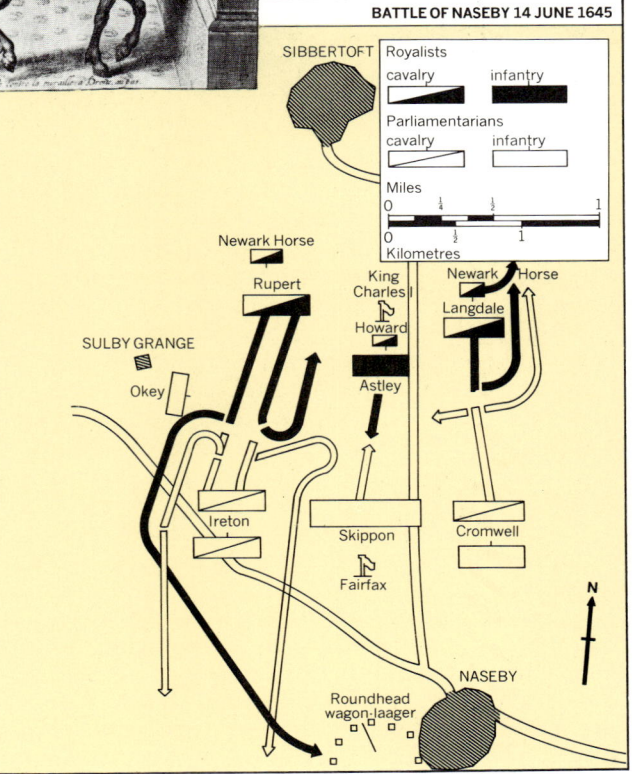

THE CAVALRY

two equal bodies on the flanks, and the King's Lifeguard, 130 strong, was in the centre of the reserve.

The battle began at about 10 am. The Cavaliers, who suspected that Sir Thomas Fairfax, the Parliamentarian commander, intended to withdraw, made a general advance. Not all the Parliamentarians were ready for this. Colonel Okey was still issuing ammunition in a meadow half a mile in rear of the line when Cromwell rode up and ordered him to mount with all speed and flank the left wing. He was only just in time. Okey later wrote, 'By the time I could get my men to light, and deliver up their horses in a little close, the enemy drew towards us which my men perceiving, they with shooting and rejoicing received them....' The target, presumably, was Rupert's Lifeguard, the right-hand unit of the Prince's front line. A little later the Earl of Northampton's regiment, to engage the enemy's second line. Ireton, too clever by half, prematurely led his squadrons into the Royalist foot, which he could see 'pressing sore' the Parliamentary centre. His horse was shot and he himself, wounded by pike and halbert, fell into the hands of a Royalist sergeant. Vermuyden with a Roundhead squadron broke some of Rupert's second line, but there were other Cavaliers at hand, and a counter-charge drove the Roundheads back in disarray. Rupert's regiment meanwhile had disposed of the rest of Ireton's wing, and with the Parliamentary cavalry on their flank in full flight Okey's dragoons felt that their future was obscure: 'We gave up ourselves for lost men, but we resolved every man to stand to the last....'

Thus Rupert's 1,600 men put to flight Ireton's wing of some 2,750. Unhappily for the King not all the rest of his cavalry was so successful. How well Howard's brigade supported the Royalist infantry

riding perhaps 100 yards or more in rear of Rupert's troop, must also have come in for attention.

THE COMPLEX DRILL FOR LOADING A PISTOL ON HORSEBACK—THOUGH DOING IT AT THE TROT MIGHT SEEM UNDULY AMBITIOUS. FROM CRUSO. (THE SEQUENCE IS CONTINUED OVERLEAF.)

Whether the fire was destructive is not recorded. It is true that Rupert halted when he was halfway across the gap that divided the two armies, but it was not fire that stopped him. He was concerned, no doubt, that the infantry in the Royalist centre should have a chance to come up level with him. Ireton led his wing of Parliamentarians over the brow and halted opposite the Prince to let his own men 'recover their stations'. He had found some rough going and rightly took care to reform his line. The halt cannot have been a long one. One cannot imagine Rupert allowing Okey's dragoons to take pot-shots at him for long. But when he sounded the charge, Ireton came down the slope to meet him.

On the extreme right Rupert with his cavalry triumphed, but on the left of his wing Ireton's Roundheads routed the Cavaliers opposed to them. Soon both sides were in a great muddle with half the squadrons of their respective front lines triumphant, and half of them routed. Rupert pushed on in the centre cannot be said. Certainly, however, one of his colonels, Richard Bagot, the stouthearted Governor of Lichfield Close, got his death wound, perhaps whilst the Royalist centre was at push of pike with the Roundhead infantry. The latter were deployed with five regiments, each of about 800, in the front line, whilst the Cavaliers had but four, averaging about 500. No doubt Howard's men charged to prevent the extra regiment of Roundheads falling on the flank of one of the already outnumbered Royalist 'divisions'.

On the Royalist left wing Langdale led out the Northern horse (1,500) to try conclusions with Cromwell, who, like Ireton, advanced to meet his enemy. Colonel Edward Whalley's regiment, one of those formed out of Cromwell's 'Ironsides', charged two squadrons of Langdale's horse. According to Joshua Sprigge in *Anglia Rediviva* (1647) the Northerners 'made a very gallant resistance, and firing at a very close charge, they came to the sword'. The *mêlée* went against Langdale's men and, routed, the survivors spurred back to where Prince Rupert's regiment of Bluecoats, 500 strong, stood in reserve, its hedgehog of pikes prepared to receive cavalry. Covered by this solid phalanx, they rallied.

At this stage Cromwell had only launched his front line. Thus, with much of the horse on each side in disorder after the first charges, Cromwell still had a strong reserve of some 1,500 veteran troopers. The King had his Lifeguard (130) and at least half the Newarkers (400) who had not yet been launched into the attack. But they were few indeed to challenge Oliver Cromwell and 1,500 men.

The overall situation now appears to have been as follows: on the Royalist side, Prince Rupert had disposed of Ireton's wing and the latter was wounded and a prisoner. The Prince himself was somewhere in the vicinity of the Roundheads' wagon-laager (which he actually summoned to surrender). The survivors of Ireton's men, though driven from the field, were rallying, as no doubt were their victorious assailants. Okey's 'Dragoons' were still in their hedge. In the centre the Cavalier infantry, against all probability, had driven back the Roundheads. Sir Edward Walker tells us, 'I saw their colours fall, and their foot in great disorder.' But the rout of Langdale, whose broken horse were now rallying behind the reserve, had exposed the left flank of the Royalist infantry. The next move was up to Cromwell. Should he attack the King's person or, ignoring the monarch with his small reserve of horsemen, fall upon the Royalist foot?

The King himself, with so small a force at his command, was, at least for the moment, compelled to wait upon events. If Cromwell charged him, well and good: he must advance to meet him, and Langdale must give him such support as he may – though, as Sir John Urry said at Marston Moor, 'Broken horse won't fight'. If on the other hand Cromwell should attack the Royalist infantry, he might give the King and his reserve some sort of opportunity to charge his right flank. It was in moments such as these, in the smoke and confusion, with riderless horses and leaderless men on every hand, and trumpets braying at shattered troops to rally, that the cavalry commander showed his mettle. A decision of some sort was required. Cromwell made one: detailing four regiments to follow Langdale he decided – and it was a fairly risky decision – to charge with the rest into the Royalist foot. This he did with his usual vigour, doubtless at a 'good round trot'. The King, too, made a decision to counterattack; but, characteristically, he did not stick to it.

'At this instant,' writes Sir Edward Walker in *Historical Discourses*, 'the King's Horseguards and the King at the head of them were ready to charge those who followed ours, when a person of quality, 'tis said the Earl of Carnwath, took the King's Horse by the bridle, turned his about, swearing at him and saying, *Will you go upon your Death?* and at the same time the word being given, *March to the right hand*, which . . . [as most concluded] was a civil command for everyone to shift for himself, we turned and ran on the spur almost a quarter of a mile, and then the word being given to make a stand, we did so; though the body could never be rallied. Those that came back made a charge, wherein some of them fell.'

Now the Royalist infantry were left to fight unsupported. On the testimony of Joshua Sprigge, a Roundhead, at least one of the Royalist infantry brigades stood 'with incredible courage and resolution' against Cromwell's attack. It was hot work for a time. Fairfax, helmetless, rode up to his Lifeguard, to be told by Charles Doyley, its leader, 'that he exposed himself to too much danger, and the whole army thereby . . . and so many bullets flying about him. . . .' Doyley offered the general his own headpiece. 'It is well enough, Charles,' Sir Thomas replied coolly. He then asked whether the Lifeguard had charged the Royalist tertia that still held out, to be told that they had done so twice, but could not break them. Fairfax then laid on the final assault. When he gave the signal Doyley attacked the Cavaliers from the front, whilst the general himself with a 'commanded party' charged them in rear. His own regiment of foot was called

THE CAVALRY

up to support this assault. This time the Roundheads were successful, Fairfax and Doyley meeting in the midst of the broken square, where the former cut down a standard-bearer with his own hand. Now Fairfax reformed his ranks. It was a wise and soldierlike move thus to consolidate his position. However, his opponent, the King, had shot his bolt. Rupert was with him again by this time but his troopers 'having done their part . . . could never be brought to charge again . . . and so after all the endeavours of the King and Prince Rupert to the hazard of their persons, they were fain to quit the Field.' Thus ended the Battle of Naseby, in which the role of cavalry had proved decisive to the end.

It is worth mentioning in conclusion to this review of Civil War developments that the Royalists produced a 'galloping-gun'. This was a small brass piece mounted on a cart; the gunners rode alongside. Its introduction meant that a flying column of horse and dragoons could not be foiled by a handful of musketeers holed up in some strongpoint, say a church or manor house. The idea for the 'galloping-gun' should most likely be attributed to the inventive genius of Prince Rupert. However that may be, the English Cavaliers seem to have had a form of horse artillery at least 60 years before anyone else.

The legacy of the horse of Cromwell and Rupert was not unimportant in the development of the British Army, for many, both officers and men, who served Charles II after the Restoration had learned their trade on the battlefields of the Civil War. And if, at the turn of the century, Marlborough's cavalry were the envy of Europe, he owed it in some measure to the traditions of the war in which his own father, Sir Winston Churchill, had commanded a troop of horse, in the Marquis of Hertford's Regiment.

CUIRASSIER FIGHTS DRAGOON, THE WHEEL-LOCK PISTOL OF ONE BEING SET AGAINST THE OTHER'S MATCHLOCK. FROM CRUSO.

THE ENGLISH CIVIL WAR

IRONSIDES CHARGE INTO A TROOP OF ROYALIST CAVALRY. ILLUSTRATION FROM GUIZOT'S *HISTOIRE D'ANGLETERRE*.

IN 1643, the year of d'Enghien's great victory at Rocroi, Louis XIV, then aged five, acceded to the throne of France. In 1661, on the death of Cardinal Mazarin, he assumed full control of the nation. A visitor to the great Palace of Versailles is left under no illusions about the proclivities of Louis XIV for the pursuit of *la gloire*, nor about the association of the horse with concepts of military triumph. In the Grand Court stands the huge bronze equestrian statue of the famous monarch, his steed's nostrils flared, its eyes glaring, its powerful hooves pawing the ground. Within the Palace the same theme, that of the mounted conqueror riding in Roman triumph over the prostrate bodies of the vanquished, meets the eye time and time again; it is repeated in paintings, tapestries and, perhaps most strikingly of all, in the fine bas-relief by Antoine Coysevox in the *Salon de la Guerre*, which depicts the Sun King in the role of Mars. J.P.L.

LOUIS XIV. THE *ROI SOLEIL*. ENGRAVED AFTER J. DE LA HAYE.

THE AGE OF THE SUN KING by DAVID CHANDLER

The mounted arm still played an essential role in the campaigns and battles of the second half of the 17th century, but this should not disguise the fact that in more ways than one the *arme blanche*—sword or sabre—had passed its zenith and was slipping into the first stages of a slow decline. During Louis XIV's long and eventful reign the realities of the situation were often easy to disguise or overlook, but, as Professor Bodart's researches have illustrated, whereas between 1618 and 1648 mounted warriors had provided 35% of the armed power of France, over the next 70 years the proportion would drop to 30%, before plunging to little more than a fifth by 1780. This was a trend experienced by all European armies, only the forces of England, Russia and Turkey maintaining a reasonably steady and consistent level in their numbers of cavalry.

The reasons for this general decline in numerical representation are not hard to find. Armies were, at least in times of war, larger than had been experienced since the days of Rome and Byzantium. To train, equip and mount a cavalryman was far more expensive than to provide for an infantryman. Although in some countries a would-be cavalry recruit was still expected to supply his own mount in the first instance, the cost of a suitable cavalry charger in England fluctuated between £12 and £15 ($24–30) during the quarter-century following the Glorious Revolution of 1688; in Ireland a dragoon's mount cost £5, a Spanish jade £9. Similarly, the cheapest remount available to the Dutch and Imperial services in 1693 cost 90 patagons, or approximately £10. At the same time the cavalry trooper's pay and subsistence was higher than that of the *fantassin* or humble foot-soldier as the former had to feed and care for his mount as well as himself. Thus in the reign of Queen Anne (1702–14) a cavalry trooper received half-a-crown a day and 14 shillings (or 70p) a week subsistence money to the dragoon's one shilling and sixpence (17p) a day and eight shillings and twopence (41p) a week respectively. Both, however, fared far better than the infantry rank and file who received only eightpence (about 3½p) a day to include sixpence subsistence money before stoppages and routine deductions. It also took considerably longer to train a raw recruit into an acceptable cavalryman than it did to teach a country bumpkin the rudiments of foot-drill and musketry. Taking all these factors into consideration, the Marquis de Santa-Cruz, the Spanish military expert of the 1730s, estimated that 'the maintenance of 1,000 cavalry costs as much as the maintenance of 2,500 infantry'. In the French Army the situation was further aggravated where pay was concerned by the widespread practice of including a double-allocation of officers in each cavalry troop, half holding actual commands, the rest serving as *reformés* or ordinary troopers. Whatever the desirable social effects of such a system, it was indubitably an expensive one, for the *reformés* drew pay as officers.

FRENCH CAVALRY DEMONSTRATE THAT BY THE MID-17TH CENTURY SHOCK ACTION HAD EMPHATICALLY RETURNED TO THE BATTLEFIELD. THE ILLUSTRATION, BY CHARLES PARROCEL, WAS 'PRESENTED TO THE PRINCE LOUIS FRANCOIS DE BOURBON, PRINCE DE CONTY'.

If expense was one factor leading to a decline in cavalry numbers, another was the rapid advance in the effectiveness of infantry weaponry and tactics. By the beginning of the 18th century the new combination of flintlock musket and socket bayonet made the foot-soldier less vulnerable to mounted attack, and at the same time increased the vulnerability of the mounted soldier. At least until the mid-17th century the cavalry as a general rule had been the battle-winning arm, but as the technological revolution in firearms took increasing effect the cavalry's superiority began slowly but surely to wane, although its social prestige remained as high as ever. 'Firearms and not cold steel now decide battles,' Maréchal de Puységur noted with typical realism. Yet this is not to claim that the day of the cavalry was wholly passed. Such commanders as the Duke of Marlborough, Prince Eugene of Savoy and Charles XII of Sweden, as we shall see, still relied on their mounted arm to achieve the *coup de grâce* in their greatest battles; and if the French Maréchal Gouvion St Cyr could still claim a century later that 'the cavalry represent the legs and eyes of an army; the infantry and artillery are its body and arms', this was equally true of the earlier generations, if not more so.

In addition to their roles on the battlefield, the cavalry had many other duties to discharge. When an army was on the march, they reconnoitred ahead or served to guard the flanks and rear against the

THE CAVALRY

possibility of a surprise attack. When an army entered camp, they provided vedettes and patrols, conducted foraging missions, protected convoys and escorted senior officers – or undertook raids into enemy territory to place hostile districts under contribution, contract, or barefaced pillage. Other detachments hovered close to the enemy's main positions, watching for signs of reinforcements or impending movement. Still others would lie quietly concealed in wood or lane, placed in ambush ready to surprise enemy convoys or other small, isolated parties.

In peacetime the cavalry were less actively employed, but their days did not pass in complete idleness. For Guards units there was the routine of ceremonial duties and escorts for members of royal families, visiting dignitaries and other notables. In the days before the existence of any regular police forces, it also often fell to the lot of the cavalry to reinforce the magistrates and tax-collectors in the performance of their unpopular duties. Dragoons might also be required by unscrupulous monarchs and governments to oppress discordant or even mildly embarrassing minorities by means of 'dragoonades' – the forcible billeting of rough soldiers on hapless civilian families upon whom they were free to wreak every indignity and havoc short of murder, whilst authority turned a blind eye. Louis XIV used such methods against the Huguenots and later the *Camisards* (a group of Calvinist insurgents); James II of England applied the same treatment to political opponents of his pro-Catholic policies; George I and II both employed the method in attempts to quell the Jacobite aspirations of the Highlands after the Scottish rebellions of 1715 and 1745.

These were not, however, the normal peacetime roles for those cavalrymen retained in service at the end of hostilities. Dragoons would be expected to assist with road-building and bridge-improvement. Regiments of horse would form parts of fortress garrisons, or hover in large encampments near to capital cities ready to overawe the 'vulgar', or keep Parliaments and Assemblies of Notables in a proper frame of loving and respectful subservience to their God-appointed sovereigns. And, year in year out, there were the perennial tasks of training to fulfil, of horses to be taken out for grass, water and exercise, with the occasional visit to the smith or farrier to fix a loose shoe or to the leather-workers to repair some defective piece of tack.

To return, however, to the primary roles of cavalry, in the second half of the 17th century the horse of most armies comprised four distinct types. First there were what may be termed Household Cavalry, forming part of the monarch's escort, or *corps d'élite*. In England these were the Life Guards, in Sweden the *Drabants*, in Austria the *Trabans*. In France the *Maison du Roi* was made up of Horse Grenadiers, the *Gardes du Corps*, the *Gendarmes de la Garde*, the *Compagnie des Chevau-Légers*, and the two companies, or squadrons, of Musketeers – the Black and the Grey (named after the colour of their mounts). All these formations were highly privileged, and officer-posts were highly prized; many indeed were reserved almost exclusively for princes of the blood or the most senior marshals and generals.

When serving in the field these crack formations were often brigaded with the most prestigious horse regiments. Thus the English Life Guards early developed close ties with the Royal Regiment of Horse Guards ('the Blues'), and in France the *Maison* often fought alongside the *Gendarmerie*. For the rest, the horse included cuirassiers – the amount of their armour progressively reduced with the passage of time until it consisted only of helmet,

THE *MAISON DU ROI*, HERE REPRESENTED BY A MEMBER OF THE *CHEVAU-LÉGERS DE LA GARDE* AND A *GENDARME DE LA GARDE*, c.1660. FROM DE NOIRMONT AND DE MARBOT.

A HORSE GRENADIER ABOUT TO THROW A GRENADE AND A *GENDARME DE BOURGUIGNON*, c.1690. HORSE GRENADIERS WERE RECRUITED FROM PICKED MEN OF THE LINE REGIMENTS; ALTHOUGH NOT MEMBERS OF THE *MAISON DU ROI*, THEY WERE OFTEN ATTACHED TO IT. THEY FOUGHT ON FOOT AS WELL AS ON HORSEBACK. FROM DE NOIRMONT AND DE MARBOT.

THE AGE OF THE SUN KING

back- and breastplates, and, sometimes, tassets; carabineers, armed, as the title suggests, with carbines or short muskets as well as the habitual sword and pistols; and finally the numerous regiments of horse, the backbone of the line cavalry, many of which only existed in time of war whilst others were reduced to the merest cadres at the cessation of hostilities.

This too was often the fate of the third category of mounted troops, the dragoons. These troops were less well paid than the regular cavalry, and were generally treated as maids-of-all-work within the mounted arm. Dragoons, still expected to fight on foot as well as on horseback, carried carbines, bayonets and hatchets as part of their standard equipment. They might also be ordered to serve in pioneering roles, and also as storm-troops or 'forlorn hopes'. Many commanders of note, including the Austrian Montecuculi, regarded their dragoons as little more than mounted infantry, but there is no denying that they performed many necessary roles. They never wore armour, and frequently were equipped with distinguishing cross-belts which supported an ammunition pouch on the one side and sword and bayonet on the other. Their high knee-boots made them somewhat clumsy in the dismounted role, and this earned the 'jackbootmen', as they were later dubbed, some telling criticisms. Nevertheless, their numerical representation steadily developed over the years. By 1668 Louis XIV boasted 14 regiments of dragoons to 66 of horse, but by 1690 the former had been increased to 43 regiments. Peter the Great inherited only a single dragoon formation in 1700, but by 1711 he had 24. William III commanded only seven regiments of English dragoons (to 31 of horse), but between 1707 and 1711 the Army Lists of his successor contain the names of 18 units of dragoons and only 11 of native horse.

Fourthly there was the light cavalry. Usually composed of irregular mounted marauders, such as the Croats and Cossacks, these light troops were becoming increasingly important. Peter the Great attempted to integrate eight regiments of hussars within the regular Russian forces by 1710, but subsequently reduced their number. In southern Europe the rulers of Austria were not slow to copy their Turkish opponents who employed large numbers of *Beshlis* and *Delis* in fast-moving but loosely organized clouds of light horsemen whose function was to protect their main forces. The Austrians were further induced to introduce similar troops within their armies when, in 1683, the King of Poland, John Sobieski, marched to the relief of Vienna, which was besieged by the Turks. The Polish army included numbers of the famous 'winged lancers', so named because of the feathers attached to the lances. The Austrians had in fact employed Hungarian Magyar irregular horsemen since the 15th century, but only in 1688 did they formally raise their first regiments of Hungarian hussars on a semi-permanent basis. France was relatively late in adopting true light cavalry. The *Chevau-Légers* of the *Maison du Roi* were not really light cavalry at all, but patterned themselves on the musketeers, and it was only in 1692 that the French raised their first real hussar regiment, recruited from Imperialist deserters. However, it is also true that Cardinal Richelieu had raised a small unit of 'Hungarian Cavalry' in 1635, but this did not long survive. As for Great Britain, her armies included no true light cavalry formations until the mid-18th century.

Light cavalrymen were not universally admired. If the regular cavalryman tended to scorn the dragoon, both affected to despise the hussar. A Frenchman, Brigadier-General de la Colonie, described hussars as 'properly speaking, little more

FRENCH DRAGOONS. FROM LEFT TO RIGHT, THE GUIDON OF THE DAUPHIN'S REGIMENT, AN OFFICER OF THE REGIMENT OF THE QUEEN, AND A DRAGOON OF THE REGIMENT OF HAUTEFORT. AT THIS TIME, c.1698, THERE WERE 47 REGIMENTS OF DRAGOONS IN THE FRENCH ARMY. FROM DE NOIRMONT AND DE MARBOT.

A FRENCH LIGHT CAVALRYMAN MOUNTS HIS HORSE WHILE A CARABINEER HAS TROUBLE WITH HIS; c.1650. FROM DE NOIRMONT AND DE MARBOT.

THE CAVALRY

than bandits on horseback', and in 1706 William Cadogan, Marlborough's famous Quartermaster-General, congratulated himself on being captured by 'the French carabines (sic) [rather than] falling into the hussars' hands, who first came up with me'. From Louis XIV's carabineers he met 'with quarter and civility, saving their taking my watch and money'. His likely fate at the hands of the hussars is not described, but they would seem to have borne a somewhat barbarous reputation. Nevertheless, these rough, wild, undisciplined light horsemen proved very valuable for scouting, ravaging and raiding, even though no army at the time deemed them worthy of a place in the formal line of battle.

Although the organization of mounted formations at this period contained numerous variations in most armies, the cavalry regiment was the basic administrative unit. It was subdivided into two main parts: a regimental headquarters, which included the colonel, a lieutenant-colonel and a major, besides an adjutant, chaplain, surgeon and a kettle-drummer – or, in the case of dragoon regiments, a gunsmith and his servant, and a varying number of cavalry troops, called *compagnies* in the French service. These each had a captain, a lieutenant and a cornet, a quartermaster, two or three corporals of horse – or sergeants in the dragoons – and a varying number of troopers or dragoons making up the rank-and-file, not forgetting also two trumpeters, or, in dragoon formations, a pair of kettle-drummers or *hautbois* players. Guards and Household formations had more elaborate rank-structures with additional posts. Precise strengths of cavalry and dragoon troops varied considerably, but French establishments in the 1670s officially comprised 12 companies, each holding four officers and 50 troopers. Fluctuations were enormous, however, and a regiment's strength might vary between 300 and 450 men. Guards units were frequently larger, a troop in the English Lifeguards for instance holding 156 'gentlemen', and dragoon regiments tended to have rather more troops or companies than did formations of line cavalry.

It will be noticed that no mention has been made of the squadron. This formation, adopted only for use in battle, was made up by grouping two or more troops together under the command of the senior troop commander, and was never a permanent administrative organization. Thus a regiment of 12 troops might provide two or three *ad hoc* squadrons on days of action. Regiments of dragoons, being generally larger, might form four or more companies. Some countries differed from the norm. Austrian cuirassier regiments, for example, commonly contained 1,000 horsemen, who fought in some six squadrons. English regiments varied in size between 300 troopers (six troops or two squadrons) and 480 men in the case of dragoons (up to eight troops). But during periods of peace many formations were disbanded and most of the survivors then found themselves reduced to the merest cadres.

The training of cavalrymen was often a long and laborious process. Brigadier-General Kane, in his *Discipline for a Regiment of foot upon action, also the most essential discipline of the Cavalry* (1745) summarized the requirements as follows: 'It is sufficient for them to ride well, to have their horses well managed, and train'd up to stand fire; that they take particular notice what part of the squadron they are in, their right and left-hand men, and file-leaders, that they may, when they happen to break, readily know how to form. Breaking their squadrons ought to be practiced in their common discipline. That they march and wheel with a grace, and handle their swords well, which is the only weapon our British Horse makes use of when they charge the enemy; more than this is superfluous ... Dragoons should be well instructed in the use of fire-arms, having upon occasion to make use of them on foot; but when on horseback, they are to fight as the horse do.'

Kane, however, was basically an infantryman, and the production of a good troop of horse called for much hard effort. The troopers had to master four basic movements and then become proficient in the 'postures' or exercise of arms, with sword, pistol and (when carried) carbine. Troops equipped with sabres were enjoined to use the sweeping cut to left or right; those armed with the broadsword were encouraged to use the point as well as the edge. Most cavalrymen were taught to slash first at their opponent's bridle headstall in the hope of causing the bit to fall from the horse's mouth and so rendering it uncontrollable. Dragoons, of course, also had to master infantry drills.

The employment of cavalry in battle varied a great deal from country to country. In the second half of the 17th century there was considerable discussion as to whether the mounted arm should be regarded as primarily an instrument of shock or, rather, as one of sophisticated firepower. In France, the advocates of the latter course for long held the advantage. French cavalry, for instance, still practised the *caracole*, discarded by the Swedish Army since the days of Gustavus Adolphus. Use of the sword was largely restricted to the general *mêlée*, which would begin once the fire action was complete.

AN OFFICER AND A TROOPER OF THE FRENCH ROYAL CARABINEERS, 1692. FORMERLY, COMPANIES OF CARABINEERS, EACH OF 30 MEN, HAD BEEN DISTRIBUTED AMONG THE CAVALRY REGIMENTS TO GIVE THEM MOUNTED FIRE SUPPORT. IN 1692 THESE WERE CONCENTRATED INTO FIVE REGIMENTS, EACH OF FOUR SQUADRONS. FROM DE NOIRMONT AND DE MARBOT.

THE AGE OF THE SUN KING

DRESSAGE FOR 17TH-CENTURY CAVALRY HORSES; DRAWN BY CHARLES PARROCEL FOR THE MARQUIS DE LA GUÉRINIÈRE'S *ÉCOLE DE LA CAVALERIE*.

THE CAVALRY

By the beginning of the 18th century, however, shock action had generally come into favour. Marlborough, for one, practised his cavalry in twin-squadron charges delivered at a fast trot and relying on cold steel for the kill. He went so far as to ban the use of firearms by cavalry except when on outpost duty. Prince Eugene of Savoy, the celebrated Austrian commander, was of much the same mind, and so was the firebrand Charles XII, King of Sweden. His cavalry were trained to charge at the gallop in vast arrowhead formations, the troopers riding 'knee behind knee' with the ensign at the apex rather than 'knee by knee' as was the practice in most European armies. Swedish horsemen were trained to baulk at no obstacle, and eventually became proficient at manoeuvring with a decisiveness and speed that no other country could match. Only the horsemen of the Ottoman armies could rival the dash of the Swedes, but they lacked the Swedish discipline, which, like Marlborough's, enjoined the immediate rally after the charge. The Turks tended to fight in a loose cloud or swarm of individual warriors rather than in a cohesive body, and provided their opponents maintained their formations or remained within their barricades of *chevaux-de-frise* set up on the battlefield, they would generally withstand the fury of these 'Turkish storms'.

Until the 1690s, however, the French cavalry remained the best in Europe in overall terms. Their triumphs under d'Enghien (who later became 'the Great Condé') and Turenne were later emulated under the command of the elder Duc de Luxembourg, whose horsemen swept all before them in the Flanders campaigns of the War of the League of Augsburg (1688–97). At Leuze on 19 September 1691, for example, he surprised the rearguard of Waldeck's army, which was 75 squadrons and five battalions strong, and proceeded with just 28 squadrons of his own to inflict 1,500 casualties upon the enemy. And at Landen two years later (29 July 1693), the French cavalry at the fourth attempt stormed the earthworks defending Neerwinden village, thereby preparing the way for William III's defeat. Those were great and influential days for the French horsemen.

The next war, that of the Spanish Succession (1701–14) witnessed a reversal of fortune. Marlborough's well-trained and disciplined English squadrons – working at all times in close association with their foot and guns – wrought havoc upon the proud cavaliers of France who, under the less inspired leadership of the latterday marshals of France, had lost some of their old fire and dash. Nowhere was this better demonstrated than at Blenheim (13 August 1704), where, in one celebrated engagement near the outset of the battle, eight squadrons of the vaunted *Gendarmerie* were routed by a bare five squadrons of English horse under Colonel Palmes. This event was witnessed by Marshal Tallard, the French commander, and when after his cataclysmic defeat he settled down to the humiliating task of describing his reasons for the loss of the day he wrote: 'First, because the *Gendarmerie* were

A POLISH LANCER OF 1576; HE WEARS AN OSTENTATIOUSLY PLUMED HELMET AND CARRIES A WING-SHAPED SHIELD.

A CAVALRY *MÊLÉE* AT MALPLAQUET, 1709.

THE AGE OF THE SUN KING

not able to break the five English squadrons.'

In their various generations, d'Enghien (Condé), Marlborough and Charles XII were the most skilled handlers of masses of cavalry at the level of grand tactics. At Blenheim, Ramillies, Oudenarde and Malplaquet, Marlborough clinched matters by the judicious husbanding and dynamic handling of his mounted squadrons at the climax of the battle. At Blenheim, he massed 80 fresh squadrons over the River Nebel in the centre to engage, and at the second attempt overwhelm the 60 squadrons and nine battalions of Tallard's exposed centre. At Oudenarde (11 July 1708) he extemporized a double-envelopment, by the Prince of Orange's squadrons on the one flank and by Natzmer's and Eugene's cavalry on the other, of Vendôme's exposed wing of the French army; and at Malplaquet (11 September 1709), close-fought and dearly-bought victory though it proved, a massive advance by the Allied squadrons, closely supported by Orkney's battalions, swept through the abandoned redoubts in the French centre to engage, and defeat, Marshal Villar's horsemen on the plain beyond. The latter action involved no less than 30,000 horsemen, and was 'one of the greatest cavalry actions in history' in the opinion of Marlborough's famous descendant, Winston Churchill. Indeed, Marlborough's relationship with his cavalry was always rather special. After Elixhem in 1705, for example, where he had led cavalry charges in person, and almost been killed, he wrote to his wife, Sarah, that 'This gave occasion to the troops with me to make me very kind expressions, even in the height of the action, which I own to you gives me much pleasure.'

For the bold handling of cavalry in action, Charles XII of Sweden had no peer. At Klizow (2 July 1702), 21 Swedish squadrons with cold steel routed 34 pistol-armed Saxon squadrons. At Narva (20 November 1700), great wedges of Swedish horsemen had charged through a dense snow blizzard to crash through and over the Russian earthworks. Charles was also ahead of his time in his doctrine of 'pursuit to the end' after a victory. Thus, following his defeat of General Schulenburg's Saxons in 1704, the Swedish cavalry hounded the survivors for nine days without respite, eventually catching up with them at Sanitz. Without hesitation, two regiments of unsupported Swedish cavalry proceeded to charge a mixed force of several thousand Saxons and scattered them all. And in 1709, when his army faced disaster at Poltava (28 June), the Swedish squadrons again distinguished themselves despite overwhelming odds ranged against them.

All in all, the cavalry of the late 17th and early 18th centuries saw some great days and brought off some memorable achievements. One of the greatest actions of all was that of Marlborough's cavalry at the Battle of Ramillies. On Whit Sunday 1706 there took place a mighty trial of strength some 20 miles south-east of Brussels in what were then known as the Spanish Netherlands, the heartland of 'the Cockpit of Europe'. Ranged against the Duke of

A COMRADE-IN-ARMS TO THE CAVALRYMAN OPPOSITE; THIS POLISH WARRIOR HAS A CIRCULAR SHIELD AND IS ARMED WITH A BOW.

BRITISH CAVALRY ADVANCE AT A FAST TROT AT THE BATTLE OF RAMILLIES.

THE CAVALRY

Marlborough's Allied army – 123 squadrons, 74 battalions and 120 guns, approximately 62,000 men in all – were the forces of Marshal Villeroi – 132 squadrons, 70 battalions and 70 guns, making a total strength of perhaps 60,000 French, Spanish and Bavarian troops. This battle is notable for a number of reasons: it took place early in the campaign of that year, and both armies were therefore fresh; the sides were evenly matched; moreover, neither had planned to fight on that exact date or in that precise area – it was an 'encounter battle' that escalated from a minor early-morning brush.

Although both armies knew of the other's general proximity, neither anticipated a major battle on 23 May. The French, however, were smarting to avenge their great defeat at Blenheim two years earlier, and Villeroi was under specific orders from Louis XIV to force or accept a major confrontation as soon as possible. That was the situation as William Cadogan, Marlborough's Quartermaster-General and a camp-survey party escorted by 600 horse, were out seeking a site for the Allied army's next stopping-place on the Plain of Ramillies. Suddenly, in the early-morning fog, they blundered upon the enemy already occupying the ground which they had provisionally selected for their own army. The news was rushed back to Marlborough, who rode forward with his staff to confirm his Quartermaster-General's impressions. Until the mist cleared he could not decide whether he faced all or only a part of Villeroi's army, and the Duke's first order was for all his cavalry to come up in case he was opposed by only a covering force. Then, at about 10.30 am, the sun broke through and the curtains of fog rapidly rolled back revealing the full splendour of the French army occupying the ridge running from near the village of Taviers in the south past Ramillies and Offus to Autre-Eglise in the north, the whole position forming an arc some four miles long. Between the two armies was a stream, the Gheete, surrounded by marshes. Marlborough realized the possibilities of the situation for the Allies: the enemy's forces were over-extended; the Gheete's marshes would obstruct their left wing and protect his own right if he adopted a shorter front; similarly, the River Mehaigne beyond Taviers and the French-held outpost of Francqnée precluded all danger of the left of his position being turned. Most important of all, his trained eye for ground picked out a useful re-entrant running from behind Foix-les-Caves to the north to opposite Ramillies in the centre – a feature that he might well make good use of to transfer troops unseen by the foe. Soon aides were spurring east to bring up the army, which fanned out into eight columns.

The French were equally taken by surprise: their intelligence had placed Marlborough a full day's march distant, and all their tents were still pitched behind Ramillies. But now the trumpets blared and the signal-guns recalled the foragers, and the French hastened to form their lines of battle. To make the most of the open plain some 1½ miles wide to the south of Ramillies, Villeroi massed 82 squadrons, including the *Maison du Roi*, with, in support, several interlaced infantry brigades, the garrisons of Taviers and Francqnée, and 20 battalions and a dozen triple-barrelled cannon grouped around Ramillies. Less sensibly, 50 more squadrons were deployed on the French left near Autre-Eglise, where broken and marshy ground around the Gheete would effectively prevent their active employment.

All morning the French watched idly while Marlborough's eight columns deployed along the Ridge of Jeuche and the Plateau of Jandrenouille. On his right the Duke placed almost all his English formations, both horse and foot, namely 12 battalions and 54 squadrons under Lord Orkney. The mass of the Allied foot, backed by heavy batteries, filled the centre; on the left, facing the cavalry in the plain, General Overkirk drew up the 69 squadrons of Dutch and Danish cavalry, with the Dutch guards and a pair of field guns on their extreme flank. Shortly after 1 pm the batteries opened fire, so launching the action.

It is doubtful whether Marlborough had a full plan already conceived, but he was evidently aware of the opportunities the terrain and the enemy's dispositions offered. His first orders were for the troops on his extreme flanks to advance on the enemy – the Dutch guards to take possession of the two villages on the French right flank, Orkney and the red-coated battalions to press ahead over the Gheete towards their left. These probing attacks would, he hoped, test Villeroi's intentions and resolve.

And so it proved. The Dutch Guards made good progress on the left, driving the French and Bavarians out of both villages, inducing the French commanders to send troops from their right centre to the support of their unfortunate colleagues. They in turn, including 15 squadrons of dragoons, were routed by Marlborough's Danish squadrons, 21 in all, who drove the French pell-mell into the marshes. Simultaneously, on the distant right flank, Orkney and his battalions began to descend towards the Gheete. This movement served further to disrupt Villeroi's battle line, for the Marshal was

THE AGE OF THE SUN KING

BOTTOM: MARLBOROUGH'S CAVALRY TAKE THE
FIELD AT RAMILLIES.

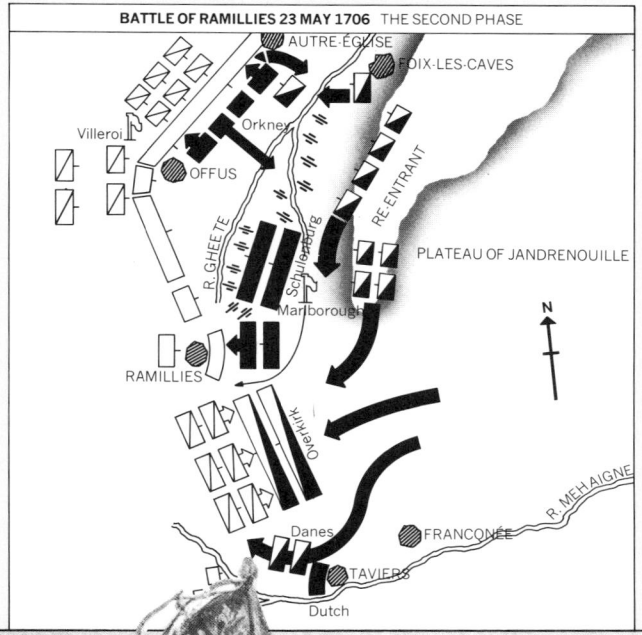

THE CAVALRY

under strict instructions from Louis XIV to pay special attention to that part of his front that would receive the first English attack. Soon more brigades of foot were moving northwards. All this Marlborough noted with satisfaction, for he had already singled out the French centre around Ramillies for his master-blow. It was almost 3.30 pm.

The Duke saw that he could use just a token force to contain the French left behind the Gheete and transfer, concealed by the convenient dip, most of the formations on his own right to build up a redoubtable strength for the blow in the centre. But two obstacles stood in way of this plan. First Lord Orkney, who had fought his way, French reinforcements notwithstanding, to the very outskirts of Autre-Eglise, turned out to be very unwilling to fall back on his original position as Marlborough's master-plan now dictated, and it took nine visits by aides-de-camp, and lastly by Cadogan himself, to induce him to relinquish his grip. Only when the English battalions had returned to their ridge near Foix-les-Caves could the full transfer movement commence.

Before this could be executed, however, the Duke's attention was drawn by anxious officers to a highly dangerous situation developing on his left centre. As General Schulenburg began to move the Allied centre towards Ramillies, Overkirk ordered his squadrons to advance on their flank. This challenge was at once accepted by the 67 remaining squadrons of Villeroi's right centre, and soon the plain south of Ramillies was filled with wheeling cavalry, as 48 Dutch squadrons and the 21 Danish attacked the *Maison du Roi*. The latter, as a French observer noted, had left over-large intervals between their squadrons, and this proved to their disadvantage. Marlborough, observing the conflict, immediately sent aides to summon 18 squadrons from his right via the dip; while their arrival was awaited the Duke and his staff rode over to join Overkirk. There they discovered a major crisis. The *Maison du Roi*, despite the presence of Dutch squadrons on their flanks and rear, had charged home with magnificent fire and discipline, and routed the Dutch right wing. Giving way, the Dutch horsemen placed in dire peril the neighbouring flank of Schulenburg's infantry, although the steady fire of four battalions earned them a brief respite to reform.

Marlborough, instantly aware that this situation must be remedied, at once summoned a further 21 squadrons from the distant right, then spurred forward with his attendants, sword in hand, to lead two successive Dutch charges. This bold, even fool-hardy, action by the Captain-General helped win time for the arrival of the cavalry from the right wing, but it almost cost him his life. In one of the eddies of combat he was knocked off or fell from his horse; worse still, his accident coincided with a French advance. For a time it seemed that the Duke must be killed or at least taken prisoner, but the Dutch rallied to his aid and he was able, despite his 57 years and cumbersome jack-boots, to run several hundred yards to the shelter of the muskets of a neighbouring friendly battalion of Dutch-paid Swiss mercenaries, where he borrowed an aide's horse. Even then his personal peril was not over. The Duke's spare charger was hurried forward, and as he was mounting this a cannon ball passed between his legs as he swung up into the saddle, and killed his equerry, Colonel Bringfield, who was holding the stirrup. However, the cavalry crisis was now averted as first the 18, and then the further 21 fresh Allied squadrons crashed into the fray, and overbore the *Maison du Roi* and their supporting squadrons with an overall superiority amounting to five to three. The French right wing began to swing back, pivoting on Ramillies.

Marlborough now sensed his opportunity. Summoning several British battalions from Orkney's silent right, which stood with its forward line of formations atop the ridge near Foix-les-Caves, the Duke began to build up forces for the *coup-de-grâce* against Ramillies. Villeroi and his staff, meanwhile, were anxiously awaiting the renewal of Orkney's onslaught on their left flank, and never thought to send their 50 useless squadrons southwards to assist their own right – but then the dip in the ground completely disguised the progressive dismantling of Orkney's command.

The fight for Ramillies was bitter, but with the collapse of the French right wing the battle was virtually won. Soon after 5 pm the Allied cavalry reformed in a new line facing north, and began remorsely to roll up the French line. Their advance was timed to coincide with a new, and decisive onslaught against Ramillies and its death-dealing batteries. This wheel, by about 100 Allied squadrons already part-spent by fierce combat, was a remarkable feat worthy of a special place in the annals of cavalry achievement. It proved decisive. The disordered French, striving to form a new line to face the advancing horsemen, found themselves hopelessly obstructed by their own tent-lines and wagon-trains behind Ramillies. Too late Villeroi ordered his 50 squadrons of the left wing to intervene: they melted away to the north and soon the whole French army, the would-be avengers of Blenheim, was dissolving across the land in a mass of fugitives.

The Allies lost 3,560 men and the French suffered some 7,000 casualties besides 5,000 prisoners. But the French had also lost their cohesion

MARLBOROUGH'S CAVALRY IN ACTION AT OUDENARDE. 1708.

THE AGE OF THE SUN KING

The SIEGE of AIRE.
Sept. 6. 1710.

THE SIEGE OF AIRE, 1710. CAVALRY PLAYED ONLY A MINOR PART IN SIEGES, ALTHOUGH HORSEMEN MIGHT BE EMPLOYED, FOR EXAMPLE, IN TAKING FORWARD BUNDLES OF FASCINES TO HELP FILL IN THE DITCH. THE FORTIFICATIONS ARE TYPICAL OF VAUBAN, THE FRENCH SIEGE-MASTER. AT RIGHT CENTRE, HEAVY SIEGE GUNS ARE IN ACTION; TO THE RIGHT THERE IS A 'ZIG-ZAG', A TRENCH ALONG WHICH ASSAULT TROOPS COULD APPROACH THE FORTRESS UNDER COVER FROM THE DEFENDERS' FIRE; THESE WERE THE FORERUNNERS OF THE TRENCHES OF 1914-18. A MORTAR BATTERY IS ALSO SEEN IN ACTION, LOBBING ITS BOMBS OVER THE CITY WALLS. ENGRAVING BY C. DU BOSC.

THE CAVALRY

and reputation. Marlborough for his part had no time to assimilate this information; he at once plunged himself into organizing his pursuit. Ramillies is unusual in this respect, for pursuits *à l'outrance* were at that time rarely attempted. The Duke himself did not pause to rest until he reached Meldert, some 12 miles from the battlefield. During the pursuit, Villeroi and the Elector of Bavaria narrowly avoided falling into the hands of the English cavalry.

If the immediate, tactical pursuit of the French after Ramillies was a notable feat, so was the strategic follow-through. Fortress after fortress and city after city of the Spanish Netherlands fell to the Allied army; no post seemed capable of withstanding the whirlwind. 'We have the whole summer before us,' exulted the victor, 'and with the blessing of God I shall make the best use of it.' This he proceeded to do: Louvain, Vilvorde, Brussels (the capital), Alost, Gavre, Bruges, Ghent, Damme, and, after sieges, Menin, Ostend and Dendermonde fell in turn to the Allies. The result was the conquest of the greater part of the Spanish Netherlands in a few short weeks. Not until Napoleon's pursuit of the Prussians after Jena a century later would this achievement be paralleled. The surrender of Ath on 2 October brought this *annus mirabilis* in Flanders to a close. Marlborough's reputation was now firmly secured, as was that of the Allied cavalry he had led to victory.

THE COSSACK

The word Cossack is an adaptation of the Russian *khasak*, literally meaning 'free' or 'freebooter'. The Cossack peoples were mainly of Tartar origin and came from settlements in the Caucasus, Black Sea and Caspian regions, including the area of the River Don. Since the 15th century these wild horsemen had played a role in Russian history, and the rulers of Muscovy, and later the Czars of Russia, had granted them land-rights and tax exemptions in return for military service, for which every Cossack male was liable. Led by their *hetman*, Cossacks proved ideally suited for reconnaissance, raiding and outpost work, but their notorious indiscipline, treacherous tendencies, and blatant disregard for authority precluded their incorporation in the formal lines of battle of Russia's 18th-century armies. Peter the Great's experiments in giving them a more formal role and status did not prove very successful, and indeed some of the Cossack peoples proved a thorn in his side. In 1709 Charles XII of Sweden hoped to inspire a revolt amongst Mazeppa's Cossacks – vainly in the event – but Peter never wholly trusted these fiercely independent peoples who never fully recognized his authority as Czar.

The Cossacks were generally armed with a lance, sabre, pistol and sometimes a carbine or musketoon. They wore fur caps, voluminous cloth or animal-skin jerkins, baggy breeches and soft-leather boots. They were organized into *sotnias*, or bands, each of which possessed a venerated *chorigoy*, or standard. They often rode to the sound of drums. In action the Cossacks usually fought as individuals rather than as members of a team. They operated in swarms or clouds of horsemen, and were particularly adept at picking off stragglers and fugitives. They were not so useful against formed bodies of horse or foot, and as often as not would flee if faced by determined resistance; this was at least true of them in the early 18th century. In later generations formations of Cossacks were incorporated into the regular Russian forces; their all-round competence was increased, and they took on standard cavalry roles. Less popularly, Cossacks were also used by later Czars as internal security troops and 'bully-boys', in much the same way as Louis XIV employed dragoons.

Of the Cossacks the Baron de Jomini, the famous military writer who served with Napoleon, wrote, no doubt from painful personal experience, 'The immense value of the Cossacks to the Russian Army is not to be estimated. These light troops which are insignificant in the shock of a great battle are terrible in a pursuit and a war of posts. They are a most formidable obstacle to the execution of a general's designs, because he can never be sure of the arrival and the carrying out of his orders, his convoys are always in danger, and his operations are uncertain.' (This version of Jomini's observations is taken from the translation by Captain G. H. Mendell, US Army.)

THE AGE OF THE SUN KING

TWO COSSACKS OF THE LINE AND A MOSLEM COSSACK, c.1830; THE FIGURE IN CHAIN-MAIL IS A MONTAGNARD OF THE CAUCASUS. FROM *COSTUMES MILITAIRES DE L'ARMÉE DE L'EMPEREUR DE TOUTES LES RUSSIES EN 1836*, by H. A. ECKERT AND CHEVALIER WEISS.

Dᴜʀɪɴɢ this period, in which Prussia began to emerge as one of the great military powers in Europe, little change occurred in the organization or tactics of the cavalry. However, two developments, the replacement of the unreliable and slow-firing matchlock by the flintlock musket and the gradual refinement of mobile quick-firing artillery, continued slowly to erode the preeminence the cavalry had hitherto enjoyed.
J.P.L.

A MEMBER OF FRANCE'S 1ST COMPANY OF MUSKETEERS. THIS INDEPENDENT UNIT, 250 STRONG, WAS FIRST RAISED IN 1622 BY LOUIS XIII (AND MADE FAMOUS AT A LATER DATE BY ALEXANDRE DUMAS). THE UNIFORM COAT WAS SCARLET AND THE SADDLECLOTH SCARLET EDGED WITH GOLD. A MUSKETEER CARRIED, IN ADDITION TO HIS MUSKET, TWO PISTOLS AND A SWORD, AND RODE A GREY.
FROM *CAVALIERS FRANCAIS*, 1756.

THE AGE OF FREDERICK THE GREAT by T. A. HEATHCOTE

Frederick the Great (reigned 1740-86) divided his cavalry into three distinct types: the cuirassiers for shock action, the dragoons to act not only as mounted infantry, but also as medium cavalry, and light cavalry for scouting and foraging. The cuirassier units remained the true regiments of horse, their role, tactics and equipment little changed from that of the previous century. They still wore the cuirass, the heavy iron breastplate which protected the troopers against sword cut or bayonet thrust in hand-to-hand combat, an iron skull-cap underneath their tricorne hat, tough leather riding boots with stiff tops covering the knees, and leather gauntlets protecting the wrist and forearm. The 'buff coat' of stout leather, worn below the cuirass in earlier times, had been discontinued, but its appearance survived in the white coat which the cuirassiers of nearly all European nations wore under their armour. The British were almost alone in not following this custom, but their regiments of horse did not become cuirassiers, being converted instead to an otherwise unknown arm, the Dragoon Guards, whereas the Austrians, Prussians, Saxons, Russians and the cuirassiers of the minor German states all wore the thick coat of white or tan-coloured woollen cloth which preserved the memory of its leather predecessor, and was almost stout enough to turn a blow.

FREDERICK THE GREAT INSPECTING HIS TROOPS. ENGRAVING AFTER CHODOWICKI.

THE CAVALRY

Frederick's cuirassiers wore no armour on their back. This was at once an official compliment and an official reminder. It also lightened the load on man and beast, already weighed down with carbine, two pistols and their holsters, pouch-belt, carbine-belt, sword and scabbard, to say nothing of the picketing-peg, valise, saddle bag, forage net, and all the other impedimenta carried about with him by the horse soldier on the line of march. The breastplate, painted black for smartness and protection against rust, was deemed to be sufficient defence in the *mêlée*, but still required its wearer to be physically strong in order to mount his horse and remain in the saddle during a long day's riding and fighting. Big men on big horses, the cuirassiers were the shock troops of the army. Their primary role was to defeat and drive the enemy's horsemen from the battlefield, and to hammer their way through any weakness in the opposing infantry line. In the Prussian Army under Frederick there were 13 cuirassier regiments including four belonging to the Household Cavalry.

As we have seen in earlier chapters, the dragoon first made his appearance in the order of battle as a mounted infantryman, corresponding to the motor rifleman or mechanized infantryman of modern times. That is to say, they rode *to* battle rather than *into* battle. They used the speed of their horses to move rapidly to seize a position or reinforce a threatened one, then dismounted and went into action on foot as musketeers. Since their horses were intended purely for transport, and not as fighting platforms, the dragoons could be mounted cheaply on low-quality nags, and did not need the big expensive war horse of the true cavalryman. But there seems to be a marked reluctance among soldiers to fight dismounted if they have the opportunity to fight in the saddle (or, nowadays, from their armoured vehicles) and the officers and men of the dragoon service increasingly sought to display their capability to fight as mounted men to the gradual exclusion of their infantry role. At the same time, governments were not averse to the emergence of a cheaper form of cavalry, able to take its place in the line of battle without demanding the expensive equipment, powerful mounts and high wages of the true horse regiments. However, the almost inevitable consequence of this process was that the dragoons, because they were employed as cavalry, came to look very like, and cost almost as much, as the horse regiments that they were now beginning to supplement.

The extent to which this process came about varied in degree and rapidity between the different armies of Europe. French dragoons served on foot on a number of occasions during the Napoleonic period, and even towards the end of the 19th century they could still be seen riding with their rifles slung across their backs. The British, at the other extreme, turned their horse into dragoons and their dragoons into horse, for by 1746 all their dragoon regiments were as much heavy cavalry as the horse; the horse were then renamed Dragoon Guards and paid the same (i.e. lower) wages as dragoons. After that there were no differences at all in the roles, equipment and tactical employment of the two branches of British heavy cavalry.

The Prussian service came halfway between these two extremes. During the reign of Frederick William I (1713–40), the Prussian dragoons were converted to battle cavalry, and, on his father's death, Frederick the Great found 10 regiments of them all capable of taking their place in the line, manoeuvring and fighting as mounted men. They wore, however, not the short jacket and breastplate of the cuirassier, but the full-skirted coat of the foot soldier, and Frederick, in 1745, changed its colour from white to sky blue. They wore the black tricorne cap which was 'universal pattern' for most Prussian soldiers of this period, and carried a straight sword like the cuirassiers but with a lighter guard. They carried a short musket slung from a cross-belt, and also a bayonet, and drilled as infantry so that if required to do so they could fight on foot as a formed body.

A FRENCH DRAGOON OF THE REGIMENT OF SEPTIMANNIE FIRING ON HORSEBACK; ON HIS RIGHT IS AN OFFICER OF THE REGIMENT OF THE KING, 1745. FROM DE NOIRMONT AND DE MARBOT.

This change in the dragoon's role certainly strengthened the cavalry in one of its major tasks, the crushing of opposition in battle, but left a gap in its capability to undertake the other conventional tasks of the mounted arm: patrolling and intelligence gathering, raids, harassment of heavy troops, pursuit of a beaten enemy, and the prevention of an enemy's horsemen from performing these tasks on behalf of their own army.

From the early years of the 18th century, step by step with the increasing weight of their dragoons, Continental armies raised bodies of light horsemen generally known as hussars to carry out this work. The name hussar is of Hungarian origin, and the reintroduction of light horsemen into European warfare came about when the hard-pressed Hapsburg monarchy decided to employ the wild mounted men of its Hungarian territory against the more conventionally drilled and attired regular soldiers of western and northern Europe. (Hussars are described in greater detail at the end of this chapter.)

Imitation is the sincerest form of flattery, in warfare as in other areas, and the impact which Austria's hussars had in battle can be judged by the

THE AGE OF FREDERICK THE GREAT

extent to which other European armies tried to copy them. If they were unable to recruit (at least in significant numbers) the genuine raw material of the original hussars, they could certainly train their own countrymen in light cavalry work, and they could certainly copy the uniforms of what were judged to be the newest and most fashionable *élite* arm. Just as, at the present time, soldiers of *élite* corps in many parts of the world affect the red or green beret (itself originally a French peasant's headdress) adopted by the Allied special forces in World War II, so then it was deemed the smartest thing to wear a stylized and tailored version of the Hungarian herdsman's workaday clothing. The reasoning behind this was apparently that to make a man fight and operate like an Austro-Hungarian hussar, it was necessary to make him dress like one. The fashion gradually spread westwards – first to the other German states, then to France, which raised its first regular hussar regiment in 1720 from volunteers levied in Ottoman territory, and finally to the United Kingdom, where the British, who with dogged insularity had in 1759 simply converted several dragoon regiments into light dragoons, began in 1811 the process of converting several light dragoon regiments into hussars. Even then, they invented a new name for the *colpeck*, or hussar's fur cap, calling it a 'busby' after the firm of London military hatters responsible for making it.

The Prussian Army raised its first hussars in 1721. At first they were merely a single troop of 30 men, but in 1729 King Frederick William was sufficiently impressed by the appearance of local hussars escorting his coach on a visit to his daughter, the Marchioness of Bayreuth, that in 1731 he formed his own Hussar Life Guard. On the accession of his son, Frederick the Great, in 1740, there were two regiments of hussars. He reorganized and strengthened them between 1741 and 1745, until by that year the Prussian Army included eight hussar regiments. Another regiment was raised in 1760, and one more in 1773. Each regiment consisted of 10 squadrons, and at full strength mustered nearly 1,500 in all ranks.

One of these regiments, the Ninth (Bosniaks), raised in 1760, were strictly speaking Lancers rather than hussars, for they were armed with that weapon, and wore the loose baggy overalls and long coats of the Cossack rather than the tight-fitting garments of the Hungarian. Indeed, they traced their descent from a group originally recruited in 1744 in the Ukraine for the Saxons. They were reduced from 10 squadrons to one after the peace of 1763, but in 1778 were again expanded to full regimental establishment for the War of the Bavarian Succession. The regiment suffered heavy casualties in that campaign at the hands of the better-trained Austrian hussars, and it was not until 1812 that lancers reappeared in the Prussian ranks.

One further body of mounted men in Frederick's army deserves a mention, the corps of mounted *Jägers*. The German word *Jäger*, like the French *chasseur*, means huntsman. The term was applied by French and German monarchs to bodies of troops, mounted or on foot, raised from the gamekeepers, woodsmen and verderers of their estates and forests, to bring to the battlefield their special skills of marksmanship, fieldcraft and individual initiative. It is difficult to find an exact translation into military English. The British Army applied the term Rifle Corps to the *élite* green-jacketed regiments which, although they originated in the forests of North America, were largely modelled on the *Jägers* – thereby distinguishing the weapon which they carried from the inaccurate but cheaper smooth-bore musket of the line – but reserved the term Mounted Rifles for units with a role similar to the original dragoons. The French *chasseurs à cheval* dressed in a style similar to that of hussars, whose work and origins were much the same. Probably 'Ranger' is the best English equivalent of *Jäger*, for the term was adopted by various provincial or auxiliary corps, both mounted and foot. Although the mounted *Jägers* would have been the best answer to the true hussars, Frederick used them entirely as guides, couriers and dispatch riders. Their number only reached 162 by the end of his reign, and strictly speaking their function remained that of a staff corps rather than a cavalry regiment.

A HUSSAR OF THE 5TH (DEATH'S HEAD) REGIMENT IN THE SERVICE OF FREDERICK THE GREAT, c.1750. HE IS CLEARLY A VEDETTE ON OUTPOST DUTY ON A COLD AND WINDY DAY; THE HORSE, TOO, LOOKS RESIGNED TO A BORING AND UNPLEASANT TASK. FROM *HEERSCHAU DER SOLDATEN FRIEDRICHS DES GROSSEN*, BY ADOLF MENZEL, PUBLISHED IN 1856.

The official manual of 1744 showed the ideal disposition of the three types of cavalry according to Prussian ideas. Each flank of the main infantry was guarded by a wing of cavalry. In front of each wing was a solid line of cuirassiers riding knee to knee, in two or three ranks. An iron-clad wall of armoured men on heavy horses, its role was to ride down any horse, over any foot or through any guns that got in its way. Behind them at a distance of some 300 paces was the second line, the dragoons, still big men on big horses, but more manoeuvrable, their squadrons separated by large intervals to enable them to switch their weight to exploit any breakthrough, or strengthen any hold-up, in the cuirassiers' attack. On the inner flank, the dragoon squadrons were moved further forward, to give close support to the cuirassiers, and to link them with, and encourage, the infantry. In the rear and on the outer flank rode the hussars, ready to gallop forward in pursuit of a defeated foe, or to harass an attacking one, so winning time for the heavies to regroup and reform after the *mêlée*.

Although Frederick was scathing in his criticism of the cavalry he inherited, arguing that its troopers and their mounts were too big and too heavy, the requirements of conventional warfare at this time demanded stature and strength in both man and beast. Frederick's major alteration in cavalry training was to introduce the fast gallop over long distances in the attack, rather than the slow trot previously practised. For this, the horses required size, speed and endurance, and the gradual introduction of lighter, east European, stock into the dragoon regiments, and the scarcity of strong Holsteiner horses for the cuirassiers, resulted by the end of his reign in a marked falling-off of their performance in the prolonged charge. Black heavy horses were reserved for the cuirassiers, black or dark roan for the dragoons, and any colour or combination of colours was accepted for the light horses of the hussars.

Certainly Frederick can claim credit for major improvements in the light cavalry, if only in numbers. From a mere 1,000 or so on his accession the Prussian hussars increased until, at his death in 1786, they totalled more than 15,000 men, nearly 10 per cent of the whole of the army's fighting strength. By contrast, the French in 1792 had only six hussar regiments; the British on the other hand had, in 1794, 10 light dragoon corps out of a total of 35 cavalry regiments.

Frederick's hussars had one special task which they were not normally trained for in other armies. This was to act as a sort of military police, and in particular to prevent desertion. When the army halted, for example, swarms of hussars would be sent out in every direction to hold every road, bridge, ford and farmstead around the camp. In this way they not only prevented enemy troops sneaking in, but Prussian deserters sneaking out. Hussars, like the other light troops in Frederick's army, were rather looked down on as *parvenus*. They, together with the technical arms, included ordinary gentlemen, or bourgeois, among their officers, whereas officers of the other arms were almost exclusively noblemen. Indeed, at one time, Frederick even advocated the occasional selection of long-serving sergeants for commissioning as subalterns in preference to some of the young fops who, attracted by the 'private army' idea, were beginning to enter the hussars – part of the common military syndrome whereby the irregulars of one generation become the fashionable *élite* of the next.

In Frederick's Army the original purpose behind the hussars' creation was gradually eroded. Even as he formed them, the King's instructions consistently urged the need for training in close-order fighting as well as the traditional hussar techniques. After the Seven Years' War (1756–63) the requirement for hussars to fight in a main battle in the same way as the heavy cavalry was accepted in theory and practice; this had resulted in part from the hussars' own creditable performance in the heavy-cavalry role. But at the end of his reign Frederick was obliged to concede that matters had gone too far, and again called for individual training of officers and men in scouting, patrolling and raids. After his death, Prussian hussars performed these duties well enough in Poland and the early Revolutionary Wars, but soon the familiar tendency of all light cavalry to become heavy cavalry reasserted itself, and in the campaign of 1806 against Napoleon the Prussian hussars virtually abandoned their true role and acted *en masse*, literally as a third-rate battle cavalry. Only with the reforms of Yorck and Scharnhorst, and with the patriotic fervour of the German War of Liberation six years later did the true light cavalry spirit return. But the very essentials of the Prussian military system – iron discipline, harsh punishments, cruel repression, instant obedience, the brutal use of stick and lung to turn thinking men into skilled automata – such were simply not conducive to producing the free and easy spirit of the true hussar.

One of Frederick's innovations, in support of the mounted arm, was the development of horse artillery. This branch of the artillery was a new departure. Unlike the light field artillery, which used the same 6-pounder gun or the even lighter 3-pounder, the horse artillerymen were all individually mounted – the three drivers riding postilion fashion on the 6-horse gun team, the eight gunners on their own horses. But while the light artillerymen had to walk behind their pieces on the march, and to manhandle them with drag ropes once they had been committed to battle, the horse gunners were able to accompany the forward cavalry units as they made contact with the enemy, then withdraw and reappear anywhere on the battlefield that artillery support was needed. Prior to this, most European armies had possessed mounted artillery of a sort – the so-called 'galloper guns', light pieces drawn by one or two horses with the gun trail forming a pair of shafts, and a light tumbril, drawn separately, to carry the ammunition. But these were essentially weapons of local close support, under command of

A TYPICAL MEMBER OF A JÄGER CORPS, STALKING THROUGH THE UNDERGROWTH WHILE A COMRADE COVERS HIS MOVEMENTS. FROM MENZEL.

THE AGE OF FREDERICK THE GREAT

the cavalry units to which they were attached in ones and twos, and not able to have the same devastating effect as a full battery of guns suddenly coming into action at a critical moment. The galloper guns really correspond to the battalion guns – the light field artillery mentioned above, which were distributed among the infantry to perform the functions of medium machine guns and light anti-tank guns in more modern times. Frederick's horse artillery adopted the blue coat with red facings which the rest of the Prussian artillery wore, but with the addition of a white plume in their cocked hats, like the cuirassiers; they also wore riding boots instead of the gaiters of the dismounted branch.

The first Prussian horse artillery was formed in 1759. This was lost in battle shortly afterwards, and its successor was captured, in the same way, from the constant temptation of this arm to gallop too far ahead of the main army, while lacking the speed to withdraw at the same rate as the cavalry if attacked. Horse artillerymen of all armies were to pride themselves on their ability to gallop up to a startled enemy, unlimber, load, fire, sponge, repeat, then limber up again and whirl away in a cloud of dust before he could make an effective reply. (The Bengal Horse Artillery once even blasted down the gates of an Indian fortress before the astonished defenders could bring a gun to bear.) Yet this scenario, to be undertaken successfully, calls for a nice degree of judgment that can only be developed after some years' experience, and it was the lack of this experience that caused Frederick's horse gunners to suffer their early misfortunes. By the end of his reign, they consisted of six troops each of nine cannon. The British copied Frederick's example by forming their own *élite* Royal Horse Artillery in 1793, which was given precedence over all other regiments in the Army. The French formed their horse artillery in the same period as the British, and Napoleon's Horse Artillery of the Guard, its men dressed in all the panoply of a mounted hussar, was one of the most brilliant units under the Emperor's command.

One of the most rapid victories in all Frederick's campaigns can be attributed to the capabilities of his cavalry and to the degree to which one commander could exploit them. The victory was that of Rossbach, on 5 November 1757. The commander was Friedrich Wilhelm von Seydlitz, justly one of the most famous cavalry commanders of his age.

Friedrich von Seydlitz was at that time 36 years old, and had seen service with all three branches of the cavalry. He first came to the notice of his king at the disastrous (for the Prussians) Battle of Kolin on 18 June 1757. In that battle the Prussian cavalry, under Major-General von Ziethen, the 'Hussar King', began well. Thirty-five squadrons of hussars, 25 of dragoons, and five of cuirassiers, attacked and routed the cavalry regiments protecting the Austrian right, handling them so severely that they did not appear in the field again that day. Frederick's plan was to support this attack with almost all the rest of his cavalry, 33 squadrons of cuirassiers and 20 of dragoons, leaving only 10 squadrons of cuirassiers to guard his own right. Unfortunately the first line of Prussian cavalry, pursuing the Austrian horse, was taken in the flank by a murderous artillery and infantry fire from Austrians posted in a group of woods, and was obliged to retire in its turn. The powerful second line of cavalry, which had been intended to strike the decisive blow, was unable to move until the woods were cleared; however, because of a series of acci-

FRENCH *CHASSEURS DE FISCHER*. THIS WAS THE FIRST REGIMENT OF *CHASSEURS* TO BE FORMED IN FRANCE, ENLISTING HUNTERS AFTER THE FASHION OF THE GERMAN *JÄGERS*. IT WAS RAISED BY FISCHER, A GERMAN SOLDIER OF FORTUNE; IN 1756 ITS ESTABLISHMENT WAS SET AT FIVE INFANTRY COMPANIES, EACH OF 40 MEN, AND FOUR COMPANIES OF HORSE, EACH OF ABOUT 75 MEN. FROM DE NOIRMONT AND DE MARBOT.

PRUSSIAN HORSE GRENADIERS PREPARE TO FORD A STREAM; IN THE BACKGROUND IS A HUSSAR OFFICER. FROM MENZEL.

THE CAVALRY

dents elsewhere on the field, the infantry of the Prussian left wing were left unsupported and unable to dislodge the Austrians. To sum up, 10,000 excellent cavalry, one-third of Frederick's army, were virtually paralysed, especially after von Ziethen was rendered unconscious by a head wound, another third was in action where it ought not to have been, and the last third, on the left, had to sustain the Austrian attack alone.

In this disaster von Seydlitz was noticed by his sovereign as one of the few cavalry commanders to have used his own initiative in getting his regiment into the fighting. He was speedily promoted to major-general and then to lieutenant-general shortly after. Few envied him his advancement, and none regretted it, for his personal chivalry, fairness and justice to those under him, and sheer technical competence were unquestionable. Above all, he was blessed with a sure *coup d'œil*, the ability so essential in cavalry leaders to sum up a situation and seize an opportunity at the fleeting instant it occurs.

Such an opportunity arose at Rossbach. There the Prussians were outnumbered two to one by an Allied army of French and various German states. The Allies began the battle by marching to outflank the Prussian left. Frederick replied by marching to his left rear, a manoeuvre interpreted by his opponents as a withdrawal, so that their advanced guard quickened its pace and drew ahead of the main force. The two columns were now converging along the sides of a V; a range of low hills ran between its two arms and the precise movements of Frederick's advance guard, under von Seydlitz, were hidden. Suddenly, as the leading Allied cavalry reached the point of the V, von Seydlitz simply wheeled his 43 squadrons into line, and supported by artillery on the hill-crest swept over and down into their unsuspecting ranks. The infantry of the Allied advanced guard tried to deploy but, with von Seydlitz's victorious troopers already on their front and rear, were unable to form in time. They and their cavalry were thrown back in disorder, while six Prussian infantry battalions marched to von Seydlitz's support. The Allied cavalry reserve of five regiments was ordered to cover their main force's deployment. This body

THE AGE OF FREDERICK THE GREAT

also failed in its mission, being promptly charged and driven back.

Meanwhile the rest of the Prussian army had crossed the hills and taken up a line diagonally across the path of the Allied troops. The Allied infantry, outflanked and exposed to heavy artillery and musketry fire, were unable to deploy on the head of their column or hold their ground, and fell back, endeavouring to deploy on the rear of their columns, protected by their own cavalry. One more charge by von Seydlitz clinched the victory. As the last of their cavalry went down before the thundering Prussian squadrons, the Allied infantry broke and ran. Thus ended the Battle of Rossbach, where in less than an hour 22,000 men, carefully controlled and brilliantly led, overcame 50,000 losing only 300 men, but killing 800, capturing 6,000, and taking 72 guns. Every crisis in the battle was resolved in the Prussian favour by the genius of von Seydlitz, first by his immediate charge against the enemy caught on the line of march, and later by his repeated attacks that prevented them from winning time to rally.

CAVALRY ON OUTPOST DUTY THE *GRANDE GARDE*. THE TROOP HAS ESTABLISHED ITS HORSE LINES IN A HOLLOW TO AVOID DETECTION; THE HORSES REMAIN SADDLED FOR INSTANT ACTION AND EACH TROOPER HAS PLACED HIS CUIRASS BY HIS HORSE'S HEAD. A SECTION OF 12 TROOPERS UNDER AN OFFICER HAS BEEN POSTED FORWARD FROM WHICH FOUR VEDETTES HAVE BEEN STATIONED ON VIEWPOINTS. IN THE RIGHT FOREGROUND, A TROOPER EITHER HAS BEEN TAKEN ILL OR IS LYING STAKED OUT FOR FIELD PUNISHMENT. FROM *TRAITÉ SUR CAVALERIES*, BY THE COMTE DRUMMOND DE MELFORT. 1786.

THE CAVALRY

AN OFFICER IN THE QUEEN'S OWN REGIMENT OF HUSSARS. 1741-80. FROM MENZEL.

MEMBERS OF THE 9TH BOSNIAK REGIMENT OF HUSSARS IN THE PRUSSIAN SERVICE. ON THE LEFT IS A TROOPER, HIS BAGGY TROUSERS VERY MUCH IN EVIDENCE. ON THE RIGHT AN OFFICER. FROM MENZEL.

A PRUSSIAN CUIRASSIER OFFICER. c.1760. FROM MENZEL.

PRUSSIAN DRAGOONS; THE AMOUNT OF IMPEDIMENTA THEY CARRIED ON THEIR HORSES WAS PRODIGIOUS. FROM MENZEL.

114

THE AGE OF FREDERICK THE GREAT

KETTLE DRUMMER AND STANDARD BEARER OF FREDERICK THE GREAT'S ROYAL BODYGUARD. FROM MENZEL.

THE CAVALRY

MARSHAL SAXE

It is relevant to follow this account of Frederick's cavalry in action with a look at the theory of cavalry as advocated by one of the foremost military minds of the age, Maurice of Saxony, Marshal of France. Marshal Saxe was born in 1696, the illegitimate son of Frederick Augustus I, King of Poland, Elector of Saxony, whence he derived his name, using its French form 'Saxe'. He served with the Allied armies in the War of the Spanish Succession, at Tournai and Malplaquet, then in Hungary against the Turks. In 1722, already distinguished, he took service in the French Army and served with credit in the War of the Polish Succession, reaching the rank of Lieutenant-general in 1734. The summit of his career was the War of the Austrian Succession. In 1745, under his command, the French armies in Flanders were successful at Fontenoy, Tournai, Oudenarde, Ostend, and in other engagements. In 1746 he added Malines, Mons, Namur and Charleroi to the list of his victories. In 1747 he was made Marshal of France. His last victory, Maastricht, in 1748, was followed by the conclusion of hostilities and the Treaty of Aix-la-Chapelle. He died in 1750 at the height of his glory. His loss was greatly to be felt by the French Army in their coming campaigns against the Prussians.

Marshal Saxe's *Rêveries* or 'musings' were composed in the 1730s, but not published until seven years after his death. They covered the whole military art in detail, from the dress and equipment of individual soldiers, and the organization, training and tactical employment of units, to the investment of fortresses and matters of grand strategy. On the subject of cavalry, he wrote that it should be mobile, mounted on horses trained to endure hardship, and that it should have little supporting transport. He had obviously suffered much in his career from what he regarded as an obsession among cavalry commanders for keeping their horses fat and sleek, and generally mollycoddling them, for he devotes a whole paragraph at the beginning of the chapter on cavalry to this subject. In his opinion, supported by his personal experience, a regiment that rode hard, trained hard, and subjected both mounts and riders to hardship, fatigue and continuous exercise, would in the end be more fit for active service than one parading on beautiful, well-covered animals.

He divided cavalry into two sections only, horse and dragoons. Light horse and properly trained dragoons were in his view of greater value than hussars. The horse, the true cavalry, should be small in numbers – 40 squadrons would be ample in any army of 30–50,000 men. Their manoeuvres should be simple and solid. They should never be taught anything resembling light cavalry work, but should concentrate on how to keep together and to fight as one. They should never be detached and used as escorts or gallopers, nor used for any other purpose than fighting in major engagements. Saxe compares them with the heavy artillery, never to be employed except as part of the main army.

Saxe's cavalry were to be mounted on strong and sturdy horses, German Holsteiners for preference, not to be under 20 hands high. The troopers were to be picked men, slim, spirited and not corpulent. He could not understand why full armour had been given up. The usual explanation, that gunpowder made it obsolete, he found unconvincing. It was, after all, used by the French until about 1667, long after the matchlock musket had made its appearance on the field. Driven to the conclusion that expense alone had been the deciding factor, he advocated a full armour made of thin iron plate. This, he said, would be inexpensive, attractive to look at, would be proof against sword cuts, and against all except direct hits from small arms fire. Most cavalry fire, he said, was in any case ineffective, the weapons being badly loaded, or the charge shaken about by the movement of the horses, so that even a direct hit might have as little penetrating power as a glancing shot. Warming to this theme, he argued that cavalry that took to using its firepower was cavalry about to be defeated. By using light armour, he would force the enemy to do just this. The enemy, finding armoured men invulnerable to sword attack, would resort to their firearms, with negligible effect. Then the armoured cavalry, having suffered the worst there was to fear, would charge home against the enemy, eager to take their revenge for the attack they had endured. What could unprotected men do against invulnerable ones? Saxe asked. His reply: nothing, unless they were very quick about it, except be killed. Even two such armoured regiments in an army would, he concluded, have an immense effect on enemy squadrons.

Like most soldiers, Saxe knew that the standard reply to requests for better equipment was the Treasury argument, objecting on grounds of cost. He therefore introduced the idea of armour by minimizing its capital cost, and went on to say that its use really represented a great saving of money. The armour, together with a low metal helmet would last the whole of a man's service. There would be no need to incur expenditure in equipping him with hat, coat or boots. All the trooper required besides his armour would be a cloak every four years, a sword-belt every six years, and his riding breeches.

Dealing with possible objections he first countered the argument that the enemy would reply by himself adopting armour and so nullifying the advantage. To begin with, for an enemy to adopt armour would be proof of its value. Then it

PORTRAIT OF MARSHAL SAXE, BY J. G. WILLE AFTER H. REGAUD.

THE CAVALRY

would take several years for any enemy to get round to doing so, out of pride, or conservatism, or bad judgment, and during this time the armoured men would have an enormous advantage. Another objection was that gunshot wounds were more serious if inflicted through armour. Saxe doubted that this was so. But, even if it were, he pointed out that having a few men more seriously wounded by bullets would be more than counter-balanced by the greater number of men who would not suffer sword injuries not to mention the considerable number of men wounded each year by the negligent or accidental discharge of their own firearms, who would be saved by their armour.

The problem about armour, he said, was the discipline required for its wear. It had been abandoned because soldiers had become soft. He admitted it was a bore to wear a cuirass or trail a pike for half a century, just to use it on a single day. But once that discipline was ignored disaster would inevitably follow. He proposed to arm his cavalry with a good strong sword, about four feet long. All ranks would carry a breech-loading carbine, chosen for its greater range and ease of loading. Ramming, required by muzzle-loaders, was difficult for mounted men, he said, and the ramrod was always getting lost or broken or cracked. Pistols he regarded as so much expensive deadweight, serving no useful purpose. The front rank would carry lances about 15 feet long. Each lance would have a large silk streamer or pennant, which he had seen the Poles use, and which had the effect of frightening the enemy's horses. (The Prussian Bosniaks depended on this technique in the charge.) In camp, the lance would serve as a tent pole. Elsewhere he proposed that infantry should be armed with pikes instead of bayonets, and that these should have a similar dual role.

In the charge, the cavalry must stay together and whatever the result of the *mêlée*, must reform around their standard and not gallop off as individuals in pursuit. The maintenance of this cohesion would govern the rate of the charge, progressing from a steady trot at about 100 yards from the enemy, and increasing in speed until at 20 yards the horses were to be spurred on to full speed. This manoeuvre, Saxe said, was to be practised over and over again; furthermore cavalry must be trained to gallop long distances without losing its formation. A squadron that could not gallop at full speed for 2,000 yards without becoming disorganized was unfit for active service.

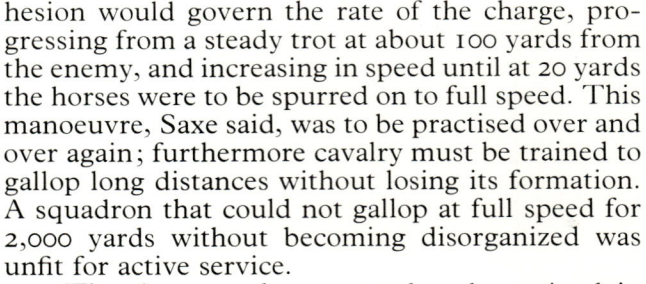

The dragoons he expected to be trained in skirmishing and also to carry out the same manoeuvres as the cavalry. In battle he allotted the duties normally given to hussars (sallying out for sudden attacks, returning and reforming at speed, etc.) to the third, or rear, rank of the dragoons. Dragoons were to be employed in the conventional cavalry tasks, *ie* as scouts, escorts, dispatch riders and so on, and moreover were to act as infantry if necessary. When dismounted, the front rank of dragoons would retain the the lance for use as a pike, and the outside files would remain mounted. All troopers would carry the long cavalry sword and the infantry musket. They were not armoured, but were to wear stout hide coats with sleeves, and leather gauntlets, and shoes and gaiters in place of the cavalry riding boots which hampered dismounted men. If properly trained, Saxe argued, dragoons were infinitely more valuable than hussars, for they would be just as fast, but more steady. To achieve this standard they were always to be out, always in contact with the enemy. Heavy cavalry couldn't catch them, hussars couldn't touch them. A troop of 50 dragoons, he maintained, had nothing to fear from a horde of hussars.

Such were the views of the great Marshal Saxe. In some ways, as with the reintroduction of full armour, or the readoption of pike and heavy lance, he seems behind his times, but in others, such as the introduction of a breech-loading carbine, and the abolition of the fashionable frills of military tailoring, he was very much ahead of them. And his insistence that all dragoons be trained to do the work of light cavalry anticipated actual developments by more than a century. His influence was considerable, and although full armour did not return, French cuirassiers wore breast- *and* backplate until 1914, while the low proportion of hussars in the army of the *ancien régime* may well have reflected his distrust of them.

A TROOPER EQUIPPED *À LA SAXE* RETURNS FROM FORAGING. HE IS ARMED WITH A RIFLED CARBINE AND PROTECTED BY A SUIT OF ARMOUR OF 'THIN IRON PLATES FIXED UPON A STRONG BUFF-SKIN'. FROM THE ENGLISH EDITION, PUBLISHED IN 1757, OF MARSHAL SAXE'S *RÊVERIES, OR MEMOIRS UPON THE ART OF WAR.*

THE AGE OF FREDERICK THE GREAT

VOLUNTEERS OF MARSHAL SAXE: AN UHLAN AND A DRAGOON ARMED WITH A CARBINE. RAISED IN 1743, THEY WERE DRAWN FROM NOBLE VOLUNTEERS OF TARTAR, POLISH AND LITHUANIAN ORIGIN; EACH UHLAN HAD A DRAGOON AS A PERSONAL SERVANT. FROM DE NOIRMONT AND DE MARBOT.

THE CAVALRY

THE HUSSAR

As has already been mentioned, the need for light irregular cavalry became evident early in the 17th century, and the Hapsburg Emperors needed to look no further than the plains of Hungary to find a race of wild horsemen for whom riding was almost as natural as walking. The employment by monarchs of their wilder subjects in a military role which preserved their distinctive appearance and personal characteristics was by no means unique to Austria-Hungary. The Russian Cossacks were another example, as were the Scottish Highlanders, whose tartan plaid, dirk and plumed headdress were regarded by 18th-century citizens of Edinburgh in much the same way as their contemporaries in Boston regarded the blanket, scalping-knife and war-bonnet of Indian braves.

An equally close parallel can be drawn between the mounted herdsmen of the east European plains and the cowboys of America's Western prairies. Both spent much of their working lives in the saddle, both were expert horsemen, mounted on clever cow ponies trained to cut in and out while their riders' hands were busy with rope or weapon. Both were accustomed to bearing arms and using them at their own discretion, against wild beasts that preyed upon their cattle, or against robbers, or marauding war parties - Indian or Turkish respectively. Both, indeed, saw articles of their working dress adopted by regular cavalrymen, in the United States the wide-brimmed hat and neck scarf, in Austria the fur-trimmed pelisse, embroidered jacket and fur cap. The virtues of these men as light horsemen, able to gallop where they wished, accustomed to act on their own initiative, and literally to ride rings round the stiff ranks of heavy cavalry, were readily apparent.

The original Hussars were raised by the Hapsburgs, wardens of Christendom's south-eastern flank against the Turks. To populate and guard these distant Marches, they established a broad belt, the Military Frontier (*Militärgrenze*), and granted the land to settlers on a system of military tenure. The frontiersmen, in return for land direct from the monarch, undertook liability for a type of militia service. This required them to turn out for local defence duties at any time, and to be embodied for full-time training or garrison duties up to four months in the year, even in peacetime. Their primary role was the immediate defence of their own provinces against border raids, and to support the regular troops in a major war by their knowledge of local conditions. The *Grenzer*, frugal, hardy and independent, formed a frontier force guarding the border from the Adriatic to Poland. They included a number of German settlers, but were mostly drawn from Hungarian, Rumanian or Slav communities. The nature of their contingents varied according to the nature of the terrain in which they dwelt. The men of the hilly and forested regions took the field as light infantry, the men of the plains as light cavalry, the hussars. All had the characteristics of light troops - the ability to operate independently or in small bands in broken country where the serried and disciplined ranks of the line were at a disadvantage, and the skill and knowledge to wage guerrilla or irregular warfare against equally mobile opponents.

The *Grenzer* system continued throughout the 17th and 18th centuries. It produced units with a high *esprit de corps* and sense of historical continuity, and, because of the circumstances in which they held their land, soldiers with a strong feeling of personal loyalty to their monarch. It was soon apparent to the Austrian generals that these military virtues could be as readily used in conventional war as in border skirmishes, and the frontiersmen were increasingly called on to support their regular comrades in campaigns against their European foes. By 1740 they numbered over 45,000 men, of whom 20,000 took part in the campaign against Prussia out of a total Austrian force of 153,000. At the beginning of the Seven Years' War they totalled 40,000 men, including 6,000 mounted troops, out of a total Austrian force of 160,000. They were available, if necessary, to thicken up the line of battle, but were primarily employed in the conventional duties of light troops - outpost work, defensive and reconnaissance patrols, scouting, raids and pursuit tasks. Because their loyalty to their land and their ruler was so firm, they were allowed a sketchier form of discipline than the soldiers of the line. They were permitted, when on detached duty, to forage for themselves, and to be free of ponderous convoys and supply magazines - those leg-irons which shackled the movement of 18th-century armies. Thus freed, they could move over the country almost at will, even in considerable force. In October 1757 Count Hadek's brigade of 3,500 troops, half of them hussars and frontier force infantry, even penetrated into Berlin, where his moderation and the good behaviour of his troops during the 24 hours they were in possession of the enemy capital attracted general admiration. Just as the inhabitants of northern and central England had been pleasurably surprised to find in 1745 that the wild Highlanders marching south with Bonnie Prince Charlie were not the savages they had expected, so too the Berliners of 1757 found the hussars were not the unscrupulous bandits which their reputation more than hinted at, but disciplined and seasoned troopers.

THE AGE OF FREDERICK THE GREAT

HUSSARS IN THE FRENCH ARMY c.1724: A *MARÉCHAL DES LOGIS* AND AN OFFICER OF THE HUSSARS OF RATTKY. FROM DE NOIRMONT AND DE MARBOT.

THE Mongols were the last of the mounted multitudes disgorged from the steppes of southern Russia to sweep into eastern Europe. Farther east, and on a more southerly front, the cavalry traditions of central Asia were carried into India by the Moguls, who invaded that subcontinent in the 16th century. Their authority was to be fiercely challenged by the Hindu Mahrattas, one of the world's great races of light horsemen. J.P.L.

STYLIZED CONTEMPORARY PRINT OF A MOGUL ARMY STORMING THE FORT AT MERTA IN 1562. QUARTER HAD BEEN OFFERED AND ACCEPTED BUT A RAJPUT, DAS DEO, TOOK IT UPON HIMSELF TO 'EXALT' SEVERAL OF EMPEROR AKBAR'S SOLDIERS 'TO THE DIGNITY OF A MARTYRDOM' WHEREAT HE AND SOME 200 OTHER RAJPUTS WERE 'EXALTED' IN SIMILAR FASHION.

THE MOGULS AND THE MAHRATTAS by JAMES LAWFORD

In the 16th century the invading Moguls imposed a Moslem rule on a Hindu India already largely ruled by Moslem princes. The early Mogul Emperors practised a religious toleration remarkable by the European standards of the day, but were more circumspect in military matters, preferring to employ Moslem mercenaries in their armies, often recruiting them from countries outside India. For the next century and a half India was largely untroubled by wars with foreign aggressors. Instead it was riven by periodic civil wars; the sons of the reigning Emperor, if they did not rebel during his lifetime, invariably contested the succession after his death.

The resulting battles in some respects resembled large-scale personal duels in which each prince, mounted on his elephant, typically sought to engage his rival in single combat; the death of one was sufficient to ensure the victory of the other, almost irrespective of the military situation at the time. Gunpowder was viewed with distaste. Foot soldiers armed with unreliable matchlock muskets were regarded as little more than menials, fit only to guard forts and encampments. Cannon were treated like ornaments, as necessary to a well-dressed army as pearls to a princess, and, as with pearls, the bigger the better. Indian cannon grew to such size they were almost immovable, and capable of firing only one round every 15 minutes; they furnished, as it were, the orchestra to the battle, sounding a rousing overture to the main performance and a suitable martial accompaniment. It was, however, the cavalry with scimitar, spear and shield, and the princes duelling on their elephants, whose task it was to decide the issue.

For such formalized encounters, the rigours of campaigning were clearly unnecessary. A Mogul army on the march carried magnificent pavilions for the princes and great nobles, and innumerable tents for those of lesser importance; with its host of servants, followers and shopkeepers of all kinds, wives and concubines, it was nothing less than a city on the march, superb in its pageantry, but slow and clumsy to manoeuvre.

In the second half of the 17th century, under Aurangzebe, the last of the great Mogul Emperors, conditions began to change. A zealous and bigoted Moslem, the Emperor drove many Hindus to revolt, and among the most notable was a Mahratta named Sivaji (pronounced See-var-jee). He created out of the hitherto peaceable Mahrattas, Hindu by persuasion, an army that came to challenge the might of Aurangzebe himself. To bolster up his strength Sivaji professed a considerable degree of piety, thus lending his wars a religious as well as a nationalistic character.

Although he was a rebel commanding an improvised army, there was nothing amateur about Sivaji's organization. He introduced a regular system of subordination with a *havildar* commanding every 25 troopers, a *jumladar* every 50, an *ek hazari* every 1,000 and a *panch hazari* every 5,000. Discipline was stern: any trooper found introducing a woman into camp faced instant execution. His tactics were based on mobility and speed. His troopers lived off the country, carrying bags attached to their saddles for food for themselves and their horses and one for plunder. They had no specific uniform, but generally wore tight cotton leggings and breeches, quilted cotton tunics, although the poorer sometimes went naked to the waist, and turbans. In a sash wound round their waists they threaded one or two light swords or scimitars; they carried shields, but their chief weapon was a spear. They rode with a long stirrup and their bridles consisted of a single headstall with a fierce bit; they used another as a martingale.

A MOGUL ARMY ON THE MARCH. DARA, THE ELDEST SON OF SHAH JAHAN, THE EMPEROR WHO BUILT THE TAJ MAHAL, IS SHOWN SEATED ON HIS ELEPHANT. HE MET A FATE NOT UNUSUAL FOR A MOGUL PRINCE, BEING DEFEATED AND EXECUTED WHEN BATTLING FOR THE SUCCESSION.

THE CAVALRY

Their horses, bred near the upper reaches of the Godaveri, were small but hardy. The Mahrattas cherished their horses and were reluctant to drive them against the musketry and grape of European armies, but in cavalry combat they were fearless. Although organized in troops they tended to fight as individuals.

They lived hard, and Sivaji set the example in frugal living. It is told that an enemy general, anxious to study the features of his opponent, commissioned an artist to paint him. The artist successfully gained an entry into the Mahratta camp, but searched in vain for the trappings of royalty. At last he asked a soldier where he would find the great Sivaji; the soldier pointed out a trooper who, with his spear slung across his back, was sitting nearby on his horse munching some grain, while his horse fed from a nosebag.

Sivaji based himself on a number of inaccessible mountain strongholds built in the Western Ghauts of the Indian peninsula. From these he issued with his cavalry to enclose the slow-moving Mogul armies in a shifting ring of light horsemen too fleet for the heavier Moguls to catch. When the Mogul armies, their foraging parties ruthlessly cut down by their elusive foe, were eventually forced to retreat, the Mahratta cavalry swooped down in a series of deadly charges.

Sivaji died, and his generals, become great princes, broke away from his dynasty to form a loose alliance known as the Mahratta Confederacy. By following his guerrilla tactics, however, they made the Confederacy one of the most formidable powers in 18th-century India. But with success came dissension. The successful generals founded dynasties of their own; their heirs began to succumb to luxurious living and to forget the precepts of their great founder. Then on 14 January 1761 at Panipat (pronounced Par-nee-putt) the Confederacy fought one of the great cavalry battles of the age against the Afghans.

In August 1759, Ahmad Shah Abdalli, the fierce marauding King of Afghanistan, made one of his periodic invasions of India. In part he came to aid his fellow countrymen, known as Rohillas, who had settled in the hill areas of Rohilcund to the north and east of Delhi and were being mercilessly harried by the Mahrattas. He swept through northwest India driving the armies of two Mahratta chieftains, Holkar and Sindia, before him like sheep before wolves. The heartland of the Mahrattas lay in the Deccan to the south and here the aged Peshwa, Balaji Rao, the head of the Confederacy, issued a clarion call to the Mahratta princes to forget their differences and unite against the invader. They answered the call and the most magnificent of all Mahratta armies assembled. Balaji Rao placed his young cousin, not yet 30 years old, Sadashiv Rao, in charge of it and dispatched his young son and heir, the 19-year-old Vishwas Rao, nominally to command it.

Sadashiv Rao, commonly called the Bhao (pronounced like the bough of a tree), arrived fresh from triumphs in southern India; and on 25 March 1760, he confidently marched north. But his was no army such as Sivaji would have recognized. Its main strength still lay with about 50,000 Mahratta horsemen, but the Bhao took with him a heavy train of artillery and nine regiments of finely disciplined infantry under Ibrahim Khan Gardi;

ADVANCED GUARD OF A MAHRATTA ARMY NEAR SERINGAPATAM.

these were armed with flintlocks and had been trained by the French under Bussy. In addition an immense baggage train and a multitude of followers, women and children accompanied the army.

The Bhao's army slowly wandered towards Delhi. By 30 May he reached Gwalior to find that Ahmad Shah Abdalli had crossed the Jumna into the Doab, the area between that river and the Ganges, to succour the Rohillas still harassed by a Mahratta force of irregulars under an elderly general called Govind Pant. The monsoon broke early that year; the rivers rose and the Jumna became impassable. The Bhao, after a long halt by the Chambal River, resumed his leisurely progress towards Delhi, which, being on the left bank of the Jumna, was now cut off from the Afghans. He announced triumphantly to the Peshwa, 'My capture of Delhi has broken his waist.' And indeed the Afghan king at Anupshahar, east of the Jumna

THE MOGULS AND THE MAHRATTAS

and now nearly isolated from Afghanistan, looked lost.

He wrote to the Bhao asking for terms, but met with a lofty refusal. However, as the monsoon rains poured down, no Indian princes came in to join the Mahrattas; meanwhile Shuja-ud-daula, the ruler of the powerful State of Oudh, had declared for the Afghan. Despite this defection the Bhao remained supremely confident. In October, as the monsoon died away, he left a garrison at Delhi and struck northwards to Kunjpura, a fortress on the west bank of the Jumna where Ahmad Shah Abdalli had stored immense quantities of food and equipment. With the fortress (the main base of the Afghans) in his hands and the river line held, the invaders would face eventual starvation. On 17 October the Mahrattas stormed Kunjpura, massacring most of the garrison. Then, fatally, the Bhao paused to plunder the area thoroughly and enjoy the provisions of which his army stood in some need.

The Afghan, though agonisingly powerless to aid his garrison, contrived shrewdly to exploit the Mahratta move. Reconnaissance parties searching the eastern bank of the Jumna found a deep, narrow but unguarded ford at Baghpat, 26 miles north of Delhi. Gambling on the careless watch kept by the Mahrattas, the Afghan king drove his army across; thousands were reported drowned, but in two days he was established on the western bank of the Jumna and next day, 27 October 1760, he thrust northwards, scattering a weak Mahratta patrol in his path. Now he had dramatically turned the tables on his adversary. He had partially opened his own communications to the west and trapped the Mahrattas in the north.

Following this reverse the Bhao, certain that his enemy lacked the means to sustain himself, moved south 40 miles to the town of Panipat and set about constructing an enormous fortified camp there. On 1 November the Afghans came in sight. The Abdalli halted and started to erect a fortified camp about three miles south of the Mahrattas and astride the road to Delhi. Both sides, being across each other's main line of communication, settled down to starve each other out.

The space between the two camps might have been designed as an arena for cavalry combat. Seven miles to the east of Panipat flowed the broad Jumna, its main stream beginning to contract from its monsoon limits; to the west of the river and south of the town stretched a wide and level plain, spotted here and there by huddled, mud-walled, empty villages, the occasional copse of trees, and the gleaming white tombs or shrines of Moslem holy men. Perhaps 15 or 20 miles to the west the plain came to an end.

During November, in almost daily combats the Afghans on their heavier Turki horses gradually came to dominate the arena. In December an attack by Rohilla tribesmen just before sunset penetrated the Mahratta camp, and they were only expelled after a bloody combat in which Mehendale, one of the Bhao's best generals, was killed. Then in the Doab came disaster: Govind Pant had been collecting food there for the Mahratta army, and preventing provisions from reaching the Afghans; now the Abdalli sent 5,000 Afghan horse across the river, and they, moving with incredible speed, surprised the Mahratta force, not least their general who at the time was having a bath. Govind Pant was killed scrambling half-naked onto his horse, his troops were dispersed in confusion and his less mobile convoy of supplies captured.

After this success the Afghans adopted the tactics that in the past had so often brought the Mahrattas success. Masses of their cavalry day and night hung about the outskirts of Panipat, cutting up foraging parties and preventing the passage of supplies. Conditions inside the Mahratta camp, where more than 100,000 men, women and children were cooped up, steadily deteriorated. Food became scarce and costly, animals died, sanitation ceased to exist and a miasma of putrefaction everywhere tainted the atmosphere. The Mahrattas began to starve and disease was rife. Tethered by his host of followers and enormous baggage train, there was no escape for the Bhao save by decisively beating his adversary. As he hesitated, the Afghan king coolly waited for the Mahrattas to disintegrate. The Bhao sent envoys to

THE CAVALRY

the Abdalli to plead for almost any terms. The Afghan soldiers crowded round them shouting that the infidels must perish and that Islam should not be robbed of its triumph for a handful of gold. The envoys departed empty-handed. By 13 January 1761 the conditions in the camp had become utterly intolerable. The Mahratta chiefs came in a body to the Bhao and pointed out that they must fight or die where they stood; they concluded, 'Let us make a valiant struggle against the foe, and then what fate has ordained will be.' The Bhao declared they would fight next day. At midnight he sent a last despairing message to Shuja-ud-daula, the ruler of Oudh, appealing for a change of heart: 'The flood has risen above my head; if anything can be done, do it, or else inform me plainly at once, for hereafter there will be no time for writing or speaking.' There was no reply.

An hour before a bitterly cold dawn, the Mahratta army began to file out of their camp to form up on the plain to the south. The brilliant stars paled and disappeared; light from the east spread across the clear dark sky. The Bhao, sitting with Vishwas Rao in the howda of his elephant, the great yellow Royal banner of the Confederacy floating overhead, halted his elephant by a black mango tree in the middle of the wide plain to watch his army deploy. His early arrogance had gone, replaced by a fatalistic resolve to die in a manner befitting his birth. As the skies lightened, rank on rank, a host of horsemen filed out of the fortified camp behind him, the riders silent and stern, the ends of their turbans hanging loose and their faces daubed with saffron to signify that they would conquer or die. Over a distance of seven miles the battle line gradually formed on the grassy plain. On the left or eastern flank Ibrahim Khan Gardi with his finely drilled infantry battalions some 8,000 strong took post, supported by Damaji Gaekwar, Prince of Gujerat, with his cavalry. In the centre 20,000 picked Mahratta horsemen formed up, line on line, under the personal command of the Bhao. On the right or western flank the ruling princes of the Houses of Holkar and Sindia arrayed their troops, hanging a little back from the line.

Then a vast train of artillery crawled across the plain; 200 heavy cannon and carts bearing rockets, with the rocketeers stepping beside them, swung ponderously into action ahead of the battle line. By now the sun had risen on the restless multitude of horsemen, the foot soldiers, the elephants, the bullocks and the cold dark metal of the guns thronging the plain outside the camp, while inside it thousands of women, some with their children, and a crowd of followers wondered with foreboding what nightfall would bring.

Two miles to the south, Ahmad Shah Abdalli strode out of the little red tent in which he had been sleeping and mounted

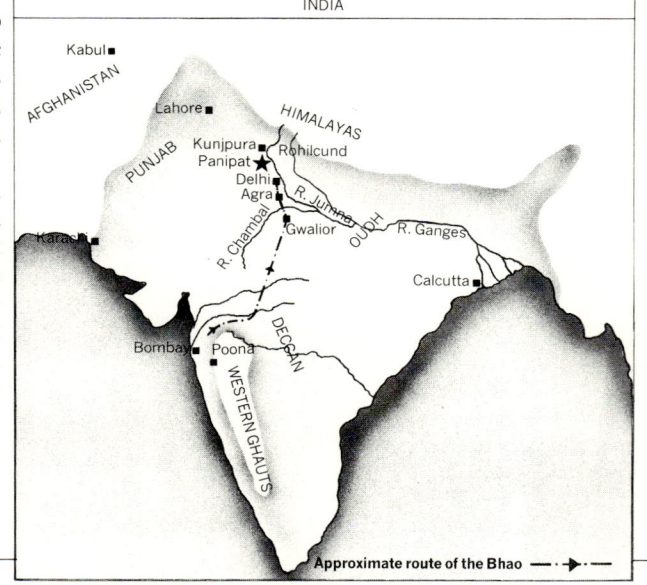

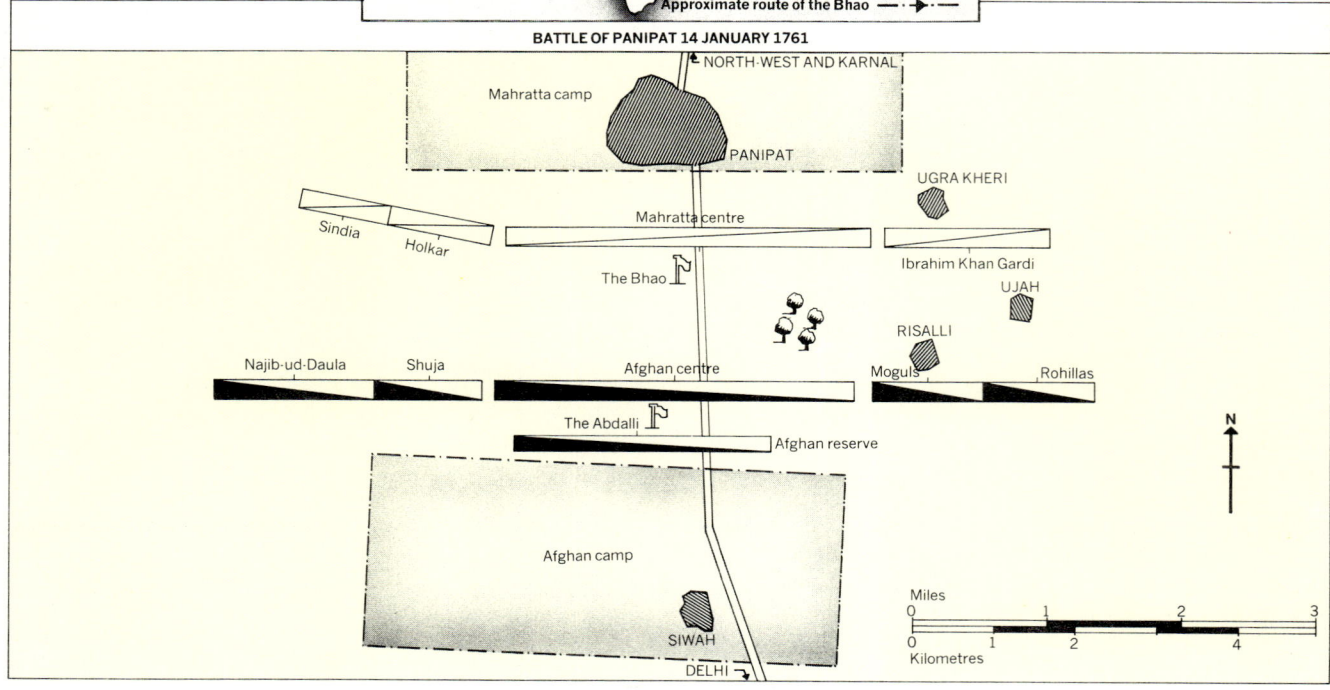

126

the horse always tethered ready and saddled outside it. As away to the north he saw the shadowy host assembling, he recognized that the day of decision had arrived. Scorning to skulk behind his entrenchments, he summoned his host to form in the plain. He placed on his right or eastern flank Rohilla and Mogul horse and foot, in the centre 10,000 Afghan cavalrymen, their sturdy Turki horses backed by 7,000 Persian musketeers, the whole under his chief minister, the Grand Vizier Shah Wali Khan, and on the left the infantry and cavalry of the inflexible Shuja-ud-daula of Oudh and more troops from Rohilcund under their prince, Najib-ud-daula. Najib had a long and bitter score to settle with Jankoji Sindia, whose banners he could now see waving across the plain in front of him.

The Afghan king himself commanded no part of the battle line. He remained in the rear where he could observe undisturbed how the battle progressed, and kept under his hand a reserve consisting of the 2,000 horsemen of the Royal Guard, 10,000 Afghan cavalry, and a corps of 1,000 camels bearing swivel guns on their backs. His artillery, numbering about 40 cannon, were deployed in front of his troops. The Afghan army consisted in total of about 60,000 men, that of the Mahrattas, wasted by battle and disease, little more than 45,000.

In the early sunlight the long line of Mahratta guns spouted flame and smoke, but the clear air deceived the gunners; they fired high, and the spluttering rockets, pursuing their usual uncertain course, inflicted little damage. Impatiently the Mahrattas surged forward, masking their cannon. On their right Ibrahim Khan Gardi's infantry clashed with the Rohillas and Moguls; although outnumbered their regular volleys tore gaps in the ranks of their foes; by midday, at the cost of a third of their number, they had triumphed; save for a few Rohillas packed round their chiefs, the rest of that wing were streaming away to the safety of their camp.

In the centre, wave after wave of Mahratta horse swept down on the Afghans. Some 30,000 horsemen became locked in mortal combat; the dust rose in white, powdery clouds cloaking the scene; a group of horsemen would suddenly loom out of the murk with only their harsh battle cries to identify them, the 'Din, Din' or 'Ya Ali' of the Muslims being answered by the 'Hur, Hur, Mahardayv' of the Mahrattas. As charge succeeded charge, the Afghan centre began to break up. By midday the Grand Vizier, clad from head to foot in armour, had dismounted and with a remnant of his men was fighting desperately to hold his ground. Only on the Mahratta left the soldiers of Holkar and Sindia, remembering their earlier defeats, hung back, while Najib-ud-daula, dreading the fierce charge of the Mahrattas, entrenched his position and awaited their assault.

The Abdalli, dispassionately watching the battle, judged that the crisis had arrived. The wild Mahratta charges were losing their impetus. He sent his royal guards round the camp with their whips to chase every soldier they could find back onto the battlefield, ordered his reserve of 10,000 Afghan horse and 1,000 camel swivel gunners to charge into the dust-wreathed chaos in the centre, and directed Najib-ud-daula to advance as soon as he saw the reserve move forward.

The stroke proved decisive. The strength of the half-starved Mahrattas, without food since before the dawn, was draining away. The fresh Afghan horse wielding sword, spear and battle-axe spread havoc in their ranks. The young prince Vishwas Rao died from a musket ball. The Bhao, descending from his elephant, mounted a horse and disappeared into the maelstrom, never to be seen again. On the right, Ibrahim Khan Gardi's infantry reeled back before fresh waves of Rohillas and Moguls. Damaji Gaekwar, his flank exposed by the crumbling Mahratta centre, withdrew, leaving the infantry to their fate. On the left Najib's and Shuja-ud-daula's men surged forward. Holkar early quitted the field; Jankoji Sindia was wounded, captured and later executed. Now the Mahratta centre was partially surrounded. To complete their ruin the Afghan king encircled them with mounted musketeers who poured in a volley then galloped away to reload. By 3 pm the Mahrattas were streaming away in a disorganized mob, while in a huge crescent the Afghans rode them down. Before nightfall perhaps 20,000 Mahrattas had fallen, and their camp lay at the mercy of a merciless foe.

Far to the south of the Indian subcontinent, Balaji Rao received the terrible news in a cryptic letter that stated: 'Two pearls have been dissolved, 27 golden mohurs have been lost and of silver and copper the total cannot be cast up.' It was too much for him; he was seized by fits of melancholia and on 23 June he expired. In March the Abdalli, his own army terribly mauled, returned to Afghanistan never to invade India again. Mahratta power was resurrected; but although not yet entirely ended, the great days of the Mahratta cavalry had already passed, and soon it was the red-coated British infantry that were to dominate the dusty plains of central India.

THE TAKING OF DELHI BY THE PERSIAN KING, NADIR SHAH, IN 1739. ELEPHANTS WERE RARELY SO EFFECTIVE AS THEY HAVE BEEN PORTRAYED IN THIS PICTURE.

TOWARDS the end of the 18th century military organizations and tactics reached a peak of efficiency probably never surpassed. But as the infantry and artillery came increasingly into their own so the role of the cavalry diminished in importance; cavalry remained an essential ingredient of an army, but the latter now depended for effective action on the harmonious blending of all three arms. The stirrup had given cavalry nearly total supremacy for all but 1,000 years; in the 15th and 16th centuries that supremacy suffered an eclipse only to re-emerge in the 17th its lustre scarcely dimmed. But in the latter part of the 18th century, thanks to the flintlock and field gun, the cavalry slipped back to the position it had held before the invention of the stirrup. Cavalry now hesitated to charge a steady column of infantry, as in Alexander's day it had hesitated before the long pikes of the phalanx. But just as Alexander gained his victories by keeping a judicious balance between the various arms and using each to best advantage, so Napoleon, whose judgment was no less sure, for long seemed equally invincible. Indeed, after taking into account the differences between the weapons of both periods, the organization and tactics of the cavalry of both these great commanders show striking similarities. J.P.L.

CAVALRY FROM THE LAST DAYS OF THE OLD ROYAL FRENCH ARMY, c.1786. ON THE LEFT IS A COLONEL OF THE DRAGOONS OF CHARTRES, ON THE RIGHT A TROOPER OF THE DRAGOONS OF PONTHIEVRE. FROM DE NOIRMONT AND DE MARBOT.

THE NAPOLEONIC WARS by PETER YOUNG

The Emperor Napoleon was a mediocre horseman. According to a contemporary, 'he never used the spur, nor the pressure of the calves to set his horse at a gallop, he started it with a touch of his whip'. It is also recorded that he rode with a loose rein. But until he began to get stout after his second marriage, he was an indefatigable rider and a bold one. For example, at 7 am on 17 January 1809 he left Valladolid for Paris. At noon he passed through Burgos, having made some 80 miles in six hours on his own horses, which had been disposed beforehand in relays. Pushing on by way of Vittoria, he passed through Tolosa the next day, reaching Bayonne on the 19th, only 45 hours after leaving Valladolid; by then he had travelled more than 260 miles.

NAPOLEON I. AT THE RETREAT FROM LEIPZIG, 1813.

He rode Arab horses which were specially trained for him by his head groom, Jardin *père*, who accustomed them to all sorts of sounds and to the sight of all kinds of objects. It was reported that 'they even went as far as driving dogs or pigs between the horses' legs'. But if he himself was no great horseman Napoleon took great trouble to reorganize the mounted arm he inherited. His main reform, an astute one, was to ensure that his heavy cavalry really were big men mounted on big chargers.

In place of the 24 regiments of heavy cavalry he formed two regiments of carabineers and 12 of cuirassiers. His medium cavalry consisted of 30 regiments of dragoons, of which six were converted in 1811 into *chevau-légers*, or lancers; in all, Napoleon formed nine such regiments. His light cavalry included 31 regiments of chasseurs and 15 of hussars. In addition the Grand Army at various times embraced comparatively large numbers of Italian and German regiments. In their establishment a carabineer or cuirassier regiment had some 1,040 men in four squadrons each of two companies. A dragoon regiment had five squadrons each of two companies, some 1,200 altogether; from 1812 onwards there were sometimes two dismounted squadrons in a dragoon regiment. Light cavalry regiments also had four squadrons of two companies (troops). A company usually had 18–20 files, two deep, or about 40 men and horses.

THE CAVALRY

When, in 1805, Napoleon's Grand Army took the field for the first time it was well supplied with cavalry. The Imperial Guard had its own cavalry: the First, Second and Sixth Corps each had its own division of light cavalry; the Third, Fourth and Fifth Corps each had a brigade: only the Seventh Corps had no cavalry of its own. In addition there was the Reserve of Cavalry, 22,000 sabres, under Prince Murat, comprising seven divisions, two heavy, composed of cuirassiers and carabineers, four medium (dragoons), and one of dismounted dragoons.

The cavalry was organized in divisions, brigades and regiments, but the tactical unit was really the squadron. This consisted of two companies, each of two platoons composed of 36–40 troopers. A squadron formed in line, or in column, by platoons. It was a simple matter for a properly drilled squadron to form line of battle from column, or to resume column. The charge was made at the gallop, and usually in echelon of squadrons, regiments or brigades. Sometimes attacks were made in close columns, for though this offered the enemy a splendid target, it was sometimes useful when cavalry sought to exploit a tactical opportunity.

Strictly contemporary cavalry manuals have nothing to say about security or reconnaissance: Napoleon's generals learned what he required of them by the light of nature. Then, as ever, the success of a regiment depended not so much on the training manuals as on the skill of its officer corps. Even though there were no regulations for training in outpost duties, Napoleon's writings show that he himself had a very clear idea of what he expected from his outpost commanders.

'General Steingel, an Alsatian, was an excellent Hussar Officer; he had served under Dumouriez in the campaigns of the North, and was skilful, intelligent, and vigilant; he combined the qualities of youth with those of mature age; he was a true general of out-posts. Two or three days before his death he was the first to enter Lezegno; the French General arrived there a few hours later, and whatever he wanted he found ready. The defiles and fords had been reconnoitred, guides secured, the curé and postmaster had been questioned; good understanding had already been established with the inhabitants; spies had been sent out in several directions; the letters in the post had been seized, and those affording military information translated and analysed; all the necessary measures had been taken to form magazines of provisions for the refreshment of the troops.'

Thus Napoleon in his *Campaign of Italy* described the duties of a general of light cavalry. The officer of whom he wrote was Henri-Christian-Michel, Baron de Steingel (1744–96), who in 1795 rose to become a divisional general commanding the cavalry of the Army of Italy. He was succeeded by a brilliant band of young cavalry commanders that included Lasalle, Montbrun, Edouard Colbert and Curély. Of these the most outstanding was General Lasalle.

A FRENCH STAFF OFFICER VIEWS THE COUNTRYSIDE, WHILE A TROOPER OF THE *CHASSEURS* OF THE GUARD HOLDS HIS HORSE. PAINTING BY MEISSONNIER.

A FRENCH CARABINEER. ENGRAVED FROM A PAINTING BY GÉRICAULT.

AN OFFICER OF THE *CHASSEURS À CHEVAL* OF THE IMPERIAL GUARD IN ACTION. FROM A PAINTING BY GÉRICAULT.

THE NAPOLEONIC WARS

Antoine-Charles Louis Comte de Lasalle was born at Metz on 10 May 1775, and numbered Maréchal Abraham de Fabert, Marquis d'Esternay (1599–1662) among his ancestors. He became a *sous-lieutenant* in the Alsace infantry in 1786, transferring to the 24th Regiment of Cavalry in 1791. After the Revolution he had to begin again: in 1794 he was just a trooper in the 23rd Chasseurs, but he became a *maréchal des logis* in the same year. In 1796 he served on the staffs of Generals Kellermann (father and son) in the Army of Italy. There is not room here to describe the many occasions upon which he distinguished himself. Bonaparte recognized his value and put him up for promotion to squadron commander, a compliment which he repaid by capturing an Austrian battalion at Rivoli a week later. He was one of those chosen for the expedition to Egypt, and performed prodigies of valour at the Battle of the Pyramids. He saved the life of Davout, the future marshal, at Redemieh (17 January 1800). Promoted general (1 February 1805) he commanded a brigade of the 4th and 14th Dragoons (Klein's Division, Reserve Cavalry) and led them at Austerlitz. In 1806 he had a Hussar Brigade (5th & 7th) with whom he compelled the Prussian Gendarmes of the Guard to surrender at Schleiz (9 October 1806). It was he who compelled General Hohenlohe and 6,000 men to capitulate at Prentzlow (28 October). Pushing on, he took the fortress of Stettin two days later. These exploits won him the rank of general of division (30 December 1806). He was 31. At Heilsburg he saved the life of Murat–who had managed to get himself routed (10 June 1807). In 1808, now a Count of the Empire, and enjoying an income of 50,000 francs a year from the resources of Westphalia and Hanover, he was posted to Spain where he distinguished himself in half-a-dozen

THE COMTE DE LASALLE. PAINTING BY FRANCOIS FLAMENG.

THE CAVALRY

fights, and especially when he broke Cuesta's right wing at Medellin (29 March 1809). Recalled to Germany, he then served at Essling.

Lasalle once said: 'Un hussard qui n'est pas mort à trente ans n'est qu'en Jean Foutre' (A hussar who isn't dead at thirty is a blackguard). He himself lived to be 34, as it happened. But at Wagram (5–6 July 1809) he had a presentiment. As General Thiébault's *Mémoires* record, 'He was a man to whom a battle was a treat, a charge positive enjoyment, yet, when he mounted his horse that day, he had the conviction that he would be killed. . . . Being unable to overcome his gloomy mood or to conceal his foreboding, he would have none of his officers near him; and in this frame of mind, unintelligible to his aides-de-camp . . . he received the expected musket ball in his forehead.' It was one of the last shots of the day. With the habits of a hussar, fond of women, wine, duelling and practical jokes, Lasalle was as witty as he was valiant. Count Roederer, the economist and politician, who met him at Thiébault's headquarters in 1809, thought him a man of high ability, and said so. 'He is a man of surpassing talent; his mind and his learning are no less deep than brilliant.'

Cavalry work falls under various headings which, generally speaking, include reconnaissance and outpost duty; advanced guards and flank guards; rearguards and flank guards; attack and defence, and pursuit. It may be useful by describing certain battles and combats of the Napoleonic era to show how the cavalrymen went about their work in those days.

Sergeant Parquin's account of the fight at Amstetten (6 May 1809) throws some light on the activities of an advance guard. At 10 am his regiment, which was leading General Colbert's *Brigade Infernale*, caught up with the rearguard of the Austrians, who were withdrawing on Vienna. In the next hour there was a sharp fight, but about 11 o'clock a white flag appeared and Colbert granted the enemy an hour's truce.

'The regiment had been in the saddle since daybreak; both men and horses were in need of a halt. Colonel Castex immediately gave orders for the horses to be unbridled and to be given the feed of oats which every chasseur always carried in a small sack on his mount when in the field.

'Not far from the spot where we had halted there was a swiftly flowing stream of which we made good use. We did not waste a moment of our halt. The chasseurs, since they had no wine, drank the small quantity of brandy which they always carried with them in the field. A crust of bread, flavoured with garlic, constituted their modest lunch, but they ate this cheerfully for they were certain that at noon battle would be joined with the enemy.

'Five minutes before the hour had passed, the trumpeters sounded for the regiment to mount and the colonel ordered the men to roll their cloaks and wear them in bandoleer fashion; this was the signal to the regiment that we were about to charge.' Skirmishers were sent out and just as the regiment was moving forward Colonel Castex rode past and shouted, 'Sergeant Parquin! I have your *sous-lieutenant's* commission in my sabretache!'

'Long live the Emperor!' cried Parquin, and turning to his men, who were congratulating him, said: 'Now that I am an officer I must have two horses. If I cannot take one from the Uhlans myself, I am counting on you to get me one.'

'Rest assured, sir,' they answered, 'we'll see you have some horses for your stable.' They proceeded to capture 22 Uhlans and hussars, and Parquin himself captured two excellent horses, but got himself wounded in the process—a pistol shot from one of the Barko Hussars. The enemy were 12 squadrons of lancers, recruited in Austrian Poland, and the Barko Hussars, rightly regarded as one of the best Austrian cavalry regiments. The

AN AUSTRIAN UHLAN, c.1806. FROM *MILITARY COSTUMES OF THE IMPERIAL AUSTRIAN ARMY, 1800–12*, BY J. AND H. MANSFELD.

THE NAPOLEONIC WARS

defeated Austrians lost some 300 men in this rough bout. Parquin's captures were a black horse with a short tail which had belonged to an officer of the Barko Hussars, whom he had shot and killed, and the charger of an Uhlan whom he had wounded. He left the charger in the care of Trumpeter Saron, aged 12.

Next is a description of a rearguard action which took place at Benavente in Spain on 29 December 1808, five days after the British commander, Sir John Moore, had begun his retreat on Corunna. General Lefèbvre-Desnoüettes, commanding the cavalry of the Imperial Guard, decided to cross the River Esla and press Moore's withdrawal. Finding a ford he crossed with the Chasseurs of the Guard, perhaps 550 strong. The British piquets, mainly 18th Light Dragoons, concentrated to resist him. As soon as he had collected about 130 sabres Lieutenant-Colonel Loftus William Otway charged the leading French squadrons with indifferent success.

Reinforced by Major Burgwedel and a troop of the 3rd Dragoons, King's German Legion, the British returned to the charge. They broke through the front rank of the Chasseurs, and though very nearly cut off by the second line, carved their way out. The brigade commander, Charles Stewart, rallied them and fell back on his supports. Lord Paget, with the 10th Hussars (450 sabres) under cover of the houses of the southern suburbs of Benavente, was invisible to Lefèbvre-Desnoüettes. When Paget came spurring out, Stewart's men (200 sabres) wheeled about, cheered and charged as well. The chasseurs, 'fine big fellows in fur caps and long green coats', put up a brave fight, but in vain. Within a few minutes they were routed, and pursued two miles to the ford. Lefèbvre-Desnoüettes, whose wounded horse refused to swim the river, fell into the hands of a German dragoon named Bergmann and of Private Grisdale of the 10th. Two captains and 70 unwounded chasseurs were taken, and Larrey, the Emperor's surgeon, had to treat another 70 wounded. The Mamelukes also suffered on this occasion; an officer was killed and another wounded.

Napoleon consoled himself with writing to his Empress that the British were 'flying in panic'. To his brother Joseph, he was more candid: 'This affair has cost me some 60 of my chasseurs. You can imagine how disagreeable that has been to me.' It may be doubted whether this favourite *corps d'élite* was ever more roughly handled, though it was to suffer heavily in charging the squares at Waterloo. The British, meanwhile, had suffered some 50 casualties, mostly among the piquets. The German, Burgwedel, was the only officer wounded.

By the time of the Napoleonic Wars it had become exceptional for cavalry to break properly formed squares of infantry. One such exception took place on 23 July 1812 at Garcia Hernandez in Spain. The French were retreating after being heavily defeated at Salamanca on the previous day. Their rearguard was led by a young general of outstanding ability, Baron Foy. The 1st Division, which he commanded, was the only one which had not suffered heavily on the previous day. It had the support of a brigade of chasseurs from General Baron Curto's light cavalry, and was further strengthened by the guns of a battery of artillery.

Wellington himself, the victor of Salamanca, rode with Major-General George Anson's brigade, the advanced guard of the pursuit, and was well forward when at about 10 am the light dragoons came upon Foy's rearguard behind the Caballero brook and in and around the village of Garcia Hernandez. Wellington, seeing only the chasseurs, determined to dispose of them without delay in order to push on in pursuit of the French infantry. Anson had only four squadrons up, two each from the 11th and 16th Light Dragoons, but Major-General Bock's brigade was not far behind. Anson was to attack the chasseurs from the front, and Bock would turn their right flank.

Wellington sent an aide-de-camp, Lieutenant-Colonel John May. He found the Germans galloping up a narrow valley in sections of threes. On hearing what he was to do Bock gave the command, 'On the move – Line to the front!', which considering the ground, was not really possible. It does seem, however, to have got the column into a sort of echelon of squadrons. Bock, who was very short-sighted, then said to May: 'But you will show us the enemy?' They galloped on with the leading squadron making straight for the right flank of the French cavalry. These, shaken by their experiences at Salamanca, for the most part decided that it was time to be gone, and, when the Light Dragoons attacked, rode to the rear in some confusion. Bock's leading squadron pushed on in pursuit, and was thrown into disorder when a French square fired into its flank.

Foy, meanwhile, had begun to retreat, but when the British cavalry advanced, he halted. He had two battalions from each of the 76th Line and 6th Light: some 2,400 bayonets. The German squadron leaders could have asked for orders from Bock had they wanted to; instead they simply used their initiative, of which they had plenty. The 3rd squadron (120 strong) was already getting up speed, when Captain Gustavus von der Decken shouted the order to throw forward the right wing and ride home on the French square. They received two vollies from one of the battalions of the 76th, at 80 and 20 yards, and the captain and a number of men fell. A mortally wounded horse, rearing and kicking, came down on the kneeling front rank of the French, knocking the men to right and left. Leaping over them the dragoons broke into the rear ranks and the square disintegrated. Many were cut down and more surrendered: perhaps 50 out of 600 got away. Of course, not more than about 200 could bring their muskets to bear, but 400 rounds at close range might have been expected to stop a single squadron. Instead the battalion had ceased to exist.

Observing this disaster, Colonel Molard of the 6th Light ordered his men to withdraw uphill. He hoped to reach ground inaccessible to cavalry. The 6th had not formed square, and now struggled in two columns up the steep slope. Seeing what they were up to, Captain von Reizenstein, commanding the second squadron of the 1st Dragoons, King's German Legion, put on the pace. Two of the rearmost French companies turned about and fired a volley. Before they could reload, however, the dragoons were among them and they were cut up. Their action saved the rest of the battalion, which

THE CAVALRY

scrambled up the hill in a mass and joined their other battalion, this having now managed to form some sort of square on the crest. A squadron or so of chasseurs was drawn up on one flank.

The difficult slope did not stop the German dragoons. The leading squadrons of the 2nd Heavy Dragoons, King's German Legion, and part of the 1st, galloped 300 yards uphill and charged home. The French chasseurs did not wait for them: the ill-formed square of the 6th broke up, many of the men throwing down their muskets, others running in droves towards the rest of the division. On swept the dragoons, sabring fugitives, and eventually charging the squares of the 69th Line. This regiment held firm. Captain von Uslar was killed and eventually the Germans withdrew under a withering fire.

We turn now to the art of the pursuit. On 14 October 1806 the Emperor Napoleon and Marshal Davout shattered the Prussian Army at Jena and Auerstadt, capturing some 25,000 men and 200 guns. The remnants of King Frederick William III's army withdrew in horrid disorder. At 5 am on the 15th Napoleon issued his orders for a general pursuit. By that time Murat was already at Weimar, while Bernadotte, whose corps – to his shame – had played no part in the battles of the 14th, was near Apolda. The Emperor's plan was to press the Prussians with his main body, consisting of Murat (Reserve Cavalry), Soult and Ney (IV and VI Corps), whilst enveloping them with the corps of Bernadotte, Davout, Lannes and Augereau (I, III, V and VII).

Murat reached Erfurt on 16 October, rounding up some 10,000 prisoners on the way. General Blücher narrowly avoided being trapped by Klein and Lasalle. Next day the Duke of Württemberg, whose 13,000 men were virtually the only intact Prussian force remaining, imprudently accepted battle at Halle. General Dupont, with Bernadotte's leading division, came up with him after a swift advance of 17 miles, and inflicted a loss of 5,000 men upon him. The French estimated their losses at 800. Meanwhile the King of Prussia had fled, leaving the unfortunate Prince Hohenlohe to concentrate what remained of his field army at the fortress of Magdeburg. On 21 October the Prince began to retreat on Stettin, a strong garrison remaining in Magdeburg. On the 25th Davout's Corps entered Berlin at the head of the Grand Army; but the pleasure of making a triumphal entry into the enemy capital did not diminish the momentum of the pursuit. Hohenlohe, pressed by Murat, Bernadotte and Lannes, was not to be permitted to reach the comparative safety of the

THE BATTLE OF JENA (1806). THE BATTLEFIELD IS SEEN FROM THE LOW HILL CALLED THE WINDKNOLLE, RIGHT FOREGROUND, NEAR WHICH NAPOLEON HAD HIS HEADQUARTERS, THE VIEW EXTENDING NORTH-WEST TO THE DORNBERG, MIDDLEGROUND CENTRE, HELD BY THE RUSSIAN GENERAL TAUENZIEN. THE DIVISIONS OF SUCHET AND GAZAN ARE ATTACKING THE DORNBERG IN ORDER TO GAIN ROOM FOR NAPOLEON TO DEPLOY THE 150,000 FRENCHMEN NOW MASSED AGAINST PRINCE HOHENLOHE'S 38,000 PRUSSIANS. IN THE FOREGROUND NAPOLEON IS ISSUING ORDERS; A BATTALION OF THE GUARD IS ON HIS RIGHT WHILE THE GUARD ARTILLERY IS IN ACTION ON THE WINDKNOLLE ITSELF.

THE NAPOLEONIC WARS

AT JENA, THE PRUSSIANS ARE GIVING WAY UNDER HEAVY FRENCH PRESSURE. NAPOLEON HAS ORDERED MURAT TO CHARGE WITH ALL AVAILABLE CAVALRY. HERE HE IS LEADING SEVEN REGIMENTS OF LIGHT CAVALRY, TWO OF DRAGOONS AND TWO OF CUIRASSIERS DOWN ON THE PRUSSIANS. SCORNING TO DRAW HIS SABRE, MURAT IS BRANDISHING A RIDING CROP. PAINTING BY H. CHARTIER.

fortress of Stettin. The Prussians were slowed down by combats at Zehdenick (26th) and Passewalk (28th), where Milhaud with some 700 French cavalry induced 4,000 Prussian horse to surrender; the Gascon Murat persuaded Hohenlohe that he was surrounded by 100,000 Frenchmen, and on 28 October he surrendered at Prentzlau with 10,000 men and 64 guns. On the 29th Lasalle (V Corps) appeared before Stettin with his brigade (5th and 7th Hussars) and General von Romberg capitulated without more ado. History affords few examples of the capture of fortresses by brigades of light cavalry.

Meanwhile Blücher, having failed to effect a

THE CAVALRY

junction with the Duke of Weimar, had thrown himself into the Danish port of Lübeck, where he in turn was compelled to surrender (7 November). On 10 November General von Kleist capitulated at Magdeburg: 22,000 men with 600 guns fell into the hands of the French. Thus in little more than a single month the Prussian Army, and its Frederician legend of invincibility, was wiped out. The casualties of the French in these operations were remarkably light. As for the cavaliers who lived through those astonishing weeks, they had one very practical reward for their long rides, their hard work and their bluff: thousands of excellent Prussian chargers found their way into the remount depots.

Extraordinary as were the incidents just described, the real cavalry climax of the age occurred on 18 June 1815 at the Battle of Waterloo. This monumental battle, in which the fate of Napoleon's empire was finally decided, may be described as falling into six phases. (The timings given below are approximate.)

Phase I. 11.30 am. The attack by units of II Corps (Reille) on the Château of Hougoumont, which went on throughout the battle.

Phase II. 1.30 pm. The attack by I Corps (d'Erlon) on the sector of Wellington's position east of the Charleroi–Brussels road, This followed a preliminary bombardment by a battery of 84 guns, which lasted about an hour and a half.

Phase III. 3.30 pm. Ney's cavalry attacks between La Haie Sainte and Hougoumont.

Phase IV. 6–6.30 pm. The capture of La Haie Sainte. By the time the French captured La Haie Sainte the Prussians had taken Plancenoit, which changed hands again twice thereafter.

Phase V. General assault on Wellington's line, whose left has now been joined by von Ziethen's Prussian Corps.

Phase VI. The pursuit of the defeated French army.

The only French cavalry involved in Phase I were Piré's Division, covering Reille's left flank, which was observed by the vedettes of the 15th Hussars. There was some fighting, especially when at about 4 pm Wathiez's Brigade tried to make a diversion in favour of Ney's cavalry. The French lancers were attacked by the 13th Light Dragoons and the 15th Hussars from Major-General Sir Colquhoun Grant's 5th Light Brigade. But Grant recognized a diversion when he saw one, and leaving a squadron of the 15th to observe Piré, concentrated his brigade in support of the infantry squares.

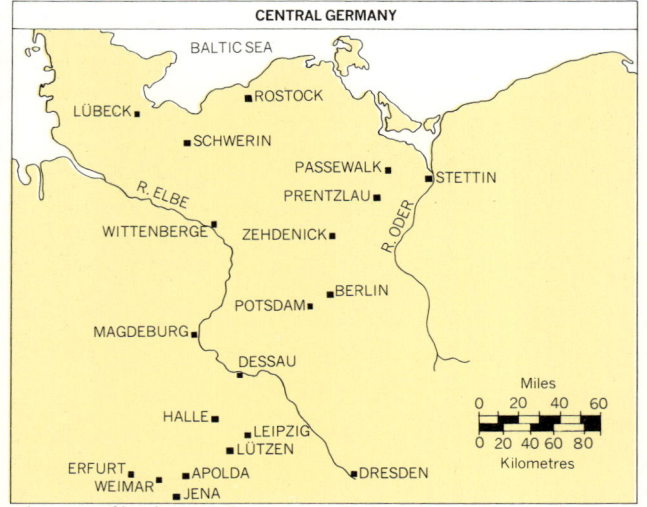

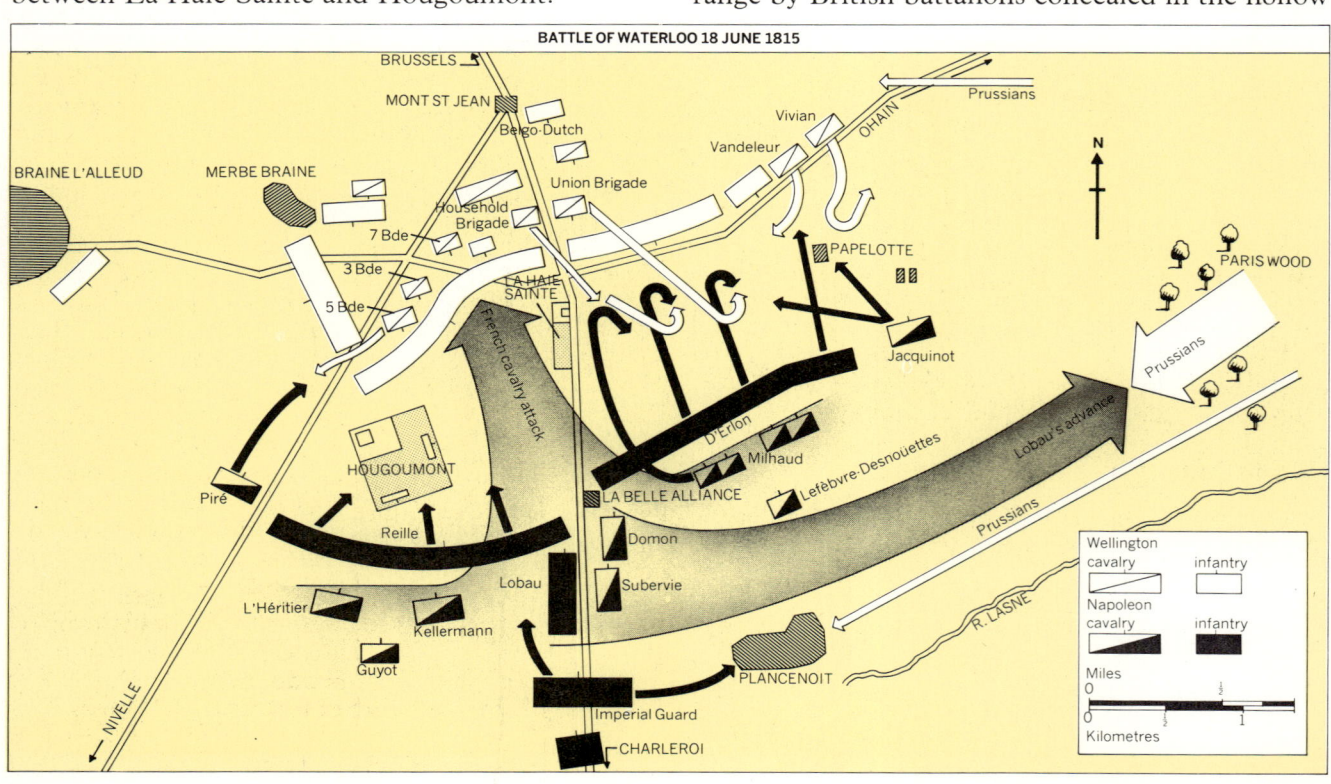

At the beginning of Phase II, when d'Erlon's Corps advanced to the attack, it had the support of the leading brigades of each of Milhaud's two divisions of cuirassiers (Farine and Travers). D'Erlon had three infantry divisions; on the right that of Durutte, charged by the brigade of Vandeleur, extricated itself fairly lightly, and in addition captured Papelotte Farm. The divisions of Marcognet and Donzelot, advancing in clumsy columns, were suddenly fired on at close range by British battalions concealed in the hollow road. They had just reached the crest of the British position, when they were charged by the Union Brigade (Major-General Sir William Ponsonby) and routed with heavy casualties and the loss of three eagles. The Union Brigade, carried away by the excitement of the moment, galloped on down the slope and, instead of endeavouring to rally, rode into the grand battery, sabring the gunners and drivers.

Meanwhile, Travers, having ridden down a German battalion advancing to reinforce the farm-house of La Haie Sainte, was charged and routed by the Household Cavalry Brigade (Major-General Lord Edward Somerset). Farine counter-attacked the Union Brigade, and Napoleon, reacting with admirable promptitude, sent in Gobrecht's brigade of Jacquinot's cavalry division, which counter-charged the disordered British dragoons, inflicting heavy casualties and killing Ponsonby. With the greatest difficulty the survivors made their way back to the British position. The two brigades had lost something like 1,000 of their 2,500 men, but they had wrecked two of d'Erlon's three regiments of dragoons, and had also hit Travers's brigade extremely hard. But of Ponsonby's brigade after the charge 'there did not remain efficient above a squadron'.

Lieutenant Charles Wyndham, who was wounded twice in the charge, described the counterattack of Gobrecht's brigade. 'The Lancers of the French, in open column, came close by me, and were evidently going in pursuit of our wounded and dismounted men, but did not attack the small main body of our Regiment. If we had been supported here, many of our poor fellows would have been saved; these Lancers did much havoc, and at Brussels, some weeks afterwards, I found many of our men with 10 or 12 lance wounds in them, and one man, Lock, had 17 or 18 about his person, and lived afterwards to tell the story.'

The lancers were themselves attacked in the flank by the 4th Light Cavalry Brigade (Major-General Sir John Vandeleur), first by the 12th Light Dragoons, which had broken Durette's column, the only one of d'Erlon's Corps remaining intact after Ponsonby's charge; and a second time by Vandeleur himself at the head of the 16th Light Dragoons. He had, very sensibly, left the 11th Light Dragoons in reserve on the brow of the hill. The 12th sustained heavy losses, Colonel the Hon. F. C. Ponsonby being severely wounded. Lieutenant-Colonel James Hay (16th) was so badly wounded that he could not be moved from the field for eight days.

Without the intervention of Vandeleur's brigade the losses in the Union Brigade would have been even more severe. In Somerset's brigade the Royal Horse Guards, originally in support, were 'kept well in hand, and being comparatively in good order, facilitated the drawing off of the remainder of the brigade from further pursuit'.

Captain Tomkinson in his *Diary* paid tribute to the French cavalry engaged in this phase. 'Their heavy cavalry and Lancers were fine, and being principally opposed to us, we had not an opportunity of ascertaining the state of the remainder.' These would have been Gobrecht's and Farine's men.

The fate of d'Erlon's Corps seems to have put the Emperor off that sector of Wellington's front that lay east of the Brussels–Charleroi road. His next great effort (Phase III), entrusted to Marshal Ney, was a cavalry assault upon the sector between La Haie Sainte and Hougoumont, where the Allied infantry was formed in 20 two-battalion rectangles known to history as the squares. They were placed in chequerboard fashion, so that anyone penetrating the first line would come under fire from the second.

Ney began by moving the 5,000 men of Milhaud's corps of cuirassiers and Lefèbvre-Desnoüettes's light cavalry west of the highway. The move had to be made under artillery fire, and was not accomplished without loss. This force now assailed the Allies on an 800-yard front. The going was heavy and the cuirassiers found it hard to raise a gallop as they closed on the squares. Ensign Rees Howell Gronow (1st Foot Guards, Maitland's brigade) wrote: 'The charge of the French cavalry was gallantly executed; but our well-directed fire brought men and horses down, and ere long the utmost confusion arose in their ranks. The officers were exceedingly brave, and by their gestures and fearless bearing did all in their power to encourage their men to

BRITISH PRIVATE OF THE 18TH LIGHT DRAGOONS. DRAWING BY C. HAMILTON SMITH

form again and renew the attack.' Captain Tomkinson relates this story: 'An officer of cuirassiers rode close to one of our squares with a detachment of men. He saw he had no chance of success, and by himself rode full gallop against the square, was shot and killed. Our men and officers regretted his fate.'

The cuirassiers probably suffered even more severely from artillery fire than from musketry. Captain Cavalié Mercer (Royal Horse Artillery) wrote: 'Our first gun had scarcely gained the interval between their squares, when I saw through the smoke the leading squadrons of the advancing column coming on at a brisk trot, and already not more than one hundred yards distant, if so much, for I don't think we could have seen so far. I immediately ordered the line to be formed for action—*case-shot!* and the leading gun was unlimbered and commenced firing almost as soon as the word was given: for activity and intelligence our men were unrivalled. The very first round, I saw, brought down several men and horses. They continued, however, to advance. I glanced at the Brunswickers [positioned on either side of him] and that glance told me it would not do; they had opened a fire from their front faces, but both squares appeared too unsteady, and I resolved to say nothing about the Duke's order [to take cover in the squares] . . . a resolve strengthened by the effect of the remaining guns as they rapidly succeeded in coming into action, making terrible slaughter, and in an instant covering the ground with men and horses. Still they persevered in approaching us (the first round had brought them to a walk), though slowly, and it did seem they would ride over us. We were a little below the level of the ground on which they moved—having in front of us a bank of about a foot and a half or two feet high, along the top of which ran a narrow road—and this gave more effect to our case-shot, all of which almost must have taken effect, for the carnage was frightful.'

'I suppose,' he continued, 'this state of things occupied but a few seconds, when I observed symptoms of hesitation, and in a twinkling, at the instant I thought it was all over with us, they turned to either flank and filed away rapidly to the rear. Retreat of the mass, however, was not so easy. Many facing about and trying to force their way through the body of the column, that part next to us became a complete mob, into which we kept a steady fire of case-shot from our six pieces. The effect is hardly conceivable, and to paint this scene of slaughter and confusion impossible. Every discharge was accompanied by the fall of numbers, whilst the survivors struggled with each other, and I actually saw them using the pommels of their swords to fight their way out of the *mêlée*. Some, rendered desperate at finding themselves thus pent up at the muzzles of our guns, as it were, and others carried away by their horses, maddened with wounds, dashed through our intervals—few thinking of using their swords, but pushing furiously onward, intent only on saving themselves. At last the rear of the column, wheeling about, opened a passage, and the whole swept away at a much more rapid pace than they had advanced, nor stopped until the swell of the ground covered them from our fire. We then ceased firing; but as they were still not far off, for we saw the tops of their caps, having reloaded, we stood ready to receive them should they renew the attack.'

The Emperor considered Ney's charge premature; nevertheless he decided to support it. At about 5.30 pm he sent in the 5,400 men of Kellermann's III Cavalry Corps and the Heavy Cavalry of the Guard under Guyot. Captain Samuel Rudyard (Lloyd's Battery) wrote of the scene: 'The Cuirassiers and Cavalry might have charged through the Battery as often as six or seven times, driving us into the squares, under our Guns, waggons, some defending themselves. In general, a Squadron or two came up the slope on our immediate front, and on their moving off at the appearance of our Cavalry charging, we took advantage to send destruction after them, and when advancing on our fire I have seen four or five men

A BRITISH LIFEGUARD ATTACKS TWO FRENCH CUIRASSIERS AT WATERLOO

FRENCH CAVALRY AT WATERLOO CHARGE THE BRITISH SQUARES. PAINTING BY W. B. WOLLEN.

FROM A CONTEMPORARY PRINT OF THE BATTLE

and horses piled upon each other like cards, the men not having even been displaced from the saddle, the effect of canister.'

In one of the charges L'Héritier's division penetrating between the squares crossed the Nivelles road and swinging left regained the French lines by riding down to the west of Hougoumont. Sergeant William Wheeler (1/51st Foot, Colonel Mitchell's Brigade) saw some of them. 'Not choosing to return by the way they came they took a circuitous route and came down the road on our left. There were nearly one hundred of them, all Cuirassiers. Down they rode at full gallop, the trees thrown across the bridge on our left stopped them. We saw them coming and was prepared, we opened our fire, the work was done in an instant. By the time we had loaded and the smoke had cleared away, one and only one, solitary individual was seen running over the brow in our front.'

Gronow says that by 4 pm the square of the 1st Foot Guards was a perfect hospital. But the Allied line, shaken more by the artillery than the cavalry, was intact; the squares were unbroken. In vain Ney had shattered 10,000 cavalry against them. The losses of the French were terrible. In IV Corps Generals Delort, Dubois, Travers and Farine had all been wounded. In the Guard cavalry Edouard Colbert was charging with his left arm in a sling, and the Marquis Jamin was mortally wounded. In III Corps, l'Héritier, Roussel d'Hurbal, Picquet, Guiton and Blancard were wounded, and Donop was missing. Not one of its seven generals was unwounded. The losses to units were no less severe. The 3rd Cuirassiers, $4\frac{1}{2}$ squadrons strong in the morning, was reduced to three platoons when, in the dusk, Marshal Ney called upon them for a last charge. From the lists of officer casualties it looks as if other regiments were even harder hit.

Phase IV began about 6 pm when the Emperor, seeing that his cavalry were exhausted, and with the Prussians pressing his right wing, ordered Ney to take La Haie Sainte; this time he succeeded. Wellington's centre was now in serious danger. In this phase, however, the French cavalry played no part.

The climax of the battle (Phase V) came when at about 7.30 Napoleon launched 5,000 men – eight battalions of the Imperial Guard – against the position Ney had assailed in vain. Had they gone in to support the first cavalry attacks they might have turned the day. They might perhaps have captured or damaged the batteries which the cuirassiers had overrun. Excellent troops though they were, to put them in now, in such relatively small numbers, was to court disaster. And indeed disaster ensued. With the cry of 'La Garde recule', Napoleon's Army of the North broke up, and only the most stout-hearted resisted the panic that followed. In this final phase the cavalry divisions of Domon and Subervie, the only ones not so far seriously engaged, supported the left wing of Lobau's Corps (VI) which was struggling to ward off the onslaught of Bülow and the Prussian IV Corps. In comparison with the rest of the French cavalry their losses were relatively light. Of the generals, only Domon was wounded.

As he had shown at Eylau in 1807, Napoleon liked on occasion to deliver a massive stroke with an immense body of heavy cavalry. At Waterloo the conditions for success were simply not there. The Allied squares were too steady, the ground was too heavy; and by a strange failure of co-ordination Reille's infantry did not press forward in support. Had the Guard been launched earlier things might have been different, but, as he had shown at Borodino, the Emperor was a miser where use of the Guard was concerned.

139

THE CAVALRY

COSSACKS OF THE BLACK SEA. FROM ECKERT AND WEISS.

THE LANCER

When in despair the cavalry of western Europe, confronted by the long pikes of the infantry, threw away their lances and took up with firearms, the Lithuanians, at that time inhabiting a spacious territory between Poland and Russia, still clung to the lance, an effective enough weapon against the lightly armed Moslem and Tartar cavalry with which they had to contend. The name Uhlan, derived from the Polish word for cavalryman, was given to the Lithuanian lancers; when their territory was amalgamated with Poland, the cavalry of both countries continued to use the lance. In 1717 August III of Poland took into his service two *polks* or regiments of *Uhlans Volontaires*. These were composed of gentlemen each accompanied by two attendants who, besides looking after the comfort of their masters, carried muskets and could function as dragoons, dismounting and covering the retreat of the noble lancers by fire when such action seemed judicious. Thus the original Uhlans were a mixture of well-born Lithuanian lancers and not quite so well-born dragoons; at that early stage neither side in this partnership was, incidentally, much concerned about what they wore.

Marshal Saxe recruited an Uhlan regiment into the French army, and other armies imitated him. The Uhlans operated much after the style of the old hussars, wandering about the countryside in small bands which suddenly coalesced to trap an unwary enemy. The lance became increasingly popular as the French Revolutionary and Napoleonic Wars progressed. No doubt the success of the Cossacks as light cavalry influenced military thinking. The French, as we have seen, converted their Polish Light Horse and a number of other regiments to lancers in the years 1809-11. The Austrians, too, had their Uhlans—the regiments of Merveldt, Schwarzenberg and the Erzherzog Karl. In addition, the Uhlans were an important arm in the reorganized Prussian Army of 1813. In the 1815 campaign there were six Uhlan regiments in the Prussian service. Generally speaking their dress and armament was much the same as that of the Polish lancers in the French Army. Officers and men wore the *czapska*, that strange-shaped headdress that is peculiarly Polish; they also wore a short jacket and overalls. There were a number of *Landwehr* cavalry regiments in Blücher's army, and these also were armed with the lance.

After the Napoleonic Wars every country adopted the lance, and lancer regiments became very fashionable, partly because the Polish lancers had shown themselves formidable opponents in battle, partly because it was hoped that the lance would enable cavalry attacking an infantry square to penetrate to the men behind the hedge of bayonets. The Lithuanians had tied pennons to their lances to make them look more awe-inspiring, a device the Cossacks disdained to employ, but most European lancer regiments followed an example which was certainly decorative if nothing else. The Germans retained the name Uhlan for their lancer regiments, and thus a name originally borne by Lithuanian irregular cavalry came to be identified with the German cavalry as a whole.

THE NAPOLEONIC WARS

MEMBERS OF THE 13TH BENGAL LANCERS. PAINTING BY H. BUNNETT.

THE Battle of Waterloo marked a watershed in the history of the cavalry. Partly this may be attributed to the failure of the French cavalry to break the British infantry squares, partly to the new idea of warfare originated by Napoleon which differed sharply from that of the 17th and 18th centuries. During those two centuries European armies had been composed of highly trained professional soldiers fighting dynastic wars in which fervent nationalistic emotions were rarely roused. Napoleon introduced, perhaps reintroduced would be more accurate, the idea of conscription and the nation in arms. Huge conscript armies now became normal in Europe, and since in general the European peasant tended to be an agriculturalist working in fields of limited size, rather than a herdsman riding an open range, the vast majority of the soldiers, their period of training necessarily limited, were more suitable for the infantry than the cavalry; moreover, the additional cost of a cavalryman was a factor not to be ignored.

During the period after Waterloo, although tremendous changes impended, weapons altered little. The two most important writers on military matters, General von Clausewitz and Baron de Jomini, based their theories on an analysis of Napoleon's strategy and tactics. Clausewitz, satirized as a 'scientific soldier' in Tolstoy's *War and Peace*, was perhaps the greatest of all military writers, but he was interested in general principles and the philosophical relationship between war and politics rather than the minutiae of tactics on the battlefield. Jomini, at one time an intellectual chief of staff to that rugged soldier, Marshal Ney, expounded what he saw as the theoretical background to Napoleon's unparalleled series of victories. Perhaps conscious that the importance of cavalry was declining he wrote: 'As a general rule it may be stated that an army in open country should contain cavalry to one-sixth of its strength, in mountainous country one-tenth will suffice.' He also suggested that 'the chief duty of the cavalry is to open the way for gaining a victory or to render it complete . . . by rapidly succouring a threatened point, overthrowing disordered infantry, covering retreats of infantry and artillery'. It is noticeable that he did not think it necessary to include the obtaining and passing of information among the principal duties. Napoleon, accustomed to forcing his enemy to conform to his movements, placed no great store on patrolling and reconnaissance; and so a role which might have been expected to gain in prominence received little consideration. Thus when in 1854 Britain and France sent an expeditionary force to the Crimea, the proportion of cavalry to infantry, particularly in the French army, was remarkably low. The British army included a weak cavalry division intended to act offensively on the battlefield, rather than to patrol, reconnoitre and use its mobility to harass the enemy's lines of communication. As for the regiments, they were if anything more richly clad but, except for the widespread introduction of the lance, their weapons and tactics differed little from those of the age of Napoleon.   J.P.L.

A COSSACK OFFICER OF THE GUARD, c.1832. FROM ECKERT AND WEISS.

THE CRIMEAN WAR by R. CROSBIE-WESTON

The Crimean War was principally an infantry campaign. On three occasions, however, the cavalry played a spectacular part, which has tended to invest their contribution with an importance not wholly in keeping with events. All three were on the same day, 25 October 1854, and in only one of them, the least well-known, did the cavalry action have any significant effect on the progress of the war. To see why this is so, it is necessary to take a brief look at the rest of the campaign.

RUSSIAN LANCER OF THE GUARD. FROM ECKERT AND WEISS.

THE CAVALRY

War had been declared against the Russians on 28 March 1854. The nominal cause was a dispute over the guardianship of the Holy Places in Jerusalem which the Turks, under French pressure, eventually decided should be held by the Roman Catholic Church instead of the Greek Orthodox Church favoured by Russia. This, of course, was only the outer aspect of a deeper struggle for power. With the Turkish Empire moving slowly towards disintegration it was obvious that strategic prizes were to be won in the eastern Mediterranean. Russia was determined not to miss what she thought was her rightful share. Various diplomatic and military blunders led to a declaration of war, and Britain and France found themselves committed to sending a joint expeditionary force to an inhospitable peninsula beset by extremes of climate and a rich store of deadly sub-tropical diseases.

18 men and women. (A small proportion of wives was allowed to each regiment because they helped with the chores and hospital work.)

Prior to attacking the Russian base at Sebastopol the Allies went into camp around Varna, in Bulgaria, on the opposite side of the Black Sea. It was a disastrous place to have chosen. Dysentery, cholera and other deadly illnesses soon appeared and every day more men died. Cardigan insisted on daily reconnaissance marches (the cavalry marches even when it is on horseback) and surprisingly enough accompanied them. Cardigan did not normally display much solicitude for his men, but on this occasion he shared their toil until he himself went down with dysentery. After that he took greater care of his own comfort.

The next move was to the Crimean peninsula itself. The Allies landed north of Sebastopol and

BRITISH CAVALRY IN THE CRIMEA. FROM LEFT TO RIGHT, A LIFEGUARD, 5TH DRAGOON, 13TH LIGHT DRAGOON, HORSE ARTILLERYMAN, 17TH LANCER, 11TH HUSSAR, 1ST DRAGOON. FROM *CAVALRY TROOPS GOING TO THE WAR*.

Although the logistics of transport, supply and remounts were to prove difficult in the extreme, a British cavalry division was sent out to the Crimea commanded by Lieutenant-General Lord Lucan; it consisted of the Light Brigade (the Earl of Cardigan) and the Heavy Brigade (The Hon. J. Scarlett). Lucan, it should be noted, was Cardigan's brother-in-law and they detested each other. The Army having been largely neglected since Waterloo, these two brigades were all that could be put in the field, and even they were understrength both in men and horses. By the time the cavalry division had passed through a storm in the Bay of Biscay and experienced the heat of the Mediterranean in June, it had still fewer horses. The worst disaster happened to the *Europa*, carrying the 6th Inniskilling Dragoons. It caught fire 200 miles out of England and lost all its horses, its commanding officer and

A TROOPER OF THE GUARD SQUADRON OF THE MONTAGNARDS OF THE CAUCASUS. c.1832. FROM ECKERT AND WEISS.

THE CRIMEAN WAR

advanced southwards. On the way they encountered the Russian army drawn up on the southern slopes of the River Alma (20 September 1854). A vigorous battle then took place, in which Raglan, the joint commander-in-chief (with Maréchal de Saint-Arnaud), became isolated from his army, and ground which had been taken was surrendered through mistaken orders and then had to be retaken. Allied cavalry was not involved in the battle but more remarkable was the fact that 3,000 Russian cavalry sat idly by watching their infantry being defeated. It was said that Raglan did not commit the British cavalry for fear that the Russians might be tempted to commit their much larger force. Much irritation was caused by the fact that when the battle was won Raglan did not allow the cavalry to pursue. In view of the lack of experience and training in some of the squadrons, and the condition of the horses, this may have been a wise decision. Raglan's decisions do not appear to have been very imaginative but he would have known from experience that a cavalry unit could soon lose itself in unknown countryside. If it did it might be ambushed and destroyed as a fighting force. Even so, Lucan and Cardigan chose to disobey the initial order not to pursue and were only recalled after further orders.

After the victory at the Alma, which had left Sebastopol open to an immediate attack which could have finished the war there and then, Raglan produced an extraordinary tactical plan. This was to march right round Sebastopol and attack it from the southern side. The best that can be said of this decision was that it gave the Allies a harbour for their supply ships. However, had Raglan attacked from the north this would not have been needed.

RUSSIAN DRAGOONS OF THE NOVGOROD REGIMENT A SUBALTERN AND A TROOPER. FROM ECKERT AND WEISS.

THE CAVALRY

The march round to the southern side was known as 'the flank march'. As it was taking place, Prince Menshikov, the Russian commander, decided to withdraw his army intact, holding it ready to attack the Allied armies in the rear once they laid siege to Sebastopol. It was a sound policy which avoided having the Russian field army locked up in a fortress. On the flank march the forward units of the British army blundered into the rear of the Russians withdrawing to the interior. Neither side was aware of the other's presence until they clashed. Minor fighting occurred but was soon broken off. The most significant feature of this curious situation was that the cavalry units of both sides were apparently so untrained and inexperienced that they did nothing to warn their own armies of the proximity of the other.

Once at Balaclava the cavalry had plenty of opportunity to make up for their lack of experience, being placed on constant patrolling duty to fend off possible Russian attacks. The Russians used Cossacks to harass the men preparing siege works but this was no more than a minor nuisance. Much more effective, although the results were not to be seen immediately, were the reinforcements the Russians were packing into Sebastopol. For a month both armies settled down to prepare for a siege which both sides knew would follow an almost ritual order. Over the previous 200 years there had developed a pattern of complex fortress-building which was matched by an equally sophisticated pattern of attack. The latter involved a complicated system of approach through trenches. The trenches were well within range of the defenders' guns and suffered accordingly. During this period, when the Russian cavalry were nosing forward towards the attacker's lines, Lucan seemed content that the British cavalry should play a passive role and not try to carry the war to the enemy. For this unenterprising attitude he was rewarded with the nickname 'Lord Look-on'.

On 24 October 1854 it became obvious that the Russians would not remain inactive while the Allies completed their preparations to capture Sebastopol. Reports came in from spies that a large Russian army was about to launch an attack and sweep the Allies into the sea. By 6 am on 25 October it seemed as if this report was substantially true. Cavalry vedettes began signalling back that a large force of Russians, including cavalry, artillery and infantry, was advancing in the direction of Balaclava. The first obstacle in their path was a force of 500 Turks manning the forward redoubts on Canrobert's Hill. Against an army of some 25,000 the resistance of the Turks was bound to be limited. They fought with great determination and courage, sustaining heavy casualties, but were eventually driven back, without their guns, which they had already spiked. (These were the guns which were mentioned in Raglan's famous order that within hours was to send the Light Brigade to its destruction.)

Raglan had positioned himself on the Sapourné Heights, where he had an excellent view of the battlefield. From this viewpoint he could see large numbers of Russian cavalry filling the plain in two bodies; the main party, some 3,000 sabres, was advancing towards the Causeway Heights; a smaller detachment of four squadrons (a total of approximately 500) was moving past the redoubts where the Turks had lost their guns and was approaching the port of

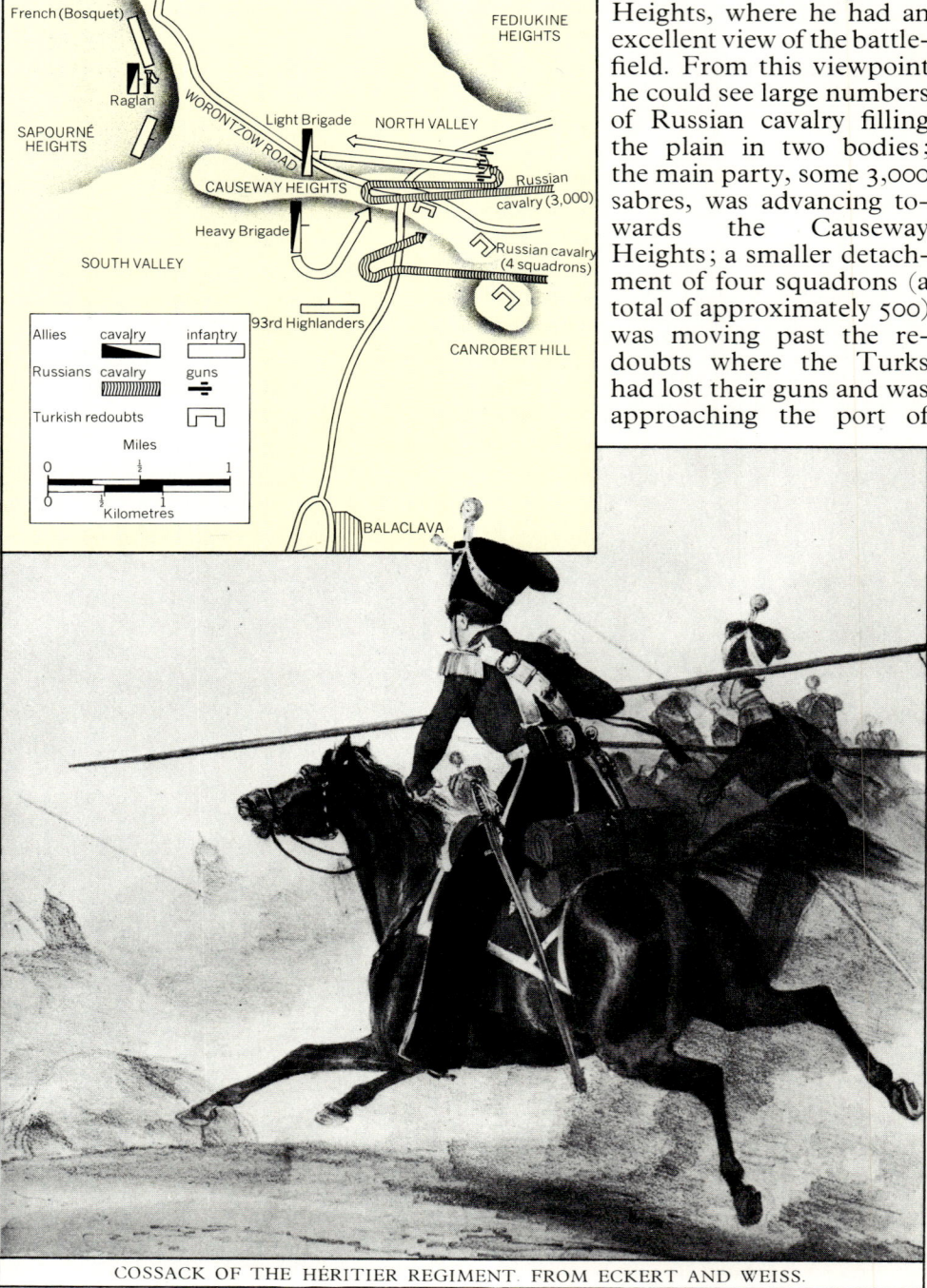

BATTLE OF BALACLAVA 25 OCTOBER 1854

COSSACK OF THE HÉRITIER REGIMENT. FROM ECKERT AND WEISS.

146

THE CRIMEAN WAR

Balaclava. Although not isolated from the battle, as he had allowed himself to become at the Alma, Raglan was too far off to be able to make any sound decisions rapidly. The only quick decision he did bring himself to make in fact turned out to be disastrous.

The four squadrons on the Russian left moved steadily forward. All that lay between them and the port was a small force of Highlanders (the 93rd, later the Argyll and Sutherland Highlanders), a few convalescents, some Guardsmen, and some of the Turks who had got away from the redoubts. Of these, the 550 Highlanders were in the best position, and condition, to face the assault. Morale was high and Sir Colin Campbell, their commander, had to restrain them with the famous remark, '93rd, 93rd. Damn all that eagerness.' Sir Colin had originally planned that the 93rd should confront the Russians from a lying-down position. However, the movements of the Russian squadrons convinced him that if they were to be intercepted it must be on the crest of the hill. Hastily he gave the necessary orders. Normally infantry would have adopted squares, or formed up four deep, to receive cavalry but there was no time for this and Campbell confronted them in a line which was only two deep. This was the origin of the famous 'thin red line'.

As the Russians approached, Campbell gave the order for the first volley, said to be at 600 yards. The Russians came on, seemingly without casulties, and at 350 yards the 93rd sent off their second volley. At this the Russian cavalry commander gave the order to wheel to the left and the squadrons veered away. No men or horses were left on the field and much controversy has occurred over whether or not the Russians sustained any casualties. The argument is immaterial for the desired effect had been achieved; this dangerous Russian probe towards Balaclava had been frustrated. Had it succeeded, it would have created a desperate situation. Campbell's view was that the Russian commander, quickly summing up the resistance in his path, wheeled away without loss. His comment was, 'That man knows his business.'

Meanwhile larger events were developing to the 93rd's left. Having marched down the North Valley, the main mass of the Russian cavalry was now coming up the Causeway Heights. Once they were over the ridge the South Valley, scene of the 93rd's spirited encounter, would be open to them. Raglan, observing this, sent orders to Sir James Scarlett, commanding the Heavy Brigade, to check the new threat. Accordingly, Scarlett with a force of 800 sabres set off to attack an army of unknown

OFFICER OF THE GUARD SQUADRON OF THE TARTARS OF THE CRIMEA. FROM ECKERT AND WEISS.

GENERAL SCARLETT LEADING THE HEAVY BRIGADE AGAINST THE RUSSIANS. PAINTING BY STANLEY BERKELEY.

THE CAVALRY

RUSSIAN HUSSAR OF THE GUARD IN ACTION. FROM ECKERT AND WEISS.

THE CRIMEAN WAR

size but which subsequently was found to be 3,000. On arrival at the Heights he drew up his force with parade-ground precision. Then he moved forward again. The Russians, surprised to find this small but determined force in their path, halted. At that moment Scarlett ordered the charge, which he himself led. This charge differed markedly from most cavalry charges in that it was performed at maximum speed, whereas they were usually performed at the trot or canter. In theory the last few yards should always be taken at a gallop, but so often had formation and cohesion been lost by a final turn of speed that most cavalry commanders were wary of using it. On this occasion the value of shock was of paramount importance and Scarlett led the charge so rapidly that he and his personal staff were several lengths ahead of the Greys and the Inniskillings. Soon the 4th Dragoons Guards, the 5th Dragoon Guards and the Royals were also in the thick of the action. Although Scarlett was over 60 he gave a fine account of himself, laying about him lustily with his sabre in spite of receiving five wounds.

The Russians were in such close formation that the Heavy Brigade was unable to penetrate to more than the fifth rank. Fortunately, too, the Russians had left no lanes between their squadrons, for any British cavalryman penetrating down one would quickly have been cut to pieces. As it happened, not only were the Russians caught at the halt, they were also about to deploy in pincer formation. In fact the wings did close in and envelop the Greys, but by this time the centre of the battlefield was such a medley, of swords whirling against a background of pistol shots, that any tactical move had become virtually impossible. Although the Russian's heavy greatcoats thwarted most of the Heavy Brigade's thrusts, the Russians sustained heavy casualties from the blades of the straight English swords.

The shock of this unexpected encounter with a small but very determined force, and the sudden incidence of heavy, though local, casualties, caused the Russian cavalry to reel backwards. At this moment the Royal Horse Artillery opened up and found useful targets in the still closely packed Russian formation. It was enough. The Russians may have thought another cavalry charge would follow, and were in no position to receive it. Without waiting for orders, the whole formation turned and went streaming backwards. Their officers tried to rally them on top of the ridge but their efforts were nullified by further bursts of accurate fire from the Royal Horse Artillery. The Heavy Brigade, which had pursued for some 300 yards, had then to call off the chase lest they too should come under the RHA fire. It had been a remarkable achievement. Eight hundred men had put some 3,000 to flight and in the process given the British cavalry a reputation which would make the Russian cavalry very careful for the remainder of the war.

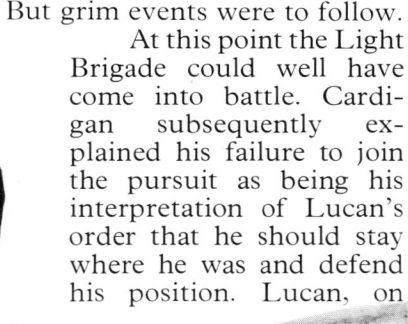

But grim events were to follow. At this point the Light Brigade could well have come into battle. Cardigan subsequently explained his failure to join the pursuit as being his interpretation of Lucan's order that he should stay where he was and defend his position. Lucan, on the other hand, said that he had instructed Cardigan to attack everything within reach. The Russian cavalry were certainly within reach. Lucan could have sent an unmistakable order to Cardigan at this juncture, but did not, so seeming to justify his nickname.

Up in his vantage point Raglan saw it all; he also saw that the Russians, in spite of their reverses, were now bringing forward artillery teams to draw away the guns they had overrun in the Turkish-held redoubts earlier in the day. Clearly this must not be allowed to happen. No commander likes to lose a gun if he can possibly prevent it. Raglan then recalled that the Light Brigade, still standing idly

GENERAL SIR JAMES SCARLETT COMMANDING THE HEAVY BRIGADE.

THE EARL OF CARDIGAN WITH THE LIGHT BRIGADE. HE IS SEEN LEADING THE 17TH LANCERS ONTO THE RUSSIAN GUNS. ON THE SABRETACHE OF THE TROOPER, CENTRE FOREGROUND, IS THE BADGE OF THE REGIMENT, SHOWING THE SKULL AND CROSSBONES FROM WHICH THEY DERIVED THEIR NICKNAME, THE 'DEATH OR GLORY BOYS'. MOST THAT DAY ACHIEVED BOTH. THE LANCE PENNONS ARE FURLED FOR ACTION.

by, were just the troops for such a task. He instructed his Quartermaster-General, Sir Richard Airey, who was virtually acting as his aide-de-camp, to write down a message. It ran: 'Lord Raglan wishes the cavalry to advance rapidly to the front, follow the enemy and try to prevent the enemy carrying away the guns. Troop Horse Artillery may accompany. French cavalry on your left. Immediate.'

This message was then torn out of Airey's notebook and handed to the one man who could deliver it quickly. This was Captain Nolan, an Irish-Italian, a brilliant horseman and cavalry expert. Nolan was a thorough-going professional, but he was also arrogant and insolent, and despised most of his senior officers and took no trouble to conceal it. He rode down the near-precipice into the valley and handed the message with an off-hand gesture to Lucan. Lucan read it with amazement. The point about the French cavalry, who were not in sight, was quite irrelevant. Even more astonishing was the fact that all Lucan could see in the way of guns were the Russian guns a mile and a quarter away at the far end of North Valley. 'What guns?' he is reported to have said, to which Nolan gave an airy sweep of his arm saying, 'There, my Lord, is your enemy, there are the guns.' Whether in fact Nolan's gesture was meant to indicate the guns in the redoubts, which he himself had seen from the Sapourné Heights, but which were invisible down in the valley, will never be known, for Nolan was killed at the beginning of the charge. Lucan, having had enough of Nolan for the time being, rode off to Cardigan and showed him the order. (Cardigan later denied seeing it, not that this would have made any difference.) A short conversation took place, surprising as the two were scarcely on speaking terms, in which Cardigan pointed out that it meant the virtual extinction of his brigade. There was, of course, no question of not obeying it. Cardigan formed up the brigade and gave the order, 'The brigade will advance.'

The Light Brigade totalled 673 men and was made up of the 11th Hussars, 17th Lancers, 13th Light Dragoons, 4th Light Dragoons and 8th Hussars. Just as the Brigade started, at a steady trot, Nolan suddenly rode obliquely across its front, waving his sword. Whether he had suddenly realized that Cardigan was heading for the wrong guns and the order had been misunderstood will never be known for a Russian shell splinter tore half his chest away, killing him almost immediately. Cardigan had noted Nolan's apparent agitation and grumbled about it subsequently. Meanwhile in perfect formation but already losing men and horses to the Russian guns, the brigade moved up the valley. As they came closer to the Russian position, the fire became more intense. One sergeant had his head taken clean off but stayed in the saddle for a further 30 yards. Eventually, at fearful cost, they reached the Russian guns, sabred the gunners and rode through the position. On the far side was the rest of the Russian cavalry including the Cossacks. There was no means of holding the objective they had reached at such cost. Those that were left turned and rode down the valley again. Losses on the return journey were even greater than on the outward one. Altogether 113 men were killed and 134 were wounded; most of the horses were killed. From beginning to end it had taken 20 minutes. Casualties would have been worse if the French 4th Chasseurs d'Afrique had not on their own initiative charged and silenced a Russian battery on the Fediukine Heights. The Heavy Brigade, which advanced to cover the Light Brigade's retreat, itself also sustained a number of casualties.

'C'est magnifique,' said General Bosquet, commanding the French 2nd Division, 'mais ce n'est pas la guerre.' The chief consequence of the devastations of 25 October was that for the rest of the war neither side again ventured far with its cavalry.

FRENCH HUSSARS OF THE 7TH, 8TH AND 9TH REGIMENTS

Interlude

COLONIAL CAVALRY by JAMES LAWFORD

IN the 19th century European imperialism reached its zenith. As the Romans had found 2,000 years before, the races in theory subject to the European powers showed little reluctance towards serving their new masters, nor did the chains of imperialism appear to enfeeble their spirit. Every colonizing power raised regiments, generally infantry, from the inhabitants of the territories they colonized, and both France and Britain formed cavalry regiments of notable quality.

Of all the Imperial cavalry regiments, perhaps the most curious were the cavalry of the Mamelukes. They were members of a Mahommedan ruling class that held power in Egypt, having imposed themselves on the native Egyptians. They achieved fame in the 13th century when they repulsed a Crusader invasion under St Louis of France, and perhaps it was not inappropriate that five centuries later it was the French under Napoleon who brought about their downfall. In essence they were a collection of feudal chieftains, called 'Beys', who recruited and maintained their private armies in a fashion typically Turkish. They purchased white boy slaves from impoverished peasant families in Georgia and Caucasus. The boys were taught to ride and handle their weapons almost from infancy and to look down on the native Egyptians. Without any form of family life and largely deprived of feminine society, they tended to become homosexual, and it is hardly surprising that the number of native-born Mamelukes increased very slowly.

The boys grew up with two overriding ideals, complete loyalty to their master and a fanatical courage in battle; the infantry soldier they despised as fit only to guard camps. At the time when Napoleon invaded Egypt, the Mamelukes wore

TROOPERS OF THE 1ST DUKE OF YORK'S OWN LANCERS (SKINNER'S HORSE) AND THE 3RD SKINNER'S HORSE. PAINTING BY A. C. LOVETT.

SCOUTS OF THE 10TH BENGAL LANCERS. PAINTING BY R. SIMKIN.

colourful robes with coats of mail underneath. Mounted on swift Arab chargers, they carried pistols, mace and sword and some carried carbines, but they knew little of drill or manoeuvre and did not fully comprehend the uses and effects of firearms. At the Battle of the Pyramids, fought outside Cairo on 21 July 1798, the Mamelukes met for the first time in a full-scale battle the cannon and muskets of the West. Again and again they charged the French squares with a gallantry that was as superb as it was futile. In an hour it was all over. The French suffered little; the Mamelukes a blow from which they never fully recovered. They survived until 1811 when Mohammed Ali, the Turkish Governor, finally disposed of them by the simple expedient of murdering all the Beys.

In the 1830s the French, engaged in subduing much of North Africa, found it desirable to raise locally recruited cavalry to aid them in their long and bitter struggle against Abd-el-Kader. Parties of the famous Turkish light irregular cavalry, the Spahis, disbanded a few years before, still remained in North Africa, and from them as well as from the Arabs the French raised regiments which retained the name Spahi long after the Turkish connection had vanished. The name, derived from the Persian *sipahi*, a cavalry soldier, was corrupted by the British into sepoy, a term which, with their usual casual attitude to foreign languages, they applied exclusively to Indian infantry.

The Spahis were essentially light cavalry, designed to supplement the Chasseurs d'Afrique, the cavalry backbone of the French colonial army in North Africa. The Chasseurs d'Afrique recruited mostly Frenchmen but included a few Arabs, while the Spahis, basically Arab, included some Frenchmen among their troopers; squadrons and regiments were normally commanded by Frenchmen. They wore Arab dress, turban, and baggy trousers (the French among them wore fezzes) and were armed and organized after the manner of their counterparts in the French Metropolitan army. In 1909 there were four Spahi regiments, each of six squadrons including a depot squadron, and six regiments of Chasseurs d'Afrique. There is little mention of the Spahis in the accounts of the Franco-Prussian War of 1870–71. They appear, in the main, to have furnished a romantic addition to the wars waged in the deserts of North Africa.

In India Britain's Honourable East India Company initially recruited only sepoys to guard its warehouses; then in 1763 it enlisted some masterless Moslem horse to form an irregular cavalry unit, the Mogul Horse, but it was not until the early 19th century that most Indian cavalry regiments were raised. After the mutiny of the Bengal army in 1857, the East India Company was dissolved, sovereignty passed to the British Crown and the Company's troops became part of the British armed forces, eventually becoming known as the Indian Army.

From the days of the Company's army, most Indian cavalry regiments had been organized and equipped much on the pattern of the British cavalry. The main difference lay in the officer structure. The troopers, known as *sowars*, and all ranks up to and including troop commander were Indian; each squadron consisted of two or more troops according to the fashion in vogue in the British Army; the Indian officer commanding a troop was known as a *jemadar*, and the senior Indian officer in a squadron was a *rissaldar*; he might command a troop, be second-in-command, or even for a limited period command the squadron. The senior Indian officer in the regiment, the *rissaldar major*, was the colonel's confidential adviser on all matters affecting the administration of the Indian personnel in the regiment. With a few exceptions the Indian officers worked their way up from trooper, wore the badges of rank of junior British officers and were entitled to a salute from their troopers. They were men of substance and greatly respected both by their soldiers and in their villages.

The British officers superimposed on this hierarchy of Indians supplied the commanding officer, the second-in-command, the squadron commanders and adjutant; in addition one or two young British officers would serve as squadron officers with no specific responsibilities. All British officers were automatically senior to all Indian ranks, although young British officers were careful to respect the years and experience of their Indian officers. The British officers held the King's Commission; they ranked with those of their own seniority in the British Army, but served exclusively in Indian Army units or formations. After World War I, limited numbers of Indians were granted King's Commissions, and to distinguish them the old-style Indian officers became known as Viceroy's Commissioned Officers.

English words of command were used, but all other orders were given in Urdu. Uniform eventually settled down to a colourful amalgam of British and Indian dress. The men in the regiments were all volunteers and there were always more volunteers than vacancies. In general regiments formed happy communities in which all ranks and

MAMELUKES, c.1808. NAPOLEON WAS SO IMPRESSED WITH THEM THAT HE RECRUITED SOME INTO THE IMPERIAL GUARD. DRAWING BY R. KNÖTEL.

SPAHIS, c.1847. FROM LEFT TO RIGHT ARE A FRENCH OFFICER, AN ARAB OFFICER AND A TROOPER. THEIR COATS ARE RED, THEIR LOWER GARMENTS BLUE.

TROOPERS OF SKINNER'S HORSE, THE SENIOR CAVALRY REGIMENT OF THE LINE, ENGAGED IN A BRISK MÊLÉE OUTSIDE BHURTPORE, c.1805. SKINNER RAISED HIS REGIMENT TO SERVE UNDER THE MAHRATTA CHIEFTAIN SCINDIA. DURING THE SECOND MAHRATTA WAR (1803–5) HE TOOK HIS REGIMENT OVER TO JOIN THE BRITISH ON CONDITION THAT HE WAS NEVER ASKED TO SERVE AGAINST SCINDIA.

races were proud to serve. The Indian cavalry had one other singular characteristic: in accordance with the *silladar* system, a practice rooted in ancient Indian history, the troopers owned their own horses. On operations, to avoid troopers feeling reluctant to risk their capital, horse casualties were replaced by the Government. The *silladar* system was abandoned after World War I.

In the period before 1914 there were 39 cavalry regiments in the Indian Army. Winston Churchill, after the Battle of Omdurman in the Sudan (1898), sighed for three regiments of Bengal Lancers to exploit the victory. In 1914 an Indian cavalry division went to France, and in 1918 some 10 Indian cavalry regiments played a major part at the Battle of Megiddo (see Chapter 14) that crowned Allenby's Palestine campaign and was perhaps the last of the great cavalry actions.

TROOPER OF THE POONA HORSE IN REVIEW ORDER. PAINTING BY LOVETT.

IN the Crimea, despite some well publicized charges, the cavalry took little effective part. Significantly, moreover, the Russian cavalry at Balaclava veered away from an infantry battalion not in square, but in line. The powers of cavalry seemed on the wane. In 1859, when the French under Napoleon III expelled the Austrians from Italy, out of an army numbering 106,000 combatants the Austrians had about 6,000 cavalry organized mostly in a single cavalry division; the French proportion was equally low. In this campaign the tendency was for cavalry regiments to be held back in reserve, their function apparently being to execute some vital, though unhappily unidentified, task – the opportunity for which never arose. Early in the campaign some Italian peasants killed an Imperial hussar with pitchforks, an act of *lèse-majesté* that so horrified the Austrian commander, Count Gyulai, that he ordered that all cavalry patrols should be accompanied by an infantry escort. As the Prussian Prince Kraft zu Hohenlohe von Ingelfingen pointed out in his letters on strategy, he might just as well have dispensed with cavalry patrols altogether. While the generals in Europe groped for a solution, it was to be in the American Civil War (1861–65) that commanders of genius were to demonstrate how, boldly handled, cavalry could yet be employed to good purpose. J.P.L.

GENERAL STAFF OF THE SAXON ARMY, 1859. FROM *GESCHICHTE DER SACHSISCHEN ARMEE.*

US CAVALRY AND THE CIVIL WAR by CURT JOHNSON

As European cavalry sought uneasily to adjust to modern conditions, a new species of cavalry appeared in America – an unique type born, in part, because the difficult, heavily wooded terrain of the eastern seaboard did not permit cavalry to be massed and manoeuvred as it had been in Europe. The earliest true American cavalrymen were shaped by the frontier experience. They first appeared as combatants in obscure backwater conflicts of the pre-Revolutionary period such as the Cherokee War. Strictly speaking, they were not cavalry but mounted infantry who rode to their objective, dismounted, and fought on foot.

PORTRAIT OF A US CAVALRYMAN, BY FREDERIC REMINGTON.

THE CAVALRY

Tactically, these indigenous American cavalrymen imitated their earliest adversaries, the Indians. Like the Indian, they frequently made long, arduous marches and penetrated deep into enemy territory where they were least expected. Drawing near to the enemy, they employed every artifice known to the woodsman to remain undetected. Then, taking advantage of whatever cover was available, they laid clever ambushes. The combat was usually short and fierce, one side or the other giving way in confusion and defeat. In the aftermath of combat the horses were employed again, either for pursuit or retreat.

The mounted rifleman flourished during the Revolutionary War (1775–83), especially in the South where irregular cavalry contributed significantly to the American war effort. 'Over-mountain men' from Virginia, Tennessee and the Carolinas, pens, where McCall's mounted militia charged alongside Lieutenant-Colonel William Washington's regular dragoons, they were launched into the thick of the fray in classic shock actions.

The regular cavalry, called light dragoons, found little employment for its talents in the Revolution. Horses were scarce and difficult to maintain, forage was non-existent, and generals such as George Washington preferred to use strong bodies of light infantry to perform the duties traditionally assigned to the light cavalry. Thus mounted actions of any significance were rare, and only a handful of cavalry regiments graced the orders of battle of either side. Later in the war there arose a preference for mixed corps of light infantry and cavalry known as legions; these, it was found, allowed commanders a degree of flexibility in their manoeuvres that they could not hope to

AN APACHE INDIAN AMBUSHES A WAGON. PAINTING BY FREDERIC REMINGTON.

for example, annihilated Major Patrick Ferguson's Tory corps at King's Mountain (7 October 1780), and Colonel Andrew Pickens's mounted militia played an important role in General Daniel Morgan's victory at the Cowpens (17 January 1781).

These untutored mounted riflemen of the Revolution established a precedent of dismounted action that later came to characterize the tactical employment of US cavalry. They were also capable of effective *mounted* action against unsupported or demoralized infantry–even though they knew nothing of manoeuvre on horseback and might have been embarrassed contending against regular cavalry in the open. The commanders of mounted rifle units recognized this aptitude for shock action in their men and generally kept a part of the command out of action for use as a mounted reserve. These men were used to improve a victory or harry the retreating foe, but sometimes, as at the Cow-

A CAVALRY MÊLÉE DURING THE ACTION AT COWPENS IN THE WAR OF INDEPENDENCE.

US CAVALRY AND THE CIVIL WAR

obtain with light infantry or light cavalry alone.

Cavalry disappeared in the general reduction of the army following the end of the war in 1783, but the legion system was resurrected for a time when General 'Mad Anthony' Wayne formed the United States Legion and led it against the Indian Federation of the Old Northwest in 1794. The cavalry of the Legion, charging in the loose order they practised for broken country, drove into the left flank of the Indian line at Fallen Timbers (20 August 1794). This blow, combined with a bayonet charge by the Legion infantry, broke the Indians. A division of mounted rifles, formed from Kentucky militia, also participated in Wayne's campaign, but with little success. Later, however, in the War of 1812, mounted rifles from Kentucky charged the British line at the Battle of the Thames (5 October 1813). This charge, which showed that mounted volunteers could fight as well on horseback as on foot, was decisive and produced one of the few American victories of the war.

The mounted volunteer continued to find employment in the numerous Indian wars of the following decades, but like all citizen-soldiers he came and went as he pleased and was never very dependable. (General Nathanael Greene deplored the fact that the Southern militia were mounted – presumably because their mobility allowed them to cut loose from the main army at will.) A reluctant Congress was ultimately forced to recognize the value of a regular establishment of cavalry over the freewheeling volunteer militia, and two regiments of regular dragoons were created in the 1830s. The First United States Dragoons, formed in 1833, were employed primarily against the Pawnees and the Comanches in the Southwest. The Second Dragoons, created three years later, fought their first action against the Seminoles in the Florida swamps. Although they were regulars, trained in the European tradition, these dragoons soon abandoned inherited European tactics and adopted the fighting style of the mounted rifleman, which was more suited to Indian fighting.

In the Mexican War (1846–47), the US Cavalry were augmented to a strength of three regiments of dragoons and one regiment of mounted rifles (regulars). In addition, seven regiments of volunteer cavalry, all mounted rifles, saw active service. In the 1840s and '50s the mounted arm matured still further with the establishment of America's first cavalry school and the publication of the 1841 tactical manual. Its combat experience and professional knowledge were then put to the ultimate test when, beginning on 12 April 1861, the nation was rent by bloody civil war.

The Southern states, the Confederates, entered the war with few advantages. They lacked war *matériel* and did not have the means to manufacture more than a fraction of what they needed to prosecute the war. Much of what they used had to be purchased in Europe and the financial strain on their wholly agrarian economy produced serious problems. In one area, though, the South was wealthy. She was blessed with a large number of experienced military officers, most of whom had been officers in the regular army, while the young men of the South, most of whom were familiar with firearms, horses and athletic pursuits from childhood, possessed a natural aptitude for warfare that was missing in their cousins of the industrialized Northern states.

It was from this reservoir of talent that the South drew the manpower for her cavalry regiments. By law they were required to furnish their own mounts, which, in the beginning at least, were drawn from the finest blooded stock in the land. Most of these 'racers' had been bred and trained for the track or the hunt, so they were intelligent, fast and nimble – qualities lacking in the stolid draught horses issued to the Northern cavalry regiments. Confederate horsemen were armed with a variety of weapons, including pistols, shotguns, carbines and Enfield rifles. The sabre was used occasionally in the East, but most of the Southern troopers preferred instead to use revolvers or sawn-off shotguns in the *mêlée*. Military rifles were used for sharpshooting or to worry the enemy at a distance, as Stuart did with advantage at Spottsylvania Court House (7 May 1864), when Fitzhugh Lee's division held off carbine-armed Northerners and secured an important road junction until Lee's infantry could establish a regular line of battle.

The Southern cavalry was generally organized in regiments of 10 companies or troops. Each company had a strength varying between 60 and 125 men. Average regimental strengths dropped markedly as the war progressed, however, and regiments which numbered 500–600 men in 1861–62 had dwindled to a strength of about 100 troopers each by 1865. Under these circumstances, brigade strengths also varied widely. At the war's greatest cavalry fight, Brandy Station (9 June 1863), Beverly Robertson's brigade of two regiments had a strength of about 2,000 men, while Wade Hampton's brigade, with six regiments, could field only 1,600 sabres.

GENERAL J. E. B. STUART, PERHAPS THE MOST FAMOUS CAVALRY COMMANDER FIGHTING FOR THE SOUTH IN THE CIVIL WAR.

THE CAVALRY

The manifest superiority of Confederate cavalry during the first two years of the war cannot be attributed wholly to the fact that the South had, initially, better personnel and horseflesh. Leadership, too, was a significant factor, and the Southern cavalry spawned commanders of conspicuous gallantry and undeniable greatness. Men like 'Jeb' Stuart, Nathan Bedford Forrest and John Hunt Morgan rank among the most gifted horse soldiers of all time. Possibly more important still was the freedom of action these commanders enjoyed. Wherever possible, Confederate cavalry were concentrated and used according to the wishes of their commander. This policy led occasionally to disaster – as in the Gettysburg campaign – but more often than not it provided resounding victories.

The Union cavalry, the Northerners, were better armed but on the whole less experienced and competent than the Confederate cavalry. This was especially true during the first two years of the war, but by the middle of 1863 the Northerners had begun to achieve parity with their grey-clad antagonists. Many of them were recruited from cities and towns, and knew little or nothing about horseback riding and weapons. They were, literally, 'Yankee tailors and shoemakers on horses', and as such were the object of much raillery in the Confederate camp. Nevertheless, their amateurism was overcome in time. The green recruits of 1861 soon learned to ride well enough, even if they were never models of equestrian grace. But, where the Confederate cavalry were eager, spirited and quick, the Union cavalry were disciplined and determined; they exhibited a cohesiveness and hitting power that eventually gained the admiration of their opponents. Their major problem during the first two years of the war was not so much lack of professionalism as the misguided views on how to use them that emanated from the Army's high command.

Beginning with General Winfield Scott, the Union Army's first General in Chief, and persisting until Ulysses S. Grant's assumption of command (12 March 1864), the army's general policy was to parcel out the available cavalry for a variety of minor duties. Scott, who thought cavalry outmoded and useless in modern warfare, set the trend when he advised the states against accepting too many volunteer cavalrymen. By early 1863 the Union cavalry, which had never been concentrated or used efficiently, was the laughing stock of the army. Forrest, Morgan, John Singleton Mosby and Turner Ashby raided and marauded at will behind Union lines, while Yankee generals argued endlessly about the size of their mounted escorts. In the East the situation was particularly grim. There Stuart led his Southern 'chivalry' on two wide-ranging rides around the entire Union army (12–15 June and 9–12 October 1862) and made numerous raids against their lines of communication. Through all this the Union cavalry looked on impotently.

Eventually, in 1863, the situation took a turn for the better. 'Fighting Joe' Hooker took command of the Union Army of the Potomac (26 January) and reorganized the cavalry, concentrating it into an independent command under General George Stoneman. This newly organized cavalry corps

US CAVALRY AND THE CIVIL WAR

AT THE BATTLE OF RESACA DE LA PALMA, TEXAS, IN 1846, US DRAGOONS CHARGE THE MEXICAN LINE.

struck hard at the Confederate picket line along the Rappahannock at Kelly's Ford (17 March 1863), but after a sharp fight the blue-coated Union troopers were forced to retreat. Later, during the Chancellorsville campaign (29 April–8 May 1863) Hooker ordered Stoneman to raid the lines of communication of Lee's Confederate army with 10,000 troopers while the main army moved on the Confederate left and rear. The Stoneman raid caused a great deal of disruption in the rear of Lee's army but was ultimately disastrous, when the South struck back. Stuart's cavalry, unopposed, found Hooker's exposed flank in the Wilderness (Stoneman had reported that cavalry could not operate in the tangled scrub and forest), and 'Stonewall' Jackson's infantry corps followed up with a devastating blow that sent the Union infantry scuttling back across the Rappahannock. In the aftermath of this calamity Stoneman was relieved of command of the cavalry corps and replaced by General Alfred Pleasonton.

Following Chancellorsville Stuart's cavalry removed to Culpeper County, whence it could guard the left flank of the Confederate army and protect the approaches to the Shenandoah Valley, Lee's favourite northern invasion route. The preceding campaigns had cost the Confederates heavily in horses and remounts were becoming scarce, so Stuart's command needed time to recuperate. At this juncture Hooker, anxious about rumoured movements of Lee's infantry, ordered Pleasonton to penetrate Stuart's covering screen and obtain information about Lee's intentions. Pleasonton, with 11,000 men, set out on his mission on 6 June. This reconnaissance in force resulted in another cavalry battle at Brandy Station – a tournament of sorts, where the vaunted supremacy to that date of the Confederate horseman was put to a severe test.

On 8 June 1863, Generals Lee and Stuart reviewed the Cavalry Corps of the Army of Northern Virginia on the rolling meadows near the hamlet of Brandy Station, Virginia. Stuart's cavalry, charged with screening the movements of the infantry corps as they slipped away from their positions opposite the Union army near Fredericksburg, was at peak strength, mustering some 8,000 sabres, and morale was high. That evening the Confederate cavalry bivouacked along the south bank of the Rappahannock River. Stuart's dispositions, made with a view to crossing the river early on the 9th, were somewhat careless. The five brigades under his command were scattered along an extended front roughly 12 miles in length. This umbrella, meant to watch the river fords and shield Lee's concentration at Culpeper, was quite brittle. The various brigades, dispersed as they were, could not easily support one another in the event of a surprise attack.

Stuart's headquarters were on Fleetwood Hill, a long prominent ridge line just north of Brandy Station. Fleetwood and the Barbour House Hill to the west commanded the plain below Brandy as well as the half-cleared area of fields and wood-lots sloping down to the river in the east. Control of this high ground was to be crucial. The northernmost of Stuart's far-flung brigades was Fitzhugh Lee's, which was posted along the upper

THE CAVALRY

reaches of the Rappahannock. Fitz Lee was ill, and command of this brigade had devolved upon Thomas T. Munford, the lacklustre colonel of the 2nd Virginia Cavalry. W. H. F. 'Rooney' Lee's brigade watched Welford's Ford farther downstream, and W. E. 'Grumble' Jones's men were posted opposite Beverly's Ford, near the point where the Hazel River empties into the Rappahannock. The southern flank was held by Beverly Robertson's North Carolinians, who picketed Kelly's Ford four miles south-east of Fleetwood. Wade Hampton's brigade alone was held back from the river line, these men remaining in the old camps about Brandy and Stevensburg. The strongest sector of the Confederate line, then, was the central area along the Fleetwood–Beverly's Ford axis, where Stuart, if need be, could concentrate up to three brigades relatively quickly; whereas Munford and Robertson on the flanks were too far away to assist their comrades in the event of an attack on the centre.

The countryside beyond the northern bank of the Rappahannock was also alive with activity that evening. General Alfred Pleasonton's Union task force, consisting of the Cavalry Corps of the Army of the Potomac and two infantry brigades, stood poised to push across the river at daybreak. Pleasonton aimed to cross at Beverly's Ford and Kelly's Ford, his objective being to penetrate as far as Brandy Station and Fleetwood Hill and from there gain information about Confederate activities around Culpeper, an important crossroads town situated some six miles south-west of Brandy Station. Pleasonton divided his command into two large battle groups of combined arms. The right-hand column, which was to pass the river at Beverly's Ford, was commanded by General John A. Buford, one of the finest fighting cavalrymen in the Army of the Potomac. Buford's force consisted of his own 1st Cavalry Division, Major Charles J. Whiting's Reserve Brigade of regular cavalry, three batteries of horse artillery, General Adelbert Ames's infantry brigade of XI Corps, and four batteries of field artillery. Six miles downstream, at Kelly's Ford, General David McMurtie Gregg's left-hand column was to drive across the river with a force consisting of General Alfred Duffie's 2nd Cavalry Division, Colonel J. Irvin Gregg's 3rd Cavalry Division, two horse artillery batteries, General

UNION CAVALRY CHARGE CONFEDERATE GUNS NEAR CULPEPER COURTHOUSE, VIRGINIA, ON 14 SEPTEMBER 1863. DRAWING BY EDWIN FORBES.

MEMBERS OF A COMPANY OF THE 6TH PENNSYLVANIA CAVALRY AT FALMOUTH VIRGINIA.

160

US CAVALRY AND THE CIVIL WAR

David A. Russell's infantry brigade of VI Corps, and two batteries of field artillery.

Pleasonton had chosen to divide his force because he was not certain about the size and disposition of Stuart's corps, which he meant to engage wherever it could be found, and because of his plan of a pincer operation converging on Brandy Station allowed one column to engage the enemy while the others (there would be three columns in all, since Gregg's column was to divide beyond Kelly's Ford) moved to its assistance by a circuitous route. If Buford, for example, were checked at Beverly's Ford, Gregg's column, marching north-west from Kelly's Ford, would arrive on the Confederate right and rear, superbly positioned to launch a decisive attack at the very point where the Confederates would least expect it.

Buford's division burst across Beverly's Ford at dawn on the 9th. The leading elements, headed by Colonel B. F. 'Grimes' Davis, a Mississippian serving in the Union cavalry, ran into resistance almost immediately as the Confederate picket, Company A, 6th Virginia Cavalry (Jones's Brigade), fought desperately to stem the tide and buy time for their comrades to the rear to saddle up. Davis's men, advancing in column of fours (a common fighting formation in Virginia, where heavy undergrowth often limited cavalry to the roads), drove the picket ahead of them and pushed inexorably forward towards the open ground north of St James's Church. At the church, Major C. E. Flournoy, commanding the 6th, barred the way with 150 hastily assembled troopers. These men charged the head of Davis's column and flung it back in a wild *mêlée*. Davis, a veteran of dozens of scraps in the course of the war, was shot in the head during this *mêlée* and killed.

The 6th Virginia's success was only temporary, however, as more Union troopers crowded forward and, eager to avenge Davis's death, redoubled their efforts against the gallant handful of Confederates. Flournoy's band was swept back but saved from annihilation when 'Grumble' Jones himself led the 7th Virginia to its rescue. Finally, the 7th too was forced to give ground and retreat as the regiments of the Union 2nd Brigade added their weight to the attack. A few score yards west of this swirling duel the men of Major R. F. Beckham's Stuart Horse Artillery hastened to limber their guns and retreat from certain capture. The loss of the horse artillery battalion might have been a severe blow to the Confederates, but Beckham's men got the guns away, covered by canister fire from Hart's two-gun battery.

The resistance of Jones's two regiments saved the horse artillery and allowed Stuart time to recover from the surprise of the Union attack and form a proper line of battle in the vicinity of St James's Church. Hampton, with four regiments (the fifth, M. C. Butler's 2nd South Carolina, was posted between Brandy Station and Stevensburg), took position on the right of the church. The horse artillery went into battery at the church, where it had a good field of fire over a plateau some 800 yards wide. Jones formed on the left of the guns, and 'Rooney' Lee's brigade extended the front to the north and east, so that the entire Confederate line resembled a vast semi-circle about two miles in length.

BATTLE OF BRANDY STATION 9 JUNE 1863

Pleasonton lost no time in testing it. Mounted attacks, covered by dismounted skirmishers and Ames's infantry, were pushed forward all along the line. Lee's position was hit first, but the sharpshooters of the 9th Virginia broke up the attack, and mounted charges by the 10th Virginia and 2nd North Carolina regiments completed its destruction. In the centre, the Union 6th Pennsylvania, which had begun the war as a lancer regiment (the lances had been discarded in 1862), seconded by the 6th Regulars, advanced on Beckham's guns in one of the grandest mounted charges of the war. Major J. F. Hart, whose guns raked this charge as it came on, described the grim determination of the Union horsemen: 'Never rode troopers more gallantly than did those steady Regulars, as under

161

a fire of shell and shrapnel, and finally of canister, they dashed up to the very muzzles, then through and beyond our guns, passing between Hampton's left and Jones's right. Here they were simultaneously attacked on both flanks, and the survivors driven back.'

Not long after this charge the fighting near the church ground to a halt. The lull, it transpired, developed when Buford shifted the Reserve Brigade to the right, where it replaced Ames's infantry brigade. Buford's concern at this point was to prevent 'Rooney' Lee's Confederates, whose line already overlapped and threatened the Union right, from getting in the rear of his division and cutting the retreat route to Beverly's Ford. Buford indeed had cause to worry at this juncture: no one had heard from David Gregg's column, and the 1st Division had been fighting hard all morning.

Gregg's column had been delayed because Duffie's 2nd Division had been inexcusably late in getting under way. This cost the column an hour of marching time and ruined Pleasonton's plans for a simultaneous attack on Brandy Station. Still later, when Gregg found Robertson's Confederate brigade blocking the most expeditious route to Brandy, he ordered his men to swing to the west in a long detour. This, of course, cost more time. Finally, at Willis Madden's house, the column split. Gregg took his 3rd Cavalry Division towards Brandy, and Duffie's division proceeded towards Stevensburg. Russell's infantry brigade, left behind to watch Robertson, took no part in the subsequent fighting.

Stuart had ample warning of Gregg's flanking movement, but he at first discounted the reports. The first warning came from Robertson but was relayed by 'Grumble' Jones, whom Stuart disliked intensely. Stuart dismissed this report out of hand and sent Jones's courier back to him with a reproach: 'Tell General Jones to tend to the Yankees in his front and I'll watch the flanks.' When Jones heard this he muttered, 'So he thinks they ain't coming, does he? Well, let him alone. He'll damned soon see for himself.' A short time later Major H. B. McClellan of Stuart's staff, was standing on Fleetwood Hill, when he spotted Gregg's column emerging from the woods to the south. McClellan knew that Fleetwood Hill was the key to the Confederate position, and his actions in the next few minutes probably saved Stuart's corps. He first dispatched a messenger to Stuart and then ordered a single howitzer, which was parked nearby, to unlimber and shell the Union squadrons. The howitzer went into action immediately, firing deliberately. Gregg, who might have taken the hill then and there, unlimbered some guns to oppose it and, just as deliberately, formed his regiments for action. Stuart, shocked out of his inexplicable lethargy by the cannonade, ordered Jones and Hampton to gallop towards the heights and repel Gregg's attack.

The closest Confederates had to traverse $1\frac{1}{2}$ miles of country to get to McClellan's position on Fleetwood, but two of Jones's units – the 12th Virginia and the 35th Battalion – arrived at the crest ahead of Colonel Sir Percy Wyndham's 1st New Jersey. Wyndham's men charged at the gallop in column of squadrons and overwhelmed the Confederates, who arrived in no particular order on tired horses. Then, just as suddenly, the 1st New Jersey were battered and forced to retire by fresh grey squadrons. In a few moments the crest of Fleetwood and the adjoining Barbour House Hill became a maelstrom of swirling cavalry squadrons as both Stuart and Gregg fed in new regiments.

Jones's regiments reformed and returned to the fray, aided by Colonel L. L. Lomax's 11th Virginia (W. H. F. Lee's brigade), which fell in on their flank and drove the Bluecoats opposite them down the Stevensburg Road. Then Hampton cleared the eastern slopes of Fleetwood in a magnificent charge which swept the Union troopers over and beyond the Orange & Alexandria railroad. Gunner Hart, who was with Hampton, recalled the charge: 'Hampton, diverging toward his left, passed the eastern terminus of the ridge, and, crossing the railroad, struck the enemy in column just beyond it. This charge was as gallantly made and gallantly met as any the writer ever witnessed during nearly four years of active service on the outposts. Taking into estimation the number of men that crossed sabres in this single charge (being nearly a brigade on each side), it was by far the most important hand-to-hand contest between the cavalry of the two armies.'

Hampton's charge was decisive. The Bluecoats, staggered, retired to lick their wounds. This action virtually ended the battle, though inconclusive fighting continued on both flanks. Buford made one last lunge at 'Rooney' Lee's embattled brigade and came within an ace of success, but Munford intervened with three of Fitz Lee's regiments and restored the situation. Duffie's division, which might have added decisive weight to the Union thrusts at Brandy and Fleetwood, was checked north of Stevensburg by Butler's 2nd South Carolina and Williams C. Wickham's 4th Virginia Regiments. Finally, at dusk, the Union squadrons retreated across the river, harried on their way by the shells of the Stuart Horse Artillery.

Brandy Station was almost entirely a cavalry combat. Nearly 18,000 horsemen clashed at St James's Church and on the slopes of Fleetwood. Casualties were quite high, totalling 523 Confederate and 936 Union officers and men. But, for all this, the battle was strangely inconclusive. Pleasonton did not get the information he had been sent to obtain, and Stuart, though eventual master of the field, was highly embarrassed at being surprised and so nearly defeated. The true significance of Brandy Station was that it *made the Federal cavalry*' (to use Major McClellan's oft-quoted phrase). Until Brandy, the Union cavalry had been an object of ridicule. Afterwards, they fought with a bold self-assurance that won field after field. The Confederates, for their part, were eventually forced to acknowledge that the Union cavalry were their equal. Hamstrung by dwindling resources, especially the scarcity of proper mounts, they were forced more and more on to the defensive.

Brandy Station was by no means a typical Civil War cavalry battle, but it does offer many illustrations of the versatility of American cavalry and the tactics used by both sides during the war. The ability to fight both mounted and dismounted in a variety of tactical configurations was an unique

US CAVALRY AND THE CIVIL WAR

attribute of American Civil War cavalry. It was prepared to meet all the exigencies of the new warfare, adjusting in particular to the changes brought about by the breech-loading rifle. Tactically, cavalry formations were looser and less compact. The Civil War cavalrymen embraced the single-rank or rank-entire system whole-heartedly and used it habitually, especially in the West. Generally, though, the single rank was screened by dismounted skirmishers and supported by squadrons in column or *en echelon,* usually on the flanks. This expedient added shock value in a charge and stability in defence. Column charges and column formations, however, were not unknown; often the terrain or the battlefield situation dictated a deviation from linear tactics. Column charges characterized the clash at Brandy Station and the cavalry fight at Gettysburg (3 July 1863).

Against infantry, cavalry were often extremely effective. Thanks to the breech-loading carbine and later the repeating magazine rifle, cavalry did not hesitate to engage infantry – even when acting independently of infantry support. This was particularly true during the last year of the war, when General Philip Sheridan's cavalry corps engaged Lee's infantry on numerous occasions. At Haw's Shop (31 May 1864), Five Forks (1 April 1865) and Sailor's Creek (6 April 1865), for example, Sheridan's cavalry fought pitched battles with Confederate infantry and emerged victorious in each instance. Of this last action the British Major Henry Havelock, a contemporary, observed: 'Had it been any European Cavalry, unarmed with "repeaters", and untrained to fight on foot, that was barring the way – any Cavalry whose only means of detention consisted in the absurd ineffectual fire of mounted skirmishers, or in repeated charges with lance or sabre – the Confederate game would have been simple and easy enough.'

Operationally, too, cavalry played an important role in screening, conducting strategic pursuits and carrying out spectacular raids deep into enemy territory. The activities of Civil War cavalry in all these areas overshadowed anything that had gone before. Indeed, cavalry have seldom been used more aggressively or boldly.

ABOVE: CAVALRY CHARGE NEAR BRANDY STATION, 1864. DRAWING BY EDWIN FORBES.

LEFT: A CAVALRY SKIRMISHING LINE IN ACTION; THE HORSES ARE KEPT WELL BACK, OUT OF DANGER. DRAWING BY ALFRED R. WARD.

THE INDIAN

In the mid-19th century the Plains Indians of the trans-Mississippi West were among the finest horsemen in the world. They were nomads, following the great buffalo herds which supplied most of their wants. Their horses provided them with mobility and were a central element in their culture.

Status within the various tribes or bands (clans) was measured by an individual's prowess at martial games. Killing or wounding an enemy was not so important in the status system of the Plains Indians as were feats of daring known as 'coups'. Thus, one warrior might kill an enemy with a rifle shot, but another, reaching the man first and touching him with his 'coup-stick' or the muzzle of his rifle, would gain the coup. The most honoured braves were 'chiefs'–accomplished warriors who were much sought-after to lead war parties but who usually had no civil authority within the tribe. Each coup was rewarded by a decorative gift which became part of the warrior's regalia. The Sioux, for example, awarded eagle feathers which were added to the warrior's war bonnet. Eventually, tribal militarism produced warrior castes, and most tribes had men's societies which sought to foster soldierly and heroic attitudes among the braves. The Dog and the Kit-Fox Societies are the most familiar of these *élites*.

The Plains Indians were skilled warriors who rarely fought the white cavalryman in tactically disadvantageous situations. They had a fine understanding of guerrilla warfare and practised many of the strategems that have characterized irregular fighting in our own time. The Fetterman Massacre (21 December 1866), for example, occurred when Indian decoys led a column of soldiers into a valley where, in the heat of the chase, the column became over-extended. As soon as the Bluecoats lost their marching order the main body of Indians struck from ambush and overwhelmed them. Similarly, at the Little Big Horn (25 June 1876) Custer's men were victims of their commander's eagerness to get at the enemy. The Custer column was hit at the precise moment when it could least resist a concerted attack. Turned back by mounted and dismounted Cheyenne, the 7th Cavalry's column was enveloped and then destroyed by dismounted Indians who infiltrated its strung-out deployment using every fold and dip in the ground.

The Indians made full use of both mounted and dismounted tactics. Firepower decided most battles, but shock tactics were not unknown. Against muzzle-loading muskets they used mounted and dismounted skirmishers. The mounted men drew the fire of the soldiers with 'squaw-riding' tactics–circling the soldiers' position and firing from under the horses' necks while using them for a shield. The main body of Indians would then charge home at the opportune moment. These tactics met with unforeseen disaster in the five-hour Wagon Box Fight (2 August 1867), where Chief Red Cloud's 1,500 Sioux were butchered because the handful of soldiers opposing them had new breech-loaders which the Indians did not understand. All Red Cloud's charges were battered back by guns which the Indians complained, 'fired themselves without stopping'. Occasionally, too, the Indians would make gross tactical errors. Roman Nose's gallant mounted charge against Major Forsyth's scouts in the Beecher's Island Fight (17 September 1868) was torn to pieces by dismounted cavalrymen firing Spencer carbines. Still, the Indians might have won if they had made a night attack, but superstition forbade them using the one expedient that would have delivered the field to them.

In the end the Indian was defeated by a combination of factors. Though well armed, he did not have the material wherewithal to resist a modern military power. The destruction of the buffalo herds by white commercial hunting was a major death-blow to the Indian's civilization. Homesteading, the railroad and the telegraph completed his defeat. Had they acted in concert, the tribes might have prevented, or at least delayed, their downfall; but they lacked unity and, for all their prowess in small-unit tactics, they had but an imperfect understanding of strategy, notably the importance of disrupting or destroying the enemy's lines of communication. In its major aspects, warfare remained for the Indian a game, which in the circumstances he was doomed ultimately to lose.

US CAVALRYMEN SKIRMISH WITH INDIANS; BOTH SIDES EVIDENTLY PREFER TO USE THEIR FIREARMS. PAINTING BY CHAS. SCHREYVOGEL.

THE INDIAN CHIEFTAIN GERONIMO RETURNS FROM A HORSE-STEALING RAID INTO MEXICO. PAINTING BY FREDERIC REMINGTON.

In elegance the cavalry during the second half of the 19th century was supreme, but its role and importance came increasingly to be questioned. The American Civil War passed largely unheeded in Europe; among the older nations the conflict was generally viewed as one between two amateur, hastily raised armies operating, moreover, in a strange environment. The tactical lessons learned by the Americans could hardly apply to the centuries-old armies of Europe; or so, at least, the French evidently thought. Denison in his *A History of Cavalry* (1877) drily observed: 'They seemed to forget that four years of continuous fighting in the field would produce professional soldiers of the highest type whose practical knowledge of the business of war would be greater than if their whole lives had been devoted to peacetime training.' Thus it was not until the Franco-Prussian War broke out in 1870 and cavalry, for the first time in Europe, faced modern, quick-firing, breach-loading weapons over a significant period, that the current tactical doctrines for mounted forces – derived from the days of the musket and muzzle-loading cannon – were seen to be hopelessly out of date. J.P.L.

MEN OF THE PRUSSIAN ARMY, *c.* 1854. FROM LEFT TO RIGHT ARE TROOPERS OF THE 2ND DRAGOONS AND 3RD UHLANS, A GUNNER OF THE 3RD ARTILLERY BRIGADE, AND TROOPERS OF THE 6TH CUIRASSIERS AND 3RD HUSSARS.

THE TWILIGHT OF THE CAVALRY by JAMES LAWFORD

At the time of the Franco-Prussian War cavalry was still divided into two categories, heavy and light. The heavy regiments, the cuirassiers and the lancers, were armed with pistol and sabre, or pistol, sabre and lance; the light cavalry and dragoons carried in addition a carbine; but the cavalryman of either category was trained primarily to cut down or spear his opponent rather than to shoot him.

It had been accepted since before Waterloo that cavalry were powerless against unshaken infantry, but the role of the heavy cavalryman remained that of the human missile, galloping down on his foe and overthrowing him by the weight of his impact. Hence, according to orthodox military theory, the cavalry ought to be kept in a mass behind the infantry, ready to repel a breakthrough, exploit a success or cover a retreat. Only light cavalry, armed with carbines, were expected to reconnoitre forward, and even these favoured charging boot-to-boot rather than acting dismounted as a species of infantry.

The Prussians, pondering their experiences against the Austrians during the Seven Weeks' War of 1866, suspected that modern weapons made such tactics outmoded. The Prussian general Prince Kraft zu Hohenlohe Ingelfingen in his letters on strategy later emphasized that in the Franco-Prussian War the Prussian High Command had reversed the traditional policy by ordering all cavalry forward. The heavy cavalry, the cuirassiers and Uhlans, co-operated with the light to interpose a massive screen of horsemen between the German armies and the French. While the outnumbered French light cavalry fell back baffled, the German cavalry, displaying great enterprise, enveloped the French battle line in a moving blanket of patrols, which blinded the French commanders while keeping the German High Command accurately informed of what their enemy was doing. (So out of touch were the French commanders that on the night before the fatal day of Sedan, 1 September 1870, they told their troops that the next day would be spent resting. Instead, they suffered 17,000 casualties and surrendered an army of 83,000.)

PRUSSIAN INFANTRY, c. 1854. FROM LEFT TO RIGHT ARE SOLDIERS OF THE 3RD, 4TH, 1ST, 5TH AND 33RD INFANTRY REGIMENTS, THE 1ST JÄGERS AND 1ST PIONEERS.

Several successful cavalry charges were executed during this period. In the war against Austria Colonel von Bredow, commanding the Prussian 5th Cuirassiers, while skilfully disposing one of his squadrons to watch a flank and keeping another in reserve, used the two remaining, deployed in open order, to charge an Austrian artillery regiment, capturing 18 guns for the loss of only 12 men and 8 horses. As a general commanding a cavalry brigade at the Battle of Mars-la-Tour (16 August 1870), he charged home on a French gun line, disrupting the artillery at a crucial stage of the battle; on this occasion, however, he himself was charged before he had fully rallied his men, and was driven off with the loss of half his brigade.

Artillery, even breach-loading artillery, was nonetheless an easier target than infantry armed with modern rifles; a line of well-drilled, steady infantry could bring down a curtain of fire that even the most gallant cavalry would find hard to penetrate when charging boot-to-boot – a development the French failed to understand in 1870–71 until far too late. In the orthodox manner they massed all their heavy cavalry behind the infantry. There the cavalry patiently waited until the closing stages of the battle when they were ordered forward like sacrificial lambs to be butchered by the German infantry while executing charges to save a day that was already lost. At the Battle of Sedan, with almost unbelievable gallantry, four times the French cavalry galloped down on the advancing German infantry, only to carpet the ground to no purpose with their dead and dying.

Denison remarked in *A History of Cavalry* (1877) that he received a letter shortly after the

167

THE CAVALRY

battle from an experienced officer who observed, 'The question of cavalry charging infantry with breach-loaders is, I think, conclusively settled by this campaign. Whenever it had been tried . . . the result has always been the same – a fearful loss of life for no result whatever.' The verdict seemed clear enough; shock tactics were finished. The function of the cavalry would still be to act as the eyes and ears of the army, but issues would be decided by the infantry and the guns. As Bernard Shaw suggested in *Arms and the Man* (1898), cavalry would only charge machine guns when the commanding officer's mount happened to bolt in an unfortunate direction.

Such seemed the opinion of the young Winston Churchill when, in 1898, as a cavalryman-turned-journalist, he rode towards Khartoum with the 21st Lancers, formerly the 3rd Bengal Light Cavalry of the East India Company's army. The regiment consisted of four squadrons, the standard organization in most armies; in each squadron there were four troops of between 20 and 25 men and horses. The men had discarded their bright uniforms for the khaki tunics and breeches that now had become fashionable for field service, and carried breach-loading, magazine carbines in place of the antiquated, muzzle-loading, rifled pistols of the 1860s. But they still had with them their sabre and lance, and few looked on dismounted action with much favour.

For the recapture of Khartoum General Kitchener commanded an army comprising a two-brigade division of British infantry and a four-brigade one of Egyptians and Sudanese; for his mounted troops he had the 21st Lancers, an Egyptian cavalry unit of nine squadrons, and a camel corps of eight companies; his army totalled 25,000 men. He used his cavalry well forward in the approved Prussian fashion, and on 1 September 1898 the 21st Lancers, riding over the desert some eight miles ahead of the infantry, and with the Nile on their left, saw suddenly looming over the horizon a yellow-brown dome to the right of the river. It was the tomb of the Mahdi in the centre of Omdurman. Then in the desert, still farther to the right and about four miles distant, there appeared an enormous dark stain, the Dervish army under the Khalifa, more than 50,000 strong.

That night Kitchener camped by the river, fortifying a perimeter that projected into the desert in the rough shape of a semi-circle with the river as its diameter. Early next morning the cavalry rode out to probe the enemy dispositions. As the sun rose they discovered the whole Dervish army in motion. Great phalanxes of spearmen with forests of flags fluttering above them and linked by lines of riflemen strode purposefully forward towards the British encampment. It was an awe-inspiring sight. Their task completed, the cavalry withdrew, and the 21st dismounted close to the bank of the river. The Battle of Omdurman was about to commence.

At a range of 3,000 yards the British artillery opened fire, but unchecked the vast horde, encircling the whole British encampment, pressed onward. Then at about 1,200 yards the British infantry started firing well-controlled volleys, while the Maxim machine guns thickened up the lethal hail with rapid bursts of fire. The slaughter was appalling. The human tide thinned out into a bloodstained froth; in a few places it came within 300 yards before it receded, leaving the plain heaped with the killed and the wounded; it had been a massacre rather than a battle. As Kitchener saw the surviving Dervishes running back, he thought they had been completely defeated, but unknown to him powerful, uncommitted reserves remained. He was anxious to avoid street fighting in Omdurman itself, which was bound to be bloody and costly; the Egyptian cavalry were embroiled in the north and he now ordered the 21st Lancers to pursue towards Omdurman and shepherd the fleeing Dervishes away from the city and into the open desert.

Eagerly the troopers mounted and trotted out after the fugitives. As they topped a rise they saw

before them a level, sandy plain stretching away to the mudwalled houses of Omdurman. It was crowded by parties of spearmen and riflemen making their way to the city. Formidable numbers faced the 400 troopers of the 21st Lancers. From the British camp a helio blinked. Kitchener ordered the cavalry to continue the pursuit. Patrols reported a Dervish rearguard 700 strong drawn up by a shallow dry watercourse. Colonel Martin, commanding the regiment, resolved first to crush it and then to drive on to Omdurman. The 21st Lancers trotted forward in a long khaki

168

THE TWILIGHT OF THE CAVALRY

column, the 16 troops, each in line, following one behind the other. The column swung round to trot parallel to the watercourse. A bugle sounded; each individual troop wheeled to its right so that the whole regiment locked into a single line facing the Dervishes, then two ranks deep the Lancers galloped down on their foe.

Suddenly, from behind an unperceived fold in the ground, a dense mass of spearmen sprang forth, 2,000 in number and 12 ranks deep. The Lancers crashed into them at a full gallop. The impact was tremendous: Dervishes, horses and riders fell sprawling to the ground. For two minutes a wild *mêlée* raged, rifle and spear, knife and sword against sabre and lance; then the surviving Lancers broke clear on the far side of their enemy, halted, turned about and reformed ready to charge again. The Dervishes faced about and closed their ranks. But among the Lancers 70 men and 119 horses had been killed or wounded. Colonel Martin led his regiment to a flank and dismounted his men; they opened fire with their magazine carbines; the Dervishes surged forward, but the fire was too intense and they wheeled about and departed swiftly but in good order. It was only 9.30 in the morning and Churchill reflected that at this hour many in Britain would be comfortably settling down to their bacon and eggs.

The charge achieved its aim and Omdurman fell virtually without resistance; but the cost had been heavy. Nearly half the British casualties in the battle came from the Lancers. Kitchener's total casualties amounted to 500; the Dervishes lost close on 10,000 killed and as many wounded; science and discipline had triumphed over ill-equipped valour. Yet, magnificent as had been the charge of the Lancers, the battle had been decided by the rifles of the infantry and the guns of the artillery. Some doubted if the cavalry charge had been either wise or necessary.

However, in the war about to start in South Africa between the British and the Boers, it was to be demonstrated that, contrary to the experience of the Prussians and the French, the cavalryman still had his place in the battlefield and that the influence he exerted might yet be decisive; but his tactics had to be adapted to the new order imposed by the breach-loading, magazine rifle. In October 1899, Boer commandos from the Transvaal and Orange Free State swept across the borders into British-ruled territory and besieged British garrisons in Ladysmith, Kimberley and Mafeking. The Commandos were composed of some hundreds of riflemen (their numbers conformed to no set pattern) mounted on ponies; they were in no sense regular soldiers but every man was a marksman, a rider and a hunter, and despite the lack of discipline inevitable in a citizen army, they made formidable opponents. During the second week of December, they inflicted a staggering succession of reverses on the British armies, bringing them to a standstill and proving that firepower linked with mobility was as yet the most potent force on the battlefield.

Reinforcements poured in from Britain including Field-Marshal Roberts and General Kitchener, fresh from his triumphs in the Sudan.

ABOVE: A RARE FRENCH SUCCESS IN THE WAR OF 1870-71: HUSSARS AT SEDAN BREAK THROUGH A GERMAN SKIRMISHING LINE. DRAWING BY STANLEY BERKELEY.

RIGHT: THE 21ST LANCERS CHARGE THE DERVISHES AT OMDURMAN (1898).

THE CAVALRY

Roberts carefully analysed the situation. One British army thrusting northwards into the Orange Free State with the dual aim of relieving the beleaguered town of Kimberley and menacing the capital, Bloemfontein, lay pinned down near the little town of Magersfontein just north of the Modder River. Rhodes, cooped up in Kimberley, wrote him piteous and largely unnecessary appeals for help. Most European nations sympathized with the Boers. Fortunately for Britain, the power of the Royal Navy prevented any possibility of European intervention, such as had occurred after the disaster at Saratoga during the American Revolution. Nevertheless Roberts required an early, spectacular and undeniable success to restore the drooping prestige of British arms. He resolved to concentrate on relieving Kimberley as a preliminary to striking against Bloemfontein.

but, as the Battle of the Somme was to show in 1916, superior numbers meant little if employed frontally against a well-entrenched enemy. Roberts, however, had no intention of indulging in expensive frontal assaults; he planned to outflank his enemy to the east, spear-heading his advance with the powerful mounted division under Lieutenant-General French. In the event the mounted infantry brigades took little part in the advance; they had been hastily improvised and some of the riders still experienced considerable difficulty in remaining on the backs of their mounts.

The cavalry consisted of the 1st Brigade with three regiments, the Scots Greys, the Carabineers, and a composite regiment made up of squadrons from the Inniskilling Dragoons, 14th Hussars and New South Wales Lancers; the 2nd Brigade with a composite Household Cavalry regiment, the 10th

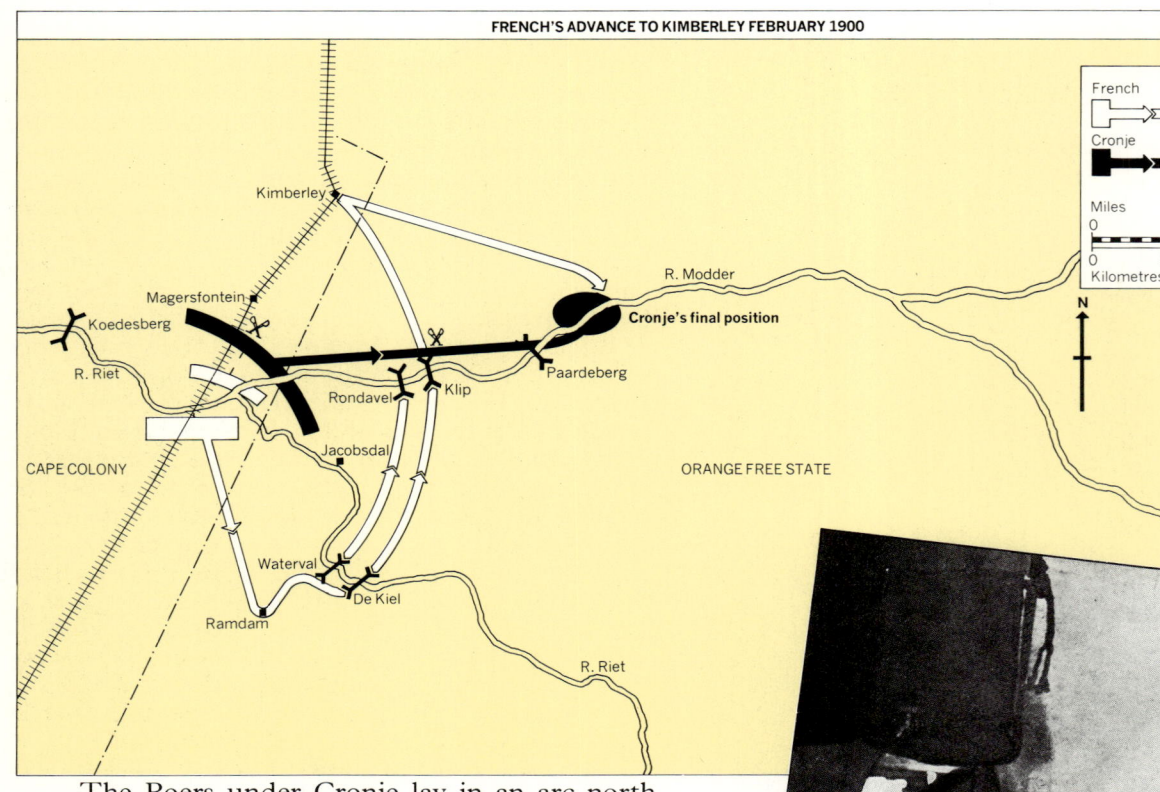

FRENCH'S ADVANCE TO KIMBERLEY FEBRUARY 1900

The Boers under Cronje lay in an arc north and east of the British bridgehead across the Modder River. In the north they guarded the approaches to Kimberley, in the east those to Bloemfontein. Cronje considered the British lacked the resources to move far from the railway and was confident that his mounted riflemen could move rapidly enough to block any shallow attempt to outflank him; any such attempt he expected to be in the west, the direction offering the shortest and easiest route to Kimberley.

Here he misjudged his adversary. Roberts first reorganized his transport to restore to his army the ability to manoeuvre. Then, ignoring the possibility of Boer risings behind him in Cape Province, he concentrated all available troops by the Modder. By this means he formed four infantry divisions, and, most important, a mounted division of three cavalry brigades and two mounted infantry brigades, bringing the number of British troops in the area to about 30,000 as against perhaps 5,000 under Cronje. The disparity in numbers was great

GENERAL ROBERTS IN SOUTH AFRICA, PHOTOGRAPHED IN HIS TRAVELLING HEADQUARTERS IN 1900.

170

THE TWILIGHT OF THE CAVALRY

Hussars and the 12th Lancers, and the 3rd Brigade with the 9th and 16th Lancers. Each was supported by two batteries (officially called troops) of Royal Horse Artillery. Most of the regiments had only three squadrons, and the numbers in a regiment ranged from 400 to 600.

Roberts planned for the division to withdraw to the south; then it was to swing east and northwards in a great loop round Cronje's left flank, and thrust directly on Kimberley. For this manoeuvre the division would have to cross two rivers, the Riet and the Modder, and the possession of the fords, known as drifts, would be of great importance. Here lay the first danger; a few riflemen on some kopjes, the low stony hills that here and there reared up over the plain or veldt, could easily frustrate a crossing. Speed and secrecy were essential. To guard the crossing, once captured, Roberts planned to send forward infantry.

On 11 February 1900, at 1.30 in the morning, leaving their bivouacs still standing to deceive the Boers, French's regiments marched to concentrate at Ramdam some 20 miles to the south. Then, in the early hours of the 12th, in bright moonlight the cavalry headed for the Waterval Drift on the Riet. They halted between moonset and dawn, then rode on to the river to find the crossing held. Leaving one brigade to occupy the Boers, French at once patrolled to the east to de Kiels Drift. Hearing that it was undefended he galloped his two other brigades there, crossing before the Boers could oppose him. Those at Waterval Drift faded away and by the afternoon, under a burning sun, the whole division was over the Riet.

On 13 February, traversing some 25 miles of parched, arid veldt French came to the Rondavel and Klip Drifts on the Modder. There he found no sign of the Boers. By 5 pm, after an exhausting ride, the cavalry had secured extensive bridgeheads across the Modder; their horses, all imported, were soft, and casualties among them from the heat and lack of water were heavy. On the 14th French paused to allow the infantry to catch up and take over the bridgehead. This pause was nearly fatal since Cronje, at last aware of what was happening, had begun dispatching troops to seal off the bridgeheads. On 15 February in the hot morning sunlight the cavalry emerged from the bed of the Modder on to the yellow dusty veldt beyond. They found to their left and right two series of kopjes linked by a low, gently sloping ridge which was about two miles in front of them. As the British approached, from both ranges of kopjes rifle fire broke out. The route to Kimberley ran straight ahead; any advance along it would be enfiladed from both flanks.

While French pondered the problem, his horse artillery batteries swung into action; at once Boer artillery replied. A cavalry brigade, acting dismounted and with every fourth man a horseholder, was if anything weaker than a normal infantry battalion. French took a bold decision. He ordered the 3rd Brigade to ride up the wide valley in front and seize the low ridge at a gallop. The 2nd Brigade would follow about 800 yards behind and the guns would support the advance until the last possible moment.

The two cavalry regiments in the 3rd Brigade only totalled four squadrons between them. They formed up in line, the 9th Lancers on the right, the 16th on the left: both were well dispersed with 8 paces between each man and 20 between front and rear ranks. Then they were off at a canter. The onlookers watched with deep anxiety; was it to be a second Charge of the Light Brigade at Balaclava? The horse artillery redoubled their fire; the two long lines of horseman cantered steadily forward. The dust rose in clouds, cloaking the tiny figures disappearing into the distance. Ahead at a gallop rode Lieutenant Hesketh with Sergeant Hale and 10 men of the 16th Lancers carrying wire cutters.

AN AUSTRALIAN LIGHT HORSE SQUADRON ON THE LINE OF MARCH NEAR PÉRONNE, 3 SEPTEMBER 1918.

THE CAVALRY

As they approached the ridge the fire from the flanks increased in intensity but that from in front was thin. The onlookers waited tensely, enthralled by the splendour of the spectacle but dreading to see at any moment the leading rank come crashing to the ground in a tangle of horses and riders. However, only here and there a horse fell or a trooper went down; then the long line of levelled lances swept over the ridge at a gallop.

The speed of the advance, the open order, making each individual trooper a separate target, and the clouds of dust had baffled the Boer marksmen; even so, the more farsighted observers of the charge reflected that a few strands of wire might have done what the enemy fire had failed to accomplish. Lieutenant Hesketh and four of his gallant band, riding into a murderous fire, had fallen, but in all British casualties numbered only about 20. With their centre broken, the Boers on the outlying kopjes withdrew and the road to Kimberley was open. That evening French dined in comfort with Rhodes at the Sanatorium Hotel.

Although the war was to continue in guerrilla form for more than two years, this was the decisive stroke. Cronje, hampered by a long train of ox-drawn transport, tried to retreat eastwards along the line of the Modder. French, striking south-east, enabled Roberts to trap him at Paardeberg; after a gallant defence, on 28 February 1900 Cronje surrendered. So, despite the experiences in Europe of the French and Germans, it seemed that cavalry could still play a dominant role on the battlefield. The argument about shock action, however, was far from concluded. The Boers, essentially mounted infantry, had demonstrated how the mobility conferred by the horse had vastly increased their effectiveness; but they almost invariably fought dismounted. The British cavalry subsequently also took to dismounted combat, using the rifle instead of the lance or sabre. In 1903 lances were withdrawn; then in 1907 they were restored, and so matters stood in 1914 when the 16th Lancers rode across France with their lances swinging round their backs.

On the Western Front, mud and wire appeared to end the argument. The cavalry dismounted and, taking up rifle and bayonet, did their stint in the trenches. Occasionally they mounted their chargers and waited wistfully for a breakthrough that never came. The cavalry era was ending, but the glow of an unexpected Indian Summer yet remained.

In Egypt a British army assembled to protect the Suez Canal against the Turks and put down an insurrection in the Western Desert; it included six mounted brigades. However, the brigades, composed of British Yeomanry regiments, Australian Light Horse and New Zealand Mounted Rifles, were intended to fight dismounted. The Australians and the New Zealanders were armed only with rifle and bayonet; the Yeomanry, exploiting an oversight in high places, had managed to retain their sabres. Thus although the mounted brigades were equipped to fight on their feet, the old cavalry spirit was by no means extinct.

In 1916 the British army in Egypt took the offensive and pushed forward along the coast of the Mediterranean towards Palestine. Holding defensive positions stretching from Gaza near the seashore to Beersheba in the east, the Turks barred the way forward and bloodily repulsed two British attacks. Stalemate ensued until on 27 June 1917 General Allenby, himself a cavalryman, arrived from France to take over command. He organized three mounted divisions, the Yeomanry, the Australian and the ANZAC (Australian/New Zealand).

Each mounted division consisted of three mounted brigades; in each brigade there were three mounted regiments and a machine-gun squadron with 12 Vickers machine guns; the regiments comprised three or four squadrons each containing four troops of 20–25 mounted riflemen. At full strength a regiment might number about 400 men, but on operations this number rapidly declined. A brigade of Royal Horse Artillery of three batteries, each equipped with four 13-pounder guns, supported each mounted brigade, but Allenby took care not to impair the mobility of his mounted corps by including any infantry.

In October 1917 he launched an offensive to break the Gaza–Beersheba Line. Initially the mounted troops fought dismounted, trying to use their mobility to compensate for their weakness in firepower. But on 31 October 1917 during the drive on Beersheba, the 4th Australian Light Horse Brigade in loose order rode across an open sandy plain towards two lines of Turkish trenches guarding the town. The enemy guns opened fire; the cavalry rode on. Machine guns clattered into action; the supporting guns of the horse artillery silenced them; then at a full gallop the Australians, in the face of heavy rifle fire, swept on and over both lines of Turkish trenches. Some Australians then dismounted to settle matters with rifle and bayonet while others dashed on into Beersheba spreading terror and panic. The brigade captured some 1,000 Turks and 9 guns at a total cost of 32 killed and 32 wounded. So fast had been the charge that neither the Turkish infantry nor their gunners had lowered their sights sufficiently quickly, and most of their fire flew high.

Then on 20 November, when the Turks were withdrawing from Gaza, a Turkish rearguard was

THE TWILIGHT OF THE CAVALRY

seen settling into a position near the village of El Huj. Scraping together an *ad hoc* force of three squadrons, half from his own regiment, the Warwickshire Yeomanry, and half from the Worcestershire, Lieutenant-Colonel Cheape led it against the Turks. The Yeomanry had outstripped their supporting arms, there were no field guns or machine guns to cover the opening stages of the charge, nor was there time to wait for any to appear. Colonel Cheape took some advantage of a rise in the ground, but much of the charge was across the open.

W. B. Mercer, who was in the leading line of one of the squadrons, wrote, as quoted in the *Official History of Military Operations in Egypt and Palestine*: 'Machine guns and rifles opened on us the moment we topped the rise.... I remember thinking that the sound of the crackling bullets was just like a hailstorm on an iron-roofed building.... A whole heap of men and horses went down thirty yards from the muzzles of the guns; the squadron seemed to melt away completely. For a time at any rate I had the impression that I was the only man left alive.' But the charge had succeeded, although at a terrible cost; all three squadron leaders were killed and nearly half the 180 men who took part in it were killed or wounded. But 11 guns and 70 Turks were captured and the rearguard dispersed. The desperate gallantry of the charge had a great effect on Turkish morale; shock action, moreover, had returned to the battlefield.

In September 1918 at the Battle of Megiddo, his last great battle in Palestine, Allenby employed his cavalry in a fashion that foreshadowed the tactics of the German Panzers in 1940. Now the cavalry carried sabres, and most the lance as well, in addition to their rifles – except for the New Zealanders who refused to change their ways. Many of the Yeomanry regiments had been shipped to France to help stem the great German offensive of that year, to be replaced by Indian cavalry regiments well versed in shock tactics.

At Megiddo Allenby utterly deceived the Turks as to his point of attack, broke through their line along the coast near Arsouf, where the Crusaders under Richard Coeur de Lion had once triumphed (see Chapter 3), and loosed his cavalry down the Plain of Sharon. Significantly, he had renumbered his two British-Indian divisions the 4th and 5th *Cavalry* Divisions. These thrust along the plain, swung across the coastal hills by the Musmus Pass, and poured into the Plain of Esdraelon to capture El Afule and Beisan far in the rear of the Turkish front line. Their communications irretrievably cut, the shaken Turkish armies collapsed.

During these operations several positions were taken at the point of the lance or sabre, but the action at the village of Samakh, situated just south of the Sea of Tiberias, perhaps best illustrates the spirit that animated the cavalry. Liman von Sanders, the German commander of the Turkish forces, desperately trying to reform his broken armies, selected Samakh as the pivot of a new line. He garrisoned Samakh with a few hundred Turkish infantry stiffened by some 150 German machine gunners, placed the whole in charge of a German officer, and then ordering him to hold out to the last, left for Nazareth.

Brigadier Grant with the 4th Australian Light Horse Brigade, less one regiment on detached duty, was directed to storm the village. Leaving Jisr el Majami at 2.30 am, he rode alongside the railway line that led northwards to Samakh. As the first streaks of dawn were appearing heavy machine-gun and rifle fire, directed down the railway line from the vicinity of the village, smote the brigade. Grant dismounted his machine-gun squadron to engage the enemy and swerved away right-handed with his leading regiment. To the right of the village he dismounted one squadron on some rising ground to support the advance, then ordered the remaining two (it was a three-squadron regiment) to charge into Samakh.

In the dim dawn light the Australians, disregarding heavy rifle fire, galloped into the village, dismounted and, assisted by some men from the second regiment in the brigade, cleared it after a grim struggle, killing or capturing 450 of the enemy of whom 150 were German. It had been a brilliantly conducted action, and the speed and reckless courage shown by the horsemen riding over unknown country in the dark were in the finest of cavalry traditions.

In 1920 when the Soviet Russian armies marched to Warsaw and disaster, General Budienny with 16,000 Cossacks caused havoc to the newly formed Polish Army. Marshal Pilsudski wrote of them, as quoted by General J. F. C. Fuller in *The Decisive Battles of the Western World*, 'For our troops who were not prepared to meet this new offensive weapon, Budienny's cavalry became an invincible, legendary force.' It was the last flicker of a not inglorious sunset. In 1939 the Polish cavalry futilely broke their lances against the iron sides of German tanks; for it was not the machine gun, the repeating rifle or the quick-firing field gun, it was wire and the internal combustion engine that spelled the ultimate doom of horsed cavalry.

And so the old type of horsed cavalryman faded away. In his peacetime pursuits there had always been an element of danger. In war he was swift into action, instant of decision, careless of the consequences. In his passing he has left behind him a tradition of light-hearted, debonair elegance, and a reckless courage in battle that is still far from dead.

POLISH LANCERS AT THE CANTER IN 1939.

INDEX

Page numbers in italics refer to illustrations

Abd-er-Rahman 48, 56
Acre 52
Adrianople, Battle of (AD 378) 44
Aemilius Paulus 39, 41
Aetius 47
Agincourt, Battle of (1415) 69
Ahmad Shah Abdalli, King of Afghanistan 124, 125, 126, 127
Air, Siege of (1710) *103*
Airey, Quartermaster-General Sir Richard 150
Aix-la-Chapelle, Treaty of (1748) 116
Ala 38, 39
Alans 47
Alaric 44
Albuquerque, Duque d' 80
Alençon, Comte Jean de 66
Aleppo 34
Alexander III, King of Macedonia, 12, 36 *37*, 37, 38, 44
Allenby, Field Marshal Viscount 14, 172, 173
Allied Army (Thirty Years' War) 74, 77, 78
Allied Army (Battle of Rossbach) 112, 113
Alma River, Battle of the (1854) 145, 147
Amazon *43*
Ames, General Adelbert 160, 162
Amstetten, Battle of (1809) 132
Ammianus Marcellinus 45
Anglia Rediviva (Joshua Sprigge, 1647) 88
Animal Management (British War Office publication, 1908) 10
Anne, Queen of England 93
Anson, Major-General George 133
Apache Indians 156
Archery
  Assyrian horse archer *32*, 33
  Arrow 50
  Bow 50, 58
  Crossbow 64, *71*
  English 64, 66, 68
  French 68
  Genoese 65
  Longbow 63, 64, 66, 70
  Mongolian 58, *59*
  Parthian 43
  Welsh 63
Armour
  Austrian 18
  Chain-mail 51–52
  Crusader *51*, 52
  Early 16
  Parts of *17*
  Plate armour *8*
  Swedish *9*, 75
  Use of 116, 118
Army
  Afghan 124, 125, 127
  Allied (Thirty Years' War) 74, 77, 78
  American Confederate 159, 161, 162, 163
  American Union 157, 159, 160, 161, 162
  Assyrian 33
  Boer 170, 171, 172
  Carthaginian 38, 39, 41
  Croat 74, 77
  Dervish 168–169
  English 52, 53, 64, 65, 66, 68, 69, 100, 102, 104, 109, 142, 144, 146, 170
  English Parliamentarian 88, 89, 90
  English Royalist 88, 89, 90
  Flemish 63
  French 64, 65, 76, 80, 82, 83, 93, 100, 140
  Genoese 65, 66
  Greek 34, 35, *36*, 37
  Hun 47
  Hungarian 60, 61
  Imperialist (Thirty Years' War) 73, 74, 77, 78, 83
  Indian 152
  Macedonian 36
  Mahratta 124, *124*, 125, 126
  Mogul 122, 123, *123*, 124, 127
  Mongol 58, 61
  Moslem 48
  Persian 34, 35, 37
  Polish 95
  Prussian 104, 108, 109, 110, 112, 113, *115*, 134, 136, 140, 167, *167*
  Roman 38, 39, *40*, 41, 43, 44, 46, 47, 48
  Russian 104, 145, 146
  Saxon 77

Spanish 80, 82
Swedish 73, 74, 75, 76, 77, 96
Swiss 63, 64
Turkish 146, 147, 172, 173
Arquebus (hackbutt) 70, *71*, 73, 85, 86
Arsouf, Battle of (1191) 52, *52*, 53, 55, 62
Artaxerxes 34, 35, 36, 38
Articles of War (Gustavus Adolphus) 74
Artillery 128
  English 64
  French 70, *71*
  Horse 90, 110, 111, 138
  Swedish 75, 78
Ashby, Turner 158
Astley, Lord 87
Ath, Surrender of (1706) 104
Athens 34
Atkyns, Captain Richard 14, 85
Attica 34
Attila 46, *46*, 47, *47*, 60
August III, King of Poland 140
Augustus 44
Aurangzebe, Emperor of the Moguls 123
Auret, Battle of (1364) *69*
Austerlitz, Battle of (1805) 131
Austrian Succession, War of the (1740–48) 14, 116

B

Babylon 35
Bagot, Richard 88
Balaclava, Battle of (1854) 146, *146*, 147, 149, 150
Balfour, Sir William 14
Bannerets 49, 69
Baseille, Alard de 68
Battle-Fields of Germany (Malleson) 78
Bavarian Succession, War of the (1778–89) 109
Beck, General 80, 82
Beckham, Major R. F. 161
Beechers Island Fight (1868) 164
Bela, King of Hungary 60, 61
Belisarius 48
Bit 12, *12*
Blackfoot Indians *9*
Black Prince, Edward the 65, 66, 68, 69
Bleda 46
Blenheim, Battle of (1704) 98, 99, 100, 102
Blois, Louis, Comte de 66, 68
Blücher, General Gebhard von 134, 135, 140
Boer War (1899–1902) 14, 25, 169, 170–71
Borodino, Battle of (1812) 18
Bosquet, General 150
Bourbon, Jacques de 66
Bourines, Battle of (1214) 50
Brandy Station, Battle of (1863) 157, 159–62, *161*, 163
Bredow, Colonel von 167
Breitenfeld, Battle of (1631) 74, 77, 78, 79
Bridle 12, *12*, 13, 14
Bringfield, Colonel 102
Buffalo 164
Buford, General John 160, 161, 162
Bulgars 56
Bulstrode, Sir Richard 86
Burgundians 46
  Estates 80
Burgwedel, Major 123
Byzantine Empire 48

C

Cadogan, Quartermaster-General William 96, 100, 102
Camel 33, *34*
Campaign of Italy (Napoleon I) 130
Campbell, Sir Colin 147
Canakhale 37
Cannae, Battle of (216 BC) 39, *40*, 41, 43, 44
Canusium 39
Caracole 30, 73, 74, 75, 96
Carbineers 74, 96, *96*, 130
Cardigan, Earl of 144, 145, 149, 150, *150*
Carrhae 43, 44
Carthage 43
Cassel, Battle of (1328) 63
Castex, Colonel 132
Catalauni 47
Cataphract 48

Catholic Imperialist Army 73, 74, 77, 83
Causeway Heights 146, 149
Cavalry 18, *18*, 50, 50, 63, 64, 65, 68, 80, 82, 93, 94, *94*, 95, *95*, 96, 97, 98, 99, 100, 102, 106, 109, 111, 113, 116, *128*, 132, 136, 137, 138, *139*, 150, 154
  Heavy 10, *11*, 129
  Light 10, *10*, 26, 95, 129
  Manoeuvres 28, *28*, 29, *29*, 30, *30*
  Afghan 124, 125, 127
  Allied (Thirty Years' War) 78
  Allied (Battle of Rossbach) 112, 113
  American 155, *155*, 156, *156*, 157, 164, *165*
    Confederate 157, 158, 159, 160, 161, 162
    Union 157, 158, 160, *160*, 161, 162
  American Indian 156, 157
  Austrian 111
  Bengal 111, *141*
  Boer 170, 172
  British 14, 18, 50, 65, 66, 69, 84, 85, 86, 88, 90, 96, 97, 98, 99, 101, 102, 104, 133, 138, 142, 144, 145, 146, 149, 168, 170, 171, 172
    Bengal Light 168
    Dragoon Guards 107, 108, 109, 149, 150
    Heavy Brigade 142, 147, 149
    Highlanders 147
    Horse Grenadiers 94, *94*
    Household 86, 94, 96, 137
    King's German Legion 133
    King's Life Guard 88, 89, 94, 96, *138*
    Light Dragoons, 13
    Light Brigade 9, 142, 146, 149, 150
    Parliamentarian 86, 87, 88, 89
    Royal Horse Artillery 111, 149, 172
    Royalist 14, 84, 86, 87, 88, 89, 90
    Royal Regiments of Horse Guards 94, 137, 149
    Union Brigade 137
  Byzantine 48
  Carthaginian 38, 39, 41, 43
  Chinese 57, 60
  Croat 83, *83*
  Danish 100, 102
  Dutch 100, 102
  European 18, 56, 140
  Frankish 48, 49, 50
  French 50, *50*, 63, 64, 66, 68, 154
    Chasseurs d'Afrique 150, 152
    Heavy 18, 167
    Imperial Guard 130, 133, 139
    Light 26, 167
    Maison du Roi 94, *94*, 95, 98, 100, 102
    Napoleon's 111
    Reserve 130
  Greek 36
  Hun 44, 46, 47
  Hungarian 95
  Imperialist 74, 77, 78
  Indian 152, 153
  Lithuanian 140
  Lydian 33
  Macedonian 36, 37, 38
  Mahratta 122, 123, 126, 127
  Mogul 122
  Mongolian 56, 57, 58, *58*, *59*, 60, 61
  Moslem 140
  Norman 51, 57
  Persian 34–35, 36, 37, 38, 43
  Portuguese *9*
  Prussian 107, 108, 109, 110, 111, 112, 113, 116, 118, 167
    Bosniaks 22, 109, 118
    Cuirassiers 18, *18*, 107, 108, 109, 111, *114*, 118, 166
    Dragoons 107, 108, 109, 111, *114*
    Hussars 109, 110
    Uhlans 22, 166
  Roman *8*, 38, 39, *40*, 41, *42*, 43, 44
  Russian 145, 146, 147, 149, 150, *150*
  Saracen 52, 53, 55
  Saxon 8, 99
  Spanish 80
  Swedish 74–75, 76, 77, 78, 84, 98, 99
  Tartar 140
  Thessalian 37
  Thracian *38*

Turkish 95, 98
Visigoth 47
Châlons, Battle of (AD 451) *47*, 48
Champagne 47
Chancellorsville, Battle of (1863) 159
Charlemagne 16, 48, 49, *49*, 50, 55, 56
Charles, Bonnie Prince 120
Charles I, King of England 84, 88, 89, 90
Charles II, King of England 90
Charles VII, King of France 70
Charles Martel 48
Charles XII, King of Sweden 93, 98, 99, 104
Chasseur 109, *111*, 129, 130, 131, 132, 150
Cherokee War 155
Chevaux de frise 49
Cheyenne Indians 164
Churchill, Winston 99, 153, 168
Civil War, American (1861–65) 157–63, 166
Civil War, English (1642–49) 14, 84–90
Clausewitz, General Karl von 142
Clearchus 35, 36
Colbert, General 132
Comanche Indians 157
Compagnies d' Ordonnance 70
Constantinople 46, 47, 48, 56
Cossacks 38, 95, 104, *105*, 109, 120, 140, *140*, 142, 146, *146*, 150
Courtrai, Battle of (1302) 63
Cowpens, Battle of (1781) 156, *156*
Crassus 40, 43
Crécy, Battle of (1346) 64, 65, 66, 66, 67, 68, 69
Crimean War (1854–56) 143–150
Croesus, King of Lydia 33
Cromwell, Oliver 84, *84*, 87, 88, 89
Cronje, General Piet 170, 171, 172
Crusaders 51, 52, 53, 54, 55
Crusades 50, 51, 52, *54*, 56
Cuirassiers 18
  Austrian 96, *134*
  English 85, 90, 139
  French 11, 18, *19*, *21*, 118, 129, 138
  Imperialist 74
  Napoleon's 86, 129
  Prussian *18*, 107, 108, 111, *114*, 167
  Weapons of 77
Culpeper County Courthouse 159, 160
Cunaxa 35, 36
Custer, General George 164
Cyrus the Great, King of Persia 33, 34, 35, 36

D

Damaji Gaekwar, Prince of Gujerat 126, 127
Dardanelles 34, 37
Darius III, King of Persia 37
Davis, Colonel B. F. 161
Decken, Captain Gustavus von der 133
Decline and Fall of the Roman Empire (Edward Gibbon, 1776–88) 47
Discipline for a Regiment of foot upon action, also the most essential discipline of the Cavalry (Brigadier-General Kane, 1745) 96
Doria, Antonio 65
Doyley, Charles 89, 90
Dragoons 25, 37, 74, 77, 85, 86, 94, 95, *95*, 96, 108
  American 156, 157
  Austrian *25*
  English 25, 95, 109, 110, 137, *137*, 150
  French 95, *95*, *108*, 129, 133, 136
  Prussian 9, 106, 109, 111, 116, 118, *119*
  Russian *145*
Duffie, General Alfred 160, 162
Düben 77
Dupplin Moor, Battle of (1332) 66

E

East India Company 152
Edgehill, Battle of (1642) 14, 85, 86, 87
Edward I, King of England 50
Edward, Prince of Wales, Black Prince 65, 66, *67*, 68, 69
Edward III, King of England 64, *65*, 68, 69

174

INDEX

Elephant 123, 126, *127*
Elixhem, Battle of (1705) 99
Enclosure Acts 85
Enghien, Louis de Bourbon, Duc d' 78, 80, 82, 92, 98, 99
Essex, Earl of 86
Eugene, Prince of Saxony 93, 98, 99
Eylau, Battle of (1807) 11, 18
Eyre, Major-General Anthony 87

F

Fabert, Maréchal Abraham de 131
Fabian strategy 39
Fairfax, Sir Thomas 88, 89, 90
Falkirk, Battle of (1298) 66
Fallen Timbers, Battle of (1794) 157
Ferguson, Major Patrick 156
Fetterman Massacre (1866) 164
Feudalism 49, 62
Firearms drill 24, *24*
Flanders campaigns 78, 98, 104, 116
Flandre, Comte de 66
Flournoy, Major C.E. 161
Fontaine, General 80
Forrest, General Nathan B. 158
Forsyth, Major 164
Foy, Baron 133
Franco-Prussian War (1870–71) 166, 167
Franks 46, 48
Frederick Augustus I, King of Poland 116
Frederick the Great, King of Prussia 12, 18, 22, 26, 107, 108, 109, 110, 111, 112, 116
Frederick William, King of Prussia 108, 109, 134
Fredericksburg 159
French, Lieutenant-General 170, 171, 172
Fürstenberg, General 77, 78

G

Gassion, Comte de 80
Gaul, Invasion of (451 BC) 47
Gaza-Beersheba Line (1917) 172
Gendarmes 70, 76, 98
George I, King of England 94
George II, King of England 94
German tribes 44, 46
German War of Liberation (1812) 110
Geronimo, Chief of the Apache *165*
Gettysburg, Battle of (1863) 158, 163
Gouvion St Cyr, Maréchal 93
Goths 46
Granicus River 37
Grant, Major-General Sir Colquhoun 136
Grant, General Ulysses S. 158
Great Military Battles (Cyril Falls ed., 1964) 82
Greene, General Nathanael 157
Grenzer 120
Gregg, General David M. 160, 161, 162
Grimaldi, Carlo 65
Gustavus Adolphus, King of Sweden 9, 70, *72*, 73, 74, 75, 76, 78, 84, 96
Gustavus Adolphus (Dodge, T. A., 1890) 74
Gyulai, Count 154

H

Hadek, Count 120
Hainault, Jean de 66, 68
Halidon Hill, Battle of (1333) 66
Hampton, Wade 157, 161, 162
Hannibal 38, 39, *39*, 41, 43, 44
Hapsburgs 78, 108, 120
Hart, Major J. F. 161
Hasdrubal 41
Herodotus 33
Hesilrige, Sir Arthur 18, 85
Hesketh, Lt. 171, 172
Historical Discourses (Sir Edward Walker, 1705) 89
History of Cavalry (Lt-Col George T. Denison, 1877) 74, 166, 167
History of the Rebellion and Civil War in England (Earl of Clarendon, 1702–4) 86
History of Gustavus Adolphus (Walter Harte, 1759) 77
Hohenlohe, General 131, 134, 135
Holkar 124, 126, 127
Holmes, Cornet Robert 85
Hooker, General Joseph 158–159
Hoplites 34, 36, 37
Horn, Field-Marshal Gustaf 78

Howard, Colonel Thomas 87, 88
Hundred Years' War 50, 63, 65, 70
Huns 44, *45*, 46, 47, *47*, 56
Hussars 95, 108, 114, 120, 140
  Austrian 108, 109
  Barko 132, 133
  French 110, 118, *121*, 129, 132, 136, *149*
  Hungarian 38, 109
  Prussian 109, *109*, 110, 111, 116
  Russian *148*
  Swedish 74

I

Ibrahim Khan Gardi 124, 126, 127
Ingelfingen, Prince Kraft zu Hohenlohe von 154, 167
Instructions on the Principles of the Cavalry (Jacobi, 1616) 73, 74, 75
Ireton, Commissary-General Henry 87, 88, 89
Ironsides 18, 86, *91*
Isembourg, Comte d' 80
Italy, Invasion of (218 BC) 39

J

Jackson, General Thomas 159
Jacobite Rebellions (1715, 1745) 94
Jäger 109, *110*
James II, King of England 94
Jena, Battle of (1806) 104, 134, *134–135*
Jenghiz Khan 57, *57*, 58, 60
Jerome 45
Jerusalem 50, 144
Johann, King of Bohemia 66, 68, 69
Johann George, Elector of Saxony 77, 78
John Sobieski, King of Poland 95
Jomini, Baron de 104, 142
Jones, W. E. 'Grumble' 160, 161, 162
Jordanes 45
Jugatai 60
Jugi 60
Jumna River 125

K

Kane, Brigadier-General 96
Khartoum 168
Khwarazmian Empire 60
Kimberley (1900) 169–170
King's Mountain (1780) 156
Kitchener, General 168, 169
Kleist, General von 136
Klingenberg, Heinrich von 68
Klizow, Battle of (1702) 99
Knight *8*, 49, 50, 63, 64, 68, 70
  Hospitallers 50, *53*, 55
  Templars 50, 51
Kolin, Battle of (1757) 111
Kunjpura, Massacre at (1760) 125

L

La Colonie, Brigadier General de 95
La Ferté, Senneterre 80
L'Hôpital, Maréchal de 80
Lance 22, *23*, *74*, 75
Lancers 22, *23*, 22, 37, 85, 98, 109, 118, 140, 143, *151*, *173*
Landen, Battle of (1693) 98
Landsknechte 70
Langdale, Sir Marmaduke 87, 88, 89
Lasalle, General Antoine-Charles, Comte de 130, 131, *131*, 132, 134
League of Augsburg, War of the (1688–97) 98
Lee, Fitzhugh 157, 159, 160
Lee, W. H. F. 'Rooney' 160, 161, 162
Lefèbvre-Desnoüettes, General Pierre 133
Leopold III, Duke of Austria 64
Leuze, Battle of (1691) 98
Lewes, Battle of (1264) 50
Little Big Horn, Battle of (1876) 164
Livy 38
Lomax, Colonel L. L. 163
Lorraine, Duc de 68, 69
Louis XIII, King of France 80
Louis XIV, King of France, 92, *92*, 93, 94, 95, 100, 102, 104
Lucan, Lieutenant-General Lord 144, 145, 146, 149, 150
Ludlow, Edmund 85
Lutzen, Battle of (1632) 73, 74, 78
Luxembourg, Duc de 98

M

Maastricht (1748) 116
McClellan, Major H. B. 162
Mafeking (1899) 169
Magdeburg, Battle of (1631) 77
Magyars 56, 95
Mahrattas 122, 123, 127
Mahratta Confederacy 124
Mâle, Louis le 66
Malines, Battle of (1746) 116
Malplaquet, Battle of (1709) 99, 116
Mamelukes 151, 152, *152*
Marathon, Battle of (490 BC) 34
Mardonius 34
Marignano, Battle of (1515) 64, *64*
Mark Anthony 43
Marlborough, John Churchill, Duke of 93, 96, 98, 99, 100, 102, 104
Marshall's Elm, Battle of (1642) 87
Mars-la-Tour (1870) 167
Marston Moor, Battle of (1644) 22, 84, 87, 89
Martin, Colonel 168–69
Master of the Horse 39
Matchlock 70, 106, 116
Maurice, Emperor 12
Maurice of Nassau 70, 73, 74
Maximilian, Emperor of Austria 18
May, Colonel John 193
Mazarin, Cardinal Jules 92
Mazeppa, Ivan Stepanovitch 104
Mediterranean 35
Megiddo, Battle of (1918) 152, *172*, 173
Mehendale, General 125
Melo, Don Francisco de 80
Mémoires (General Thiébault) 132
Memoirs (Sir John Hinton, 1679) 86
Menshikov, Prince Alexander 146
Mercenaries 34, 35, 38, 70, 74, 75, 77, 80, 83, *83*, 95, 102, 103
La Méthode et Invention Nouvelle de Dresser les Chevaux (Marquis of Newcastle, 1657) 86
Metz 47
Mexican War (1846–47) 157, *158–159*
Militärgrenze 120
Militarie Instructions for the Cavallrie (John Cruso, 1632) 85
Military Revolution 1560–1660 (Michael Roberts) 73
Mithridates 38
Mohammed Ali, Governor of Turkey 152
Moore, Sir John 133
Moguls 122, 123
Mongols 56, 57, 58, 59, 60, 61, 122
Mons, Battle of (1746) 116
Montfort, Simon de 50
Moravia, Markgraf of 68
Morgan, General Daniel 156
Morgan, General John Hunt 158
Morgarten, Battle of (1315) 64
Mosby, John Singleton 158
Munford, Colonel Thomas T. 160
Murat, Prince Joachim 130, 134, *135*
Muret, Battle of (1213) 50
Musket 77, 93
Musketeers 73, 86, 90, *106*
Muybridge, Edward 8

N

Nadir Shah, King of Persia *127*
Najib-ud-daula 127
Namur, Battle of (1746) 116
Napoleon I, Emperor of France 104, 110, 128, 129, *129*, 130, 131, 132, 133, 134, 137, 138, 142, 151
Napoleonic Wars 128–139, 140
Napoleon III *19*, 154
Naseby, Battle of (1645) 84, 86, 87–90, *87*
Ney, Marshal Michel 134, 136, 137, 138, 139
Nineveh 33, 35
Nolan, Captain 150
Northampton 65, 69, 88
Norwich, Sir Thomas 68, 69

O

Ogodai 60, 61
Okey, Colonel 86, 87, 88, 89
Omdurman, Battle of (1898) 152, 168, 169, *169*
Orange Free State 169–170
Orkney, Lord 99, 100, 102
Orleans 47
Ostrogoths 44
Otway, Lieutenant-Colonel Loftus 133

Oudenarde, Battle of (1708) 99, *102*, 116
Overkirk, General 100, 102
Oxford, Robert de Vere, Earl of 65, 69

P

Palmes, Colonel 98
Panipat, Battle of (1761) 124, 125, 126–27, *126*
Pant, Govind 124, 125
Pappenheim, Gottfried 77, 78
Parliament 84, 85
Parmenion 37
Parquin, Sergeant 132, 133
Pausanias, King of Sparta 34
Pawnee Indians 157
Peltasts 34
Pembroke, William Marshall, Earl of *52*
Peppin II, King of the Franks 48
Peter the Great, Czar of Russia 95, 104
Philip II, King of Macedonia 36, 37
Philip II, King of Spain *16*
Philippe VI, King of France 64, 65, 66, 69
Pickens, Colonel Andrew 156
Pike 63, 70, 73
Plains Indians 164
Plataea, Battle of (479 BC) 34
Pleasanton, General Alfred 159, 160, 161
Podelwitz 77, 78
Poitiers, Battle of (1357) 69
Polish Succession, War of the (1722) 116
Poltava, Battle of (1709) 99
Ponsonby, Major-General Sir William 137
Pot-de-fer *51*, 52
Prentzlow, Surrender at (1806) 131, 135
Priscus 46
Punic War, Second (219–202 BC) 38
Puységur, Marechal de 93
Pyramids, Battle of the (1789) 131, 152

Q

Quintus Fabius 39

R

Raglan, General Lord 145, 147, 149, 150
Ramillies, Battle of (1706) 99, 100, *100*, *101*, 102, 104
Rao, Balaji 124, 127
Rao, Sadashiv, 'The Bhao' 124, 125, 126, 127
Rao, Vishwas 124, 126, 127
Rappahannock River 159, 160
Rêveries (Marshal Saxe, 1757) 116, 118
Red Cloud, Chief of the Sioux 164
Redemieh, Battle of (1800) 131
Reille, General 136, 139
Reiter 70, 71, 76, *76*
Resaca de la Palma, Battle of (1846) *158–59*
Revolutionary War, American (1775–83) 156, 157
Richard I, King of England 51, 52, 53
Richelieu, Cardinal 78, 80, 95
Rifle *10*, *24*, 164
Roberts, Field-Marshal 169, 170, *170*, 171
Robertson, Beverly 157, 160, 162
Rocroi, Battle of (1643) 78, 80, *81*, 82, *82*, 92
Rohilcund 124, 125
Roman Empire 44, 46, 48
Romberg, General von 135
Rossbach, Battle of (1757) 111, 112, *112*, 113
Roundway Down, Battle of (1643) 85
Rua, King of the Huns 46
Rupert, Prince 14, 86, 87, 88, 89, 90
Russell, General David A. 161, 162

S

Sabre *15*, *27*
Saddle *10*, 12, *13*, 14, 34, 48, 148
Sajo River 60, 61
Salamis, Battle of (480 BC) 34
Saladin 53, 55
Salamanca, Battle of (1812) 133
Sanders, Liman von 173
Santa Cruz, Marquis de 93
Saracens 51, *52*, 53, *54*

INDEX

Sardis 33, 34, 37
Saxe, Marshal, Maurice of Saxony 116, *117*, 118, 140
Saxons 78
Saxony, Invasion of (1631) 77
Scarlett, General James 142, 147, *147*, 149, *149*
Schulenburg, General 99, 102
Scipio Africanus 43
Scott, General Winfield 158
Scythia 46
Sempach, Battle of (1386) 64
Sebastopol 144, 145, 146
Sedan, Battle of (1870) 167, *168–69*
Seminole Indians 157
Sepoy 152
Seven Weeks' War (1866) 167
Seven Years' War (1756–63) 14, 18, 110, 120
Seydlitz, General Friedrich von 111, 112, 113
Sheridan, General Philip 163
Shuja-ud-daula, Ruler of Oudh 125, 126, 127
Sindia, Jankoji 124, 126, 127
Sioux Indians 164
Sirot 80
Sivaji 123, 124
Slavs 56
Somerset, Major-General Lord Edward 137
Spahis 152, *153*
Spanish Netherlands 99, 104

Spanish Succession, War of the (1701–14) 18, 98, 116
Spottsylvania Courthouse (1864) 157
Spur 12, *13*
Spurs, Battle of the (1302) 63
Steingel, General Henri, Baron 130
Stettin, Battle of (1806) 134, 135
Stirrup *10*, 12, *13*, 34, 48, 148
Stoneman, General George 158, 159
Stuart, General James Ewell Brown (Jeb) 157, *157*, 158, 159, 161, 162
Subotai 60, 61
Surenas 43
Swiss League 64
Sword drill 20, *21*

T

Tacitus 44
Tallard, Marshal 98
Tartars 57, 58, 104, *147*
Tercio 73, *73*, 77, 78, 80, *81*
Terentius Varro 39, 40, 41
Thames, Battle of the (1813) 157
Thebes 37
Theodoric 47
Thermopylae (480 BC) 34, 37
Thirty Years' War 73–82
Thorismund 47

Tilly, Count Johann 74, 77, 78
Tissaphernes 35
Toulouse, Battle of (721) 48
Tournai, Battle of (1745) 99, 116
Travers, General 136, 137
Troy, Siege of (12th Cent. BC) 33, 37
Turenne 98
Turmae 38

U

Uhlan 22, 119, 132, *132*, 140
Urry, Sir John 89
Uslar, Captain von 134

V

Valens 44
Vallée aux Clercs 65
Valois, Philippe de 63
Vandeleur, Major-General Sir John 136, 137
Västgöta 76
Vendôme, Louis 99
Villar, Marshal Claude 99
Villeroi, Marshal 100, 102, 104
Visigoths 44, *44*

W

Wadicourt 65, 66
Wagon Box Fight (1867) 164
Wagram, Battle of (1809) 131
Waldeck 98
Wallenstein, General Albert von 74, 78
Warsaw, Battle of (1920) 173
Warwick, Earl of 65
Waterloo, Battle of (1815) 11, 18, 22, 133, 136–39, *136*, 142, 144, 167
Wayne, General Anthony 157
Wellington, Arthur Wellesley, Duke of 133, 136, 137, 138
Whalley, Colonel Edward 88
Whiting, Major Charles 160
William III, King of England 95, 98, 99
Winkelreid, Arnold von 64
Wyndham, Lieutenant Charles 137
Wyndham, Colonel Sir Percy 162

X

Xenophon 34, 35, 36, 43
Xerxes, King of Persia 34

Z

Zama, Battle of (202 BC) 43, *43*
Ziethen, Major-General von 111, 112, 136

ACKNOWLEDGEMENTS

ROXBY PRESS WISH TO THANK THE FOLLOWING INDIVIDUALS AND ORGANIZATIONS FOR PERMISSION TO REPRODUCE ILLUSTRATIONS APPEARING IN THE BOOK:

AMERICAN HISTORY PICTURE LIBRARY; BIBLIOTHEQUE NATIONALE, PARIS; BRITISH MUSEUM; MICHAEL CALVERT; CORPUS CHRISTI COLLEGE CAMBRIDGE; DEUTSCHE FOTOTHEK; DEPARTMENT OF THE ENVIRONMENT, CROWN COPYRIGHT RESERVED; MARY EVANS PICTURE LIBRARY; WERNER FORMAN ARCHIVE; JOHN R. FREEMAN; MICHAEL HOLFORD; IMPERIAL WAR MUSEUM; INDIA OFFICE LIBRARY; LIBRARY OF CONGRESS; MANSELL COLLECTION; MANSELL COLLECTION/GIRAUDON; NATIONAL ARMY MUSEUM; PARKER GALLERY; POPPERFOTO; PRINCE CONSORT LIBRARY, ALDERSHOT; RONALD SHERIDAN; US ARMY; VICTORIA AND ALBERT MUSEUM; WESTERN AMERICANA PICTURE LIBRARY; PETER YOUNG.

OTHER ILLUSTRATIONS WERE SPECIALLY DRAWN FOR THE BOOK BY DAVID POCKNELL AND LARS HOKANSON. DAVID POCKNELL DREW THE MAPS.